Praise for *The Platform Bu* *Navigator*

'*The Platform Business Navigator* begins with a very readable explanation of platform business structures, their types and how they work. The book then clearly answers the "so what" question by providing direct and actionable frameworks to help organisations implement platform strategies. I highly recommend this for teams and leaders who wish to understand platform business and make changes in their organisations.'

Geoffrey Parker, Charles E. Hutchinson '68A Professor of Engineering Innovation, Dartmouth College; Fellow, MIT Initiative on the Digital Economy; co-author of *Platform Revolution*

'Digital platforms are core to every business today. But how do you build and scale a successful platform business and make it a profitable business? *The Platform Business Navigator* is a great source of inspiration and an actionable toolkit to rethink your business.'

Dr. Tanja Rückert, CDO and member of the board of management, Bosch Group

'Platforms fundamentally alter the way we work, collaborate, consume and participate in society. Hence, every company needs to rethink what platform means for their business. In light of this challenge, *The Platform Business Navigator* offers a comprehensive guide to understanding and harnessing the power of platforms.'

Gerhard Oswald, supervisory board member of SAP; former member of the executive board of SAP

'The book's comprehensive approach and practical examples make it very accessible, and the platform business patterns are a great source of inspiration.'

Christoph Tonini, CEO Swiss Marketplace Group; former CEO, TX Group

'A masterful blend of academic insight and practical guidance, this book is an essential map for navigating the platform economy.'

Prof. Dr. Miriam Meckel, co-founder and CEO, ada Learning; Professor, University of St. Gallen

'*The Platform Business Navigator* is an enriching and inspiring source for understanding patterns to ideate, design and monetise in digital platform ecosystems – a book to read and revisit many times and an ideal playbook for training students and practitioners on business modeling.'

Prof. Dr. Fiona Schweitzer, Professor of Marketing, Grenoble Ecole de Management, France

'Platform business models are very important for us at Bosch. Many of our projects and growth initiatives depend on network effects, which is often only apparent at a second glance. The well-researched collection of 88 patterns helps us in our daily work to identify those opportunities early on and gives us actionable support in developing viable platform business models.'

Dr. Stefan Ferber, co-founder, TREEO; former CEO and CTO, Bosch.IO

'There is a lot of literature on platform business models, but *The Platform Business Navigator* is one of the most comprehensive and easy-to-understand guides with a clear structure and insightful examples. A must-read for any manager interested in the essentials of platform design, growth and management.'

Felicitas Geiss, Vice President Bosch Digital; former Vice President, Azena

'A comprehensive toolkit for ideating and guiding fundamental design decisions about platform business models, making the complex topic of platforms actionable.'

Dr. Jonas Böhm, Global Director Mobility, TWAICE Technologies; Platform Scholar

'We have used *The Platform Business Navigator* very successfully in several customer projects. An inspiring tool to systematically develop attractive platform business models – from ideation, design, scaling and management to monetisation. A must-have to overcome the platform paradox.'

Georg von der Ropp, CEO BMI Lab AG

'This timely book arrives amidst the sweeping transformation of industries and sectors, where platform-based business models are gaining prominence. In this era, every company finds itself influenced by these shifts, whether they embark on building their own platforms or partake in various roles within platform-based business ecosystems. As a result, effective management must equip itself to thrive in this rising age of platforms. Herein lies the value of this comprehensive tool, which adeptly unravels the multifaceted nature of platforms and their profound impact on product or service businesses, particularly considering the related network effects. This book proves indispensable in fostering a profound understanding of these dynamics, making it an essential resource for navigating the modern business landscape.'

Prof. Dr. Christoph Wecht, New Design University

The Platform Business Navigator

Pearson

At Pearson, we believe in learning – all kinds of learning for all kinds of people. Whether it's at home, in the classroom or in the workplace, learning is the key to improving our life chances.

That's why we're working with leading authors to bring you the latest thinking and best practices, so you can get better at the things that are important to you. You can learn on the page or on the move, and with content that's always crafted to help you understand quickly and apply what you've learned.

If you want to upgrade your personal skills or accelerate your career, become a more effective leader or more powerful communicator, discover new opportunities or simply find more inspiration, we can help you make progress in your work and life.

Every day our work helps learning flourish, and wherever learning flourishes, so do people.

To learn more, please visit us at **www.pearson.com**

The Financial Times

With a worldwide network of highly respected journalists, *The Financial Times* provides global business news, insightful opinion and expert analysis of business, finance and politics. With over 500 journalists reporting from 50 countries worldwide, our in-depth coverage of international news is objectively reported and analysed from an independent, global perspective.

To find out more, visit **www.ft.com**

FELIX WORTMANN
SVEN JUNG
OLIVER GASSMANN

The Platform Business Navigator

The strategies behind the most successful platform companies

Pearson

Harlow, England • London • New York • Boston • San Francisco • Toronto • Sydney • Dubai • Singapore • Hong Kong
Tokyo • Seoul • Taipei • New Delhi • Cape Town • São Paulo • Mexico City • Madrid • Amsterdam • Munich • Paris • Milan

PEARSON EDUCATION LIMITED
KAO Two
KAO Park
Harlow CM17 9NA
United Kingdom
Tel: +44 (0)1279 623623
Web: www.pearson.com

First edition published 2024 (print and electronic)

ISBN: 978-1-292-46618-7 (print)
       978-1-292-73428-6 (ePub)

British Library Cataloguing-in-Publication Data
A catalogue record for the print edition is available from the British Library

Library of Congress Cataloging-in-Publication Data
Names: Wortmann, Felix, 1977- author. | Jung, Sven, author. | Gassmann, Oliver, 1967- author.
Title: The platform business navigator : the strategies behind the most successful platform companies / Felix Wortmann, Sven Jung, Oliver Gassmann.
Description: First edition. | Harlow, England ; New York : Pearson, 2024. | Includes bibliographical references.
Identifiers: LCCN 2023047067 | ISBN 9781292466187 (paperback) | ISBN 9781292734286 (epub)
Subjects: LCSH: Multi-sided platform businesses.
Classification: LCC HD99E9.M782 W678 2024 | DDC 338.7--dc23/eng/20231108
LC record available at https://lccn.loc.gov/2023047067

10 9 8 7 6 5 4 3 2 1
28 27 26 25 24

Cover design by Nick Redeyoff

Print edition typeset in 9.75/12 Helvetica Neue by Straive
Printed by Ashford Colour Press Ltd, Gosport

NOTE THAT ANY PAGE CROSS REFERENCES REFER TO THE PRINT EDITION

Contents

PART ONE Platform business innovation 1

PART TWO 88 patterns of the Platform Business Navigator 55

List of figures

Pearson's Commitment to Diversity, Equity and Inclusion

Pearson is dedicated to creating bias-free content that reflects the diversity, depth and breadth of all learners' lived experiences. We embrace the many dimensions of diversity including, but not limited to, race, ethnicity, gender, sex, sexual orientation, socioeconomic status, ability, age and religious or political beliefs.

Education is a powerful force for equity and change in our world. It has the potential to deliver opportunities that improve lives and enable economic mobility. As we work with authors to create content for every product and service, we acknowledge our responsibility to demonstrate inclusivity and incorporate diverse scholarship so that everyone can achieve their potential through learning. As the world's leading learning company, we have a duty to help drive change and live up to our purpose to help more people create a better life for themselves and to create a better world.

Our ambition is to purposefully contribute to a world where:

- Everyone has an equitable and lifelong opportunity to succeed through learning.
- Our educational products and services are inclusive and represent the rich diversity of learners.
- Our educational content accurately reflects the histories and lived experiences of the learners we serve.
- Our educational content prompts deeper discussions with students and motivates them to expand their own learning and worldview.

We are also committed to providing products that are fully accessible to all learners. As per Pearson's guidelines for accessible educational Web media, we test and retest the capabilities of our products against the highest standards for every release, following the WCAG guidelines in developing new products for copyright year 2022 and beyond. You can learn more about Pearson's commitment to accessibility at:

https://www.pearson.com/us/accessibility.html

While we work hard to present unbiased, fully accessible content, we want to hear from you about any concerns or needs regarding this Pearson product so that we can investigate and address them.

- Please contact us with concerns about any potential bias at:
  https://www.pearson.com/report-bias.html
- For accessibility-related issues, such as using assistive technology with Pearson products, alternative text requests, or accessibility documentation, email the Pearson Disability Support team at:
  disability.support@pearson.com

About the authors

Felix Wortmann is professor, senior lecturer and vice director at the Institute of Technology Management of the University of St Gallen (HSG). Moreover, he is the scientific director of the Bosch IoT Lab, a collaboration between HSG, ETH Zurich and the Bosch Group. His research focuses on the convergence of the physical and digital worlds into an Internet of Things. Felix's current activities are geared towards platform and product-as-a-service business models, machine learning and digital innovation in mobility, health and energy. Felix received a Bachelor and Master of Science in Information Systems from the University of Münster, Germany, and a PhD in Management from the University of St Gallen. Furthermore, he gained several years of industry experience in a German-based multinational software corporation. His transdisciplinary research has been published in leading academic and practitioner-oriented journals. Felix has been recognised for his overall research performance and has received various awards for the relevance and impact of his research.

Sven Jung is currently a visiting fellow at Harvard University and a final-year PhD candidate at the University of St. Gallen. Over the last three and a half years, he has been a research associate and project manager at the Bosch IoT Lab, a research and consulting think tank. His practice-oriented research focuses on the platformisation of existing businesses and strategies for designing, scaling and managing platform business models. Previously, Sven worked for a management consultancy, in business development at a biotech start-up and at a Danish M&A advisory for technology start-ups. He received a Master of Science in Finance and Strategic Management from Copenhagen Business School and a Bachelor of Arts in Business Administration from the University of St Gallen.

Oliver Gassmann is full professor at the University of St Gallen, director of its Institute of Technology Management (ITEM) and a thought leader in the field of innovation. After completing his PhD in 1996, he was leading Corporate Research at Schindler Corporation. Oliver has published articles in leading academic journals on technology management and innovation. His book *The Business Model Navigator* became a global bestseller, he has founded several spin-off companies and he is on various boards of international companies and institutions. Oliver has been recognised as one of the most active innovation scholars (IAMOT) and as one of the leading German economists (FAZ). In 2014 he was awarded the Scholarly Impact Award by the *Journal of Management*, and in 2015 he received the Citation of Excellence Award from the *Emerald Group*. He is a widely renowned keynote speaker and advisor for several Fortune 500 companies.

Authors' acknowledgements

We would like to extend our gratitude to the individuals who played a critical role in the development of this book, particularly Wolfgang Bronner, director of the Bosch IoT Lab. He was involved from the beginning and contributed to earlier versions of *The Platform Business Navigator*. His continuous input and feedback were instrumental in shaping the patterns. We also express our appreciation to our stakeholders in the Bosch Group for their unwavering support. As a thought leader in the field of digital innovation, Bosch's support was essential in bringing this book to life.

Julius Schilling and Christoph Schink deserve special mention for their invaluable support as student assistants. Their dedication and contributions greatly enriched and improved the content. Furthermore, we would like to thank Florian Meister, Jessica Keil and Hanna Bencseky for their excellent assistance.

Our appreciation also goes to our graphic designer, Malte Belau, whose creative talent gave life to the visual aspects of this book, as well as to Diana Schnelle for her editorial feedback. Lastly, we want to thank our colleagues at the Institute of Technology Management (ITEM) of the University of St Gallen and beyond who provided us with additional feedback and suggestions. Their contributions and encouragement over the last few years have been invaluable, and we greatly appreciate their involvement.

Publisher's acknowledgements

Text credits

6 Harvard Business Publishing: Adapted from Van Alstyne, M., Parker, G. and Choudary, S. (2016) 'Pipelines, platforms, and the new rules of strategy'. Harvard Business Review, 94(4), 54–62; 6 Harvard Business Publishing: Adapted from Eisenmann, T., Parker, G. and Van Alstyne, M. (2006) 'Strategies for two-sided markets'. Harvard Business Review, 84(10), 92–101; 7 John Wiley & Sons, Inc: Gawer, A. and Cusumano, M. (2014) 'Industry platforms and ecosystem innovation'. Journal of Product Innovation Management, 31(3), 417–433.; 8 Harvard Business Publishing: Eisenmann, T., Parker, G. and Van Alstyne, M. (2006) 'Strategies for two-sided markets'. Harvard Business Review, 84(10), 92–101.; 11 Landing AI: Ng, A. (2018) 'AI transformation playbook: How to lead your company into the AI era'. Available at: https://landing.ai/wp-content/uploads/2020/05/LandingAI_Transformation_Playbook_11-19.pdf (accessed August 2023) ; 11 Harvard Business Publishing: Hagiu, A. and Wright, J. (2020) 'When data creates competitive advantage'. Harvard Business Review, 98(1), 94–101; 11 NFX Capital Management: Currier, J. (2020) 'What makes data valuable: The truth about data network effects'. Available at: https://www.nfx.com/post/truth-about-data-network-effects (accessed August 2023); 13 SAGE Publications: Adner, R. (2017) 'Ecosystem as structure: An actionable construct for strategy'. Journal of Management, 43(1), 39–58; 21 John Wiley & Sons, Inc: Gawer, A. and Cusumano, M. A. (2014) 'Industry platforms and ecosystem innovation'. Journal of Product Innovation Management, 31(3), 417–433; 59 Jeff Bezos: Jeff Bezos, The Power of Invention, amazon.com. Retreived from https://s2.q4cdn.com/299287126/files/doc_financials/annual/letter.PDF; 60 Tino Kreßner: Crowdfunding.de (2020) '"Unser Mut und die ständige Experimentierfreude haben sich über zehn Jahre ausgezahlt" – Interview zu 10 Jahren Startnext' [Translated from German, written interview]. Available at: https://www.crowdfunding.de/magazin/interview-zu-10-jahre-startnext/ (accessed August 2023); 62 Emerald Publishing Limited: Allio, R. (2004) 'CEO Interview: The InnoCentive model of open innovation'. Strategy & Leadership, 32(4). Available at:https://www.emerald.com/insight/content/doi/10.1108/10878570410547643/full/html (accessed August 2023); 63 Andrew Medal: Medal, A. (2014) 'The story of how GitHub supplied software its teeth'. Available at: https://www.linkedin.com/pulse/20141029195334-25909192-the-story-of-how-github-suppliedsoftware-its-teeth/ (accessed August 2023); 64 Hugging Face: (2023) 'Hugging Face collaborates with Microsoft to launch Hugging Face model catalog on Azure'. Available at: https://huggingface.co/blog/hugging-face-endpoints-on-azure (accessed August 2023); 65 EuroSecurityTV aktuell: EuroSecurity TV aktuell. (2018) 'SAST, neues Startup der Bosch Gruppe geht

an den Start' [Translated from German, video interview]. Available at: https://www.youtube.com/watch?v=mY8Ri1oNB2s (accessed August 2023); 66 Maximilan von Löbbecke: Jaeschke, H. (2020) [Translated from German, audio interview]. Available at: https://anchor.fm/hauke-jaeschke/episodes/Agrora-6---Maximilian-von-Lbbecke-von-365FarmNet-AgTech-Avantgarde-Wie-365FarmNet-Landwirte-untersttzt--Betriebsprozesse-zu-digitalisieren-unddadurch-profitabler-zu-werden-eietnd (accessed August 2023); 67 Landing AI: Figure adapted from Ng, A. (2018) 'AI transformation playbook: How to lead your company into the AI era'. Available at: https://landing.ai/wp-content/uploads/2020/05/LandingAI_Transformation_Playbook_11-19.pdf (accessed August 2023); 67 NFX Capital Management: Levy-Weiss, G. (2021) 'The insider story of Waze'. Available at: https://www.nfx.com/post/theinsider-story-of-waze (accessed August 2023); 70 MIPIM world: MIPIM world. (2015) 'Meet the players – Allianz and Airbnb discuss the sharing economy'. Available at: https://www.youtube.com/watch?v=AJ40c4X8ahM (accessed August 2023); 72 futurebrains: Futurebrains. (2022) 'Bernd Weidmann über Community Building im B2B' [translated from German, video interview] Available at: https://www.youtube.com/watch?v=TJwHFtrkjWc&t=174s (accessed August 2023); 74 WTWH Media LLC: Budimir, M. (2021) 'Bosch Rexroth's crtlX store offers automation and control apps'. Available at: https://www.motioncontroltips.com/bosch-rexroths-ctrlx-store-offers-automation-and-controlapps/ (accessed August 2023).; 75 Uber Technologies Inc: The history of Uber, Newsroom, Uber. Retreived from https://www.uber.com/newsroom/history/ (accessed June 2023); 76 MEDIENHAUS Verlag GmbH: Kren, S. (2019) 'Die digitale Spedition' [translated from German, written interview]. Available at: https://www.it-zoom.de/mobile-business/e/die-digitale-spedition-24457/ (accessed August 2023); 78 Thomson Reuters: Copley, C. (2014) 'Mila sees big firms using web to outsource customer support'. Available at: https://www.reuters.com/article/us-mila-sharingeconomy-idUSBREA2U0UK20140331 (accessed August 2023); 82 Inkitt: Inkitt. (2017) 'Ali Albazaz, founder and CEO, Inkitt, on BBC' [video interview]. Available at: https://www.youtube.com/watch?v=cHuPshSqTQE (accessed August 2023); 84 Penske Media Corporation: Littleton, C. (2021) 'How MasterClass CEO David Rogier brought star power to online learning'. Variety. Available at: https://variety.com/2021/digital/news/masterclass-classescovid-ceo-david-rogier-1234951028/ (accessed August 2023); 86 Zendesk: 'See how Fiverr uses Zendesk Support to serve its thriving marketplace'. Available at: https://www.zendesk.com/customer/fiverr/ (accessed August 2023).; 88 Decisive Media Limited: Warwick, M. (2021) 'Digital banking service M-Pesa now the biggest fintech platform in Africa'. Telecom TV. Available at: https://www.telecomtv.com/content/digital-platforms-services/branchless-banking-service-m-pesa-is-now-the-biggest-fintech-platform-in-africa-42322/ (accessed August 2023).; 89 Funding Societies Pte: Funding Societies. (2021) 'Funding Societies: Survey reveals 72% of MSMEs in SEA boosted revenue with digital financing'. Available at: https://fundingsociet es.com/economic-impactsurvey#:~:text=Funding%20Societies%20%7C%20Modalku%20is%20the,Thailand%2C%20and%20 registered%20in%20Malaysia (accessed August 2023); 90 Crowdinvesting Compact: (2022). 'Seedmatch Interview – Die bisherigen Erfolge soqie kritisch gesehene Fundings der Anleger' [translated from German, written interview]. Available at: https://crowdinvestingcompact.de/journal/seedmatch-interview_2022-02/ (accessed August 2023).; 92 The Seattle Times: Long, K. A. (2021) 'In the 15 years since its launch, Amazon Web Services transformed how companies do business'. The Seattle Times. 13 March, 2021. Available at: https://www.seattletimes.com/business/amazon/in-the-15-years-since-its-launch-amazon-web-serviceshas-transformed-how-companies-do-business/ (accessed August 2023); 92 Amazon.com, Inc: Amazon Web Services Launches, March 14, 2006. Retrieved from [Quote on para. 1] https://press.aboutamazon.com/news-releases/news-release-details/amazon-web-services-launches-amazon-s3-simple-storage-service (accessed August 2023); 92 Tech Xplore: Long, K. K. (2021) 'In the 15 years since its launch, Amazon Web Services transformed how companies do business'. TechXplore. Available at: https://techxplore.com/news/2021-03-years-amazon-web-companies-business.html (accessed August 2023); 93 UiPath: Reminnyi, S. (2021) 'UiPath marketplace: Enhanced for the enterprise'. UiPath. Available at: https://www.uipath.com/blog/product-and-updates/uipath-marketplace-enhanced-forenterprise (accessed August 2023); 94 Sazbean: Worsham, A. (2008) 'Interview with James Lindenbaum, CEO of Heroku'. sazbean.com. Available at: https://sazbean.com/2008/05/29/interview-with-james-lindenbaum-ceo-ofheroku/ (accessed August 2023); 95 The New Stack: Cassel, D. (2021) 'Linus Torvalds on why open source solves the biggest problems'. The New Stack. Available at: https://thenewstack.io/linus-torvalds-on-why-open-source-solves-thebiggest-problems/ (accessed August 2023); 99 Andreessen Horowitz: Lutwak, T. and Chung, Y. (2013) 'The lion, the platform, and the lesson'. a16z.com. Available at: https://a16z.com/2013/12/18/the-lion-the-platform-and-the-lesson/ (accessed August 2023); 100 Mumbrella Asia Pte Ltd: By 2036 – Alibaba wants 2 billion customers, 10 million businesses, 100 million staff, Mumbrella Asia, 2018. Retrieved from https://www.mumbrella.asia/2018/10/by-2036-alibaba-is-aiming-for-2-billion-customers-10-million-profitable-businesses-and-100-million-staff [letter to shareholders] (accessed August 2023); 100 Startbase GmbH: Gerhardt, J. (2022) 'Instafreight raises US$40 million'. Available at: https://www.startbase.com/news/instafreight-sammelt-40-millionen-us-dollar-ein/ (accessed August 2023); 101 World Economic Forum: Jacobides, M. G., Sundararajan, A. and Van Alstyne, M. (2019) 'Platforms and ecosystems: Enabling the digital economy'. In WEF Briefing Paper. Available at: https://www3.weforum.org/docs/WEF_Digital_Platforms_and_Ecosystems_2019.pdf (accessed August 2023); 102 VC Café: Vidra, E. (2009) 'Utest defines the future of quality assurance: CEO interview'. Available at: https://www.vccafe.com/2009/04/08/utest-defines-the-future-of-quality-assurance-ceointerview/ (accessed August 2023); 103 Corporate Valley: Corporate Valley. (2013) 'Exclusive interview with Pierre Omidyar – Founder of eBay Inc.' Available at: https://www.youtube.com/watch?v=Yy-p5i4Vimo (accessed August 2023);

105 Yahoo: Butcher, M. (2022) 'As our populations age, this startup is turning li-in care into a gig-economy platform'. Available at: https://techcrunch.com/2022/08/23/as-our-populations-age-thisstartup-is-turning-live-in-care-into-a-gig-economy-platform/ (accessed August 2023); 107 Skift: Oates, G. (2016) 'Airbnb CTO and 3 tech CTOs discuss the digital platform economy at Davos'. Available at: https://skift.com/2016/01/31/airbnb-cto-and-3-tech-ceos-discuss-thedigital-platform-economy-at-davos/ (accessed August 2023); 107 EnsembleIQ: Johnsen, M. (2016) 'The long game: Fitbit positioning to be key digital health partner'. Available at: https://drugstorenews.com/news/long-game-fitbit-positioning-be-key-digital-health-partner (accessed August 2023); 109 The Linux Foundation: Starting an Open Source Project, The Linux Foundation. Retreived from https://www.linuxfoundation.org/resources/open-source-guides/starting-an-open-sourceproject (accessed August 2023); 112 Business Insider Deutschland GmbH: Scherkamp, H. (2019) 'Warum Nutzer diesem Gründer Geld zahlen? Um ihre Nachbarn kennenzulernen' [translated from German, written interview]. Available at: https://www.businessinsider.de/gruenderszene/business/christian-vollmann-nebenan-de-interview/ (accessed August 2023); 113-114 Time USA LLC: Walt, V. (2022) 'It's expensive to be poor. This CEO wants to reduce "antiquated" bank fees and wait times'. Time. Available at: https://time.com/6132715/dan-schulman-ceo-paypalinterview/ (accessed August 2023); 115 Medium Corporation: Schenker, J. L. (2020) 'Interview of the week: Joerg Hellwig'. Available at: https://innovator.news/interview-of-the-week-joerg-hellwig-26637edb59a3 (accessed August 2023); 117 Compagnie Financière Richemont SA: (2022) 'Richemont, FARFETCH and Alabbar cement partnership to advance the digitalisation of the luxury industry'. Available at: https://www.richemont.com/en/home/media/press-releasesand-news/richemont-farfetch-and-alabbar-cement-partnership-to-advance-the-digitalisationof-the-luxury-industry/ (accessed August 2023); 122 Skift: Oates, G. (2016) 'Airbnb CTO and 3 tech CTOs discuss the digital platform economy at Davos'. Available at: https://skift.com/2016/01/31/airbnb-cto-and-3-tech-ceos-discuss-thedigital-platform-economy-at-davos/ (accessed August 2023); 125 Stratechery LLC: Ben Thompson (2022) 'An interview with Opendoor CEO Eric Wu about building a marketplace in a real estate slowdown'. Available at: https://stratechery.com/2022/an-interview-with-opendoor-ceo-eric-wu-about-building-a-marketplace-in-a-real-estate-slowdown/ (accessed August 2023).; 130 Wright's Media: Weintraub, S. (2022) 'Tesla App Store concept is so real you can almost touch it'. Available at: https://electrek.co/2022/02/16/tesla-app-store-concept-is-so-real-you-can-almost-touch-it/ (accessed June 2023); 132 The Linux Foundation: Starting an Open Source Project, The Linux Foundation. Retreived from https://www.linuxfoundation.org/resources/open-source-guides/starting-an-open-sourceproject (accessed June 2023); 136 Los Angeles Times: Piller, C. (1997) 'Apple may be ready to cease cloning about'. Los Angeles Times. 4 August 1997. Available at: https://www.latimes.com/archives/la-xpm-1997-aug-04-fi-19214-story.html//; https://www.macobserver.com/features/power.shtml (accessed June 2023); 138 Harvard Business Publishing: Tong, W.,

Guo, Y. and Chen, L. (2021) 'How Xiaomi redefined what it means to be a platform'. Harvard Business Review. Available at: https://hbr.org/2021/09/how-xiaomi-redefined-what-itmeans-to-be-a-platform (accessed June 2023); 140 Bosch Rexroth AG: This is just the beginning!, Ctrix Automation. Retreived from https://apps.boschrexroth.com/microsites/ctrlx-automation/en/news-stories/story/this-is-just-the-beginning/ (accessed August 2023); 142 Gizchina Media: Udin, E. (2021) 'Tim Cook explains why Apple will not open up the iOS system'. Gizchina. Available at: https://www.gizchina.com/2021/10/29/tim-cook-explains-why-apple-will-notopen-up-the-ios-system/ (accessed August 2023); 146 Dow Jones & Company, Inc: Albergotti, R. (2014) 'Instagram CEO Systrom: "We can't be just a hedge" for Facebook'. The Wall Street Journal. 10 December 2014. Available at: https://www.wsj.com/amp/articles/instagram-ceo-systrom-we-cant-be-just-a-hedge-for-facebook-1418227334 (accessed August 2023); 147 CNBC: CNBC. (2018) 'Steve Jobs 1997 interview: Defending his commitment to Apple'. Available at: https://www.youtube.com/watch?v=xchYT9wz5hk (accessed August 2023); 148 Yahoo: Arrington, M. (2009) 'Davos interviews: Etsy founder Robert Kalin'. Available at: https://techcrunch.com/2009/02/01/davos-interviews-etsy-founder-robert-kalin/ (accessed August 2023); 150 Hunt Scanlon Media: (2010) 'Interview: Indeed.com founder discusses online recruitment'. Available at: https://huntscanlon.com/interview-indeed-com-founder-discusses-online-recruitment/ (accessed August 2023); 151 Regionalmedien AG: Schurter, D. (2021) 'Threema ist das neue Whats-App – und schlägt die Konkurrenz um Längen'. Available at: https://www.watson.ch/!298079852 (accessed August 2023); 153 Starthouse Bremen and Bremerhaven: Raveling, J. (2022) 'Der Duft Asiens in einer Dose'. Starthaus. Available at: https://www.starthaus-bremen.de/de/page/mediathek/stories/yummy-organics (accessed August 2023); 154 LinkedIn Corporation: (2005) 'LinkedIn launches premium service for recruiters and researchers'. Available at: https://news.linkedin.com/2005/08/linkedin-launches-premium-service-for-recruiters-and-researchers (accessed August 2023); 156 Zalando: Bringing Our Customer Promise to the Next Level, Annual Report 2017, Zalando. Retreived from https://annual-report.zalando.com/2017/magazine/zalando-plus-bringing-our-customer-promise-to-the-next-level/ (accessed August 2023); 159 Seeking Alpha: Oakland, T. (2022) 'Opendoor: The art of winning an unfair game'. Seeking Alpha. Available at: https://seekingalpha.com/article/4490583-opendoor-the-art-of-winning-an-unfair-game (accessed August 2023); 160 TechCrunch: TechCrunch. (2011) 'Tr'pAdvisor's Stephen Kaufer – Founder stories'. Available at: https://www.youtube.com/watch?v=5JBa9ZH1i1M (accessed August 2023); 160 Recode: Recode. (2018) 'Full interview: Susan Wojcicki, CEO of YouTube, at Code Media'. Available at: https://www.youtube.com/watch?v=klQZLssoyI4&t=1063s (accessed August 2023); 163 The Business journals: Collins, L. (2018). 'Farmobile launches nationwide data marketplace for "the infinite commodity"'. Kansas City Business Journal. Available at: https://www.bizjournals.com/kansascity/news/2018/07/18/farmobile-launches-nationwide-data-marketplace.html (accessed August 2023); 164 Cable News Network: Quest Means Business, Transcripts. Retreived from https://transcripts.cnn.com/show/qmb/date/2015-03-02/segment/01 (accessed August 2023); 169 The New York Times Company: Irwin, I. (2014) 'Uber's Travis Kalanick explains his pricing experiment'. New York Times. 11 July 2014. Available at: https://www.nytimes.com/2014/07/12/upshot/ubers-traviskalanick-explains-his-pricing-experiment.html (accessed August 2023); 171 Peter Thiel: Peter Thiel: Escape the Competition, The Podcase. Retrieved from https://s3.amazonaws.com/he-product-images/docs/Podcase_transcript_A.pdf?elqTrackId=f086091397a74b1d82f8a23d4ebb0fba&elqaid=124&elqat=2 (accessed August 2023); 173 Cdixon: Come for the tool, stay for the network, Cdixon January 1,2015. Retreived from https://cdixon.org/2015/01/31/come-for-the-tool-stay-for-the-network (accessed June 2023); 173 Substack Inc: Rachitsky, L. (2019) 'How to kickstart and scale a marketplace business'. Available at: https://www.lennysnewsletter.com/p/how-to-kickstart-and-scale-a-marketplace (accessed August 2023); 174 Substack Inc: Rachitsky, L. (2019) 'How to kickstart and scale a marketplace business'. Available at: https://www.lennysnewsletter.com/p/how-to-kickstart-and-scale-a-marketplace-911?s=r (accessed August 2023); 174 W. W. Norton & Company: Parker, G., Van Alstyne, M. and Choudary, S. (2016) Platform Revolution: How Networked Markets Are Transforming the Economy and How to Make Them Work for You. New York: W. W. Norton & Company; 175 Substack Inc: Rachitsky, L. (2019) 'How to kickstart and scale a marketplace business'. Available at: https://www.lennysnewsletter.com/p/how-to-kickstart-and-scale-a-marketplace (accessed August 2023); 177 Google Inc: Google Announces $10 Million Android Developer Challenge, Google news from Google. Retrieved from http://googlepress.blogspot.com/2007/11/google-announces-10-million-android_12.html (accessed August 2023); 181 Harvard Business Publishing: Gassmann, O. and Ferrandina, F. (2021) 'Die Win-win-win Formel' [translated from German]. Available at: https://www.alexandria.unisg.ch/server/api/core/bitstreams/78ebcba9-f857-4435-9bcd-05c9923f4540/content (accessed August 2023); 184 Gisbert Rühl: (2021) 'Gisbert Rühl: Leading digital transformation at a century old German steel distributor'. Available at: https://web.archive.org/web/20220118041815/ https://kreatize.com/blog/launchpad/gisbert-ruehl-interview-digital-transformation/ (accessed August 2023); 186 TechCrunch: Lomas, N. (2022) 'Babylon Health dials back some services in the UK'. Available at: https://techcrunch.com/2022/08/09/babylon-health-nhs-contracts-ended/ (accessed August 2023); 188 VC Café: Vidra, E. (2009) 'Utest defines the future of quality assurance: CEO interview'. Available at: https://www.vccafe.com/2009/04/08/utest-defines-the-future-of-quality-assurance-ceointerview/ (accessed August 2023); 188 Substack Inc: Rachitsky, L. (2019) 'How to kickstart and scale a marketplace business'. Available at: https://www.lennysnewsletter.com/p/how-to-kickstart-and-scale-a-marketplace-911?s=r (accessed August 2023); 188 Harvard Business Publishing: Tong, T. W., Guo, Y. and Chen, L. (2021) 'How Xiaomi redefined what it means to be a platform'. Harvard Business Review. Available at: https://hbr.org/2021/09/how-xiaomiredefined-what-it-means-to-be-a-platform (accessed August 2023); 190 Substack Inc: Rachitsky, L. (2019) 'Accelerating growth at scale: Phase 2 of kickstarting and scaling a market-place business'. Lenny's Newsletter. Available at: https://www.lennysnewsletter.com/p/accelerating-growth-at-scale-phase (accessed August 2023); 192

PhoneArena: Victor, H. (2012) 'Here is why Google blocked Acer's Aliyun smartphone launch'. Phone Arena. Available at: https://www.phonearena.com/news/Here-is-why-Google-blocked-Acers-Aliyunsmartphone-launch_id34535 (accessed August 2023); 195 Vox Media, LLC: (2017) 'Full transcript: Instagram CEO Kevin Systrom on. Recode decode'. Vox. Available at: https://www.vox.com/2017/6/22/15849966/transcript-instagram-ceo-kevin-systromfacebook-photo-video-recode-decode (accessed August 2023).; 197 CustomerThink Corp: Michelli, J. (2021) 'Customer experience excellence: The Airbnb way'. Customer Think. Available at: https://customerthink.com/create-belonging-customer-experience-excellence-the-airbnb-way/ (accessed August 2023); 197 CNBC: CNBC Television. (2020) 'Watch CNBC's full interview with PayPal CEO Dan Schulman at Davos'. Available at: https://www.youtube.com/watch?v=nAM9uKJpDxM (accessed August 2023); 198 Medium Corporation: Schenker, J. L. (2020) 'Interview of the week: Joerg Hellwig'. Available at: https://innovator.news/interview-of-the-week-joerg-hellwig-26637edb59a3 (accessed August 2023); 198 Mansueto Ventures LLC: Tabaka, M. (2019) 'Amazon's 4 keys to success, according to Jeff Bezos'. Available at: https://www.inc.com/marla-tabaka/jeff-bezos-says-these-4-principles-are-key-to-amazons-successthey-can-work-for-you-too.html (accessed August 2023); 200 Charlie Rose: Rose, C. (2006) 'Preview of interview with YouTube co-founders'. Available at: https://www.youtube.com/watch?v=7E6E9q8Jebw (accessed August 2023); 202 Apple Inc: Apple's Find My network now offers new third-party finding experiences, Newsroom, Apple 2021. Retreived from https://www.apple.com/newsroom/2021/04/apples-find-my-network-now-offers-new-thirdparty-finding-experiences/ (accessed August 2023); 204 TechCabal: Adeleke, D. (2015) 'How Facebook "owned" MySpace'. Tech Cabal. Available at: https://techcabal.com/2015/11/10/how-facebook-owned-myspace/ (accessed August 2023); 204 Neue Zürcher Zeitung: (2021) 'China verhängt Milliardenstrafe gegen Internetriese Alibaba – angeblich wegen Verstoß gegen Wettbewerbsrecht'. Neue Zürcher Zeitung. Available at: https://www.nzz.ch/wirtschaft/china-verhaengt-milliardenstrafe-gegen-internetriese-alibaba-ld.1611231?reduced=true (accessed August 2023); 206 Meta: Lawsuits Filed by the FTC and the State Attorneys General Are Revisionist History, Jennifer Newstead (2020), Meta. https://about.fb.com/news/2020/12/lawsuits-filed-by-the-ftc-and-state-attorneys-general-are-revisionist-history/ (accessed August 2023); 207 NPR: Bond, S. (2020) '"The wrath of Mark": 4 takeaways from the government's case against Facebook'. NPR. Available at: https://www.npr.org/2020/12/11/945234491/the-wrath-of-mark-takeawaysfrom-the-governments-case-against-facebook?t=1660722432117 (accessed August 2023); 208 MediaNews Group: Somerville, H. (2015) 'Lyft's CEO Logan Green: On why being nice pays off, and getting back to its roots'. The Mercury News. 12 February 2015. Available at: https://www.mercurynews.com/2015/02/12/lyfts-ceo-logan-green-on-why-being-nice-pays-off-and-getting-back-to-its-roots/ (accessed August 2023); 208 World Economic Forum: Jacobides, M. G., Sundararajan, A. and Van Alstyne, M. (2019) 'Platforms and ecosystems: Enabling the digital economy'. In WEF Briefing Paper. Available at: https://www3.weforum.org/docs/WEF_Digital_Platforms_and_Ecosystems_2019.pdf

(accessed August 2023); 209 CNBC: CNBC Television. (2020) 'Watch CNBC's full interview with PayPal CEO Dan Schulman at Davos'. Available at: https://www.youtube.com/watch?v=nAM9uKJpDxM (accessed August 2023); 213 Tim Cook: Quotes from Tim Cook, Retrieved from https://twitter.com/tim_cook/status/1487100529251520512?ref_src=twsrc%5Etfw%7Ctwcamp%5Etweetembed%7Ctwterm%5E1487100529251520512%7Ctwgr%5E663a97d57b02ef0ddf0d8f69fc6ef058eb2cc96c%7Ctwcon%5Es1_&ref_url=https%3A%2F%2F www.redditmedia.com%2Fmediaembed%2Fseusxn%3Fresponsive%3Dtrueis_nightmode%3Dfalse (accessed August 2023); 214 The News Minute: Suresh, H. (2021) '"We have no data with us to sell to anyone": Signal CEO Aruna Harder to TNM'. The News Minute. 18 January 2021. Available at: https://www.thenewsminute.com/article/we-have-no-data-us-sell-anyone-signal-coo-aruna-harder-tnm-141678 (accessed August 2023); 214 Health Business group: Interview with Ben Heywood, CEO of PatientsLikeMe (transcript), health Business Group. Retrieved from https://www.healthbusinessgroup.com/blog/2008/01/interview-with-ben-heywood-ceo-of-patientslikeme-transcript (accessed August 2023); 215-216 The New York Times Company: The New York Times. (2017) 'Full interview: Uber C.E.O Dara Khosroshahi'. Available at: https://www.youtube.com/watch?v=Mo2-4sXYZxU (accessed August 2023); 218 The Singju Post: Pangambam, S. (2014) 'Apple CEO Tim Cook keynote at WWDC June 14 Transcript'. The Singju Post. Available at: https://singjupost.com/apple-ceo-tim-cook-keynote-wwdc-june-2014-transcript/?singlepage=1 (accessed August 2023); 218 Nate Moch: Fireside chat with Nate Moch VP product teams at zillow and morgan brown coo at inman news defining true growth how do you find your north star metric, Retrieved from https://www.slideshare.net/growthhackers/growthhacker-conference-16-fireside-chat-with-nate-moch-vp-product-teams-at-zillow-and-morgan-brown-coo-at-inman-news-defining-true-growth-how-do-you-find-your-north-star-metric#5; 220 KrAsia: Jingli, S. (2019) 'Despite widening losses, Pinduoduo continues to prioritize user engagement over monetization (updated)'. KrAsia. Available at: https://kr-asia.com/pinduoduo-hits-123-yearon-year-revenue-growth-narrows-gap-with-alibaba-in-user-count (accessed August 2023); 220 Handelsblatt GmbH: Interview of Christian Bertermann by Stephan Knieps in Wirtschaftswoche (1 December, 2020) [translated from German, written interview]. Available at: https://www.wiwo.de/erfolg/gruender/auto1-mitgruender-christian-bertermann-im-jahr-2000-hat-man-ja-auch-ueberlegt-ob-jemandein-buch-online-kaufen-wuerde-/26654048-2.html (accessed August 2023); 221 Investment Knowledge: Investment Knowledge. (2019) 'Jeff Bezon explains why Amazon makes no profit (2014)'. Available at: https://www.youtube.com/watch?v=Ue9uW1K_RJw (accessed August 2023).

Image credit

COV – Shutterstock : Pro Symbols/Shutterstock.

Preface

If you want to understand what platform business means for your company, derive concrete platform opportunities or develop and implement a sustainable platform business model, *The Platform Business Navigator* is here to help you.

Platform companies like Amazon, Alibaba, Apple or Google dominate today's economy. However, in our daily work we still see that companies, entrepreneurs and students are confused about platforms and their mechanisms. Most platform initiatives fail, and established companies, in particular, struggle with this new notion of doing business. The reasons are manifold. There is often no common understanding of platform business fundamentals. Platform opportunities and network effects are not recognised. Platform strategies are overwhelming and not concise enough to be effectively communicated and executed in organisations. The necessary mindset shift towards thinking in ecosystems and network effects is just not taking place.

At the same time, we see that it is no longer just digital companies that have embarked on a platform journey. Today, companies like Bosch, CLAAS, Daimler, Heidelberg, Hilti, LANXESS, Lego, Siemens, Sony and Swisscom have developed and implemented platform business models. Every product, service and retail business has a promising potential for platform models – either as a platform owner, complementor or user. Platforms will affect many traditional industries, and leveraging network effects will be vital for each and every company. The Internet of Things, for example, presents many new opportunities for traditional companies to platformise their existing business. It is no longer a matter of choosing between platforms and products. Instead, product companies are beginning to mesh their product business models with platform business models to take advantage of network effects. Every company has to understand and act upon the platform logic in order to create and sustain competitive advantage.

This evidence was the starting point for us to develop the Platform Business Navigator and to provide a toolkit for interested and engaged leaders, regardless of whether you are managing a product, a project, a business unit, a division or a whole company. Building upon the success of *The Business Model Navigator* and based on a systematic literature review and empirical study of more than 400 platform cases, we derived 88 patterns along five steps: ideate, design, monetise, scale and manage platforms. Not all patterns in the book will be helpful for your business, and the patterns are certainly not exhaustive. But we believe that every manager should be aware of the patterns to sustain competitive advantage.

There is certainly a lot of great platform literature out there, such as *Platform Revolution*, *The Business of Platforms*, *Winning the Right Game*, which inspired us when developing this book. Our objective is to focus on 'how to do platforms' and try to foster your business model journey with actionable, hands-on insights. Ultimately, you need compelling cases to derive and communicate a platform idea and convince others in your organisation that it will succeed. This is what our book is all about: It's a well-researched and easy-to-digest collection of 88 patterns with successful and insightful examples from practice. To complement the book, a physical card set is also available, which can be used in strategy, consulting or innovation workshops.

Ultimately, the Platform Business Navigator is not just relevant for those who build a platform. Every manager with P&L responsibility has to understand how platform business can help the existing product and service business to create and capture additional value. Every CEO and product manager has to reflect on how to position their offerings within the platform economy: How can you create and capture value in the networked economy? How can you create a connected business in the new world? The best way to do this is to put yourself in the driver's seat and develop your own platform business model. Therefore, after reading our book you will be able to. . .

- establish a common understanding of platform business in your company;
- illustrate the diversity of platforms to inspire others with meaningful examples;
- identify platform opportunities and leverage network effects for your business;
- make key design decisions for viable platform business models;
- define concrete implementation measures to bring a platform to life

. . .for your project, team or organisation.

We hope you enjoy reading *The Platform Business Navigator* and wish you every success in the implementation of your platform initiatives!

St. Gallen/Boston, Summer 2023

Felix Wortmann
Sven Jung
Oliver Gassmann

How to use the book

This book is not intended simply to be read from front to back. Based on our platform business teaching and consulting experience, we have learned that it is most effective to follow a three-step approach: (1) learn the platform fundamentals, (2) understand the logic of the Platform Business Navigator and (3) let the patterns inspire your innovation and strategy work. Where you start depends on your previous experience and your current situation:

- **Chapters 1 and 2 in Part One** introduce platform thinking and the fundamentals of platform business models. These chapters are important for someone who has not had many touchpoints with platforms yet. Our goal was to summarise the essence and core concepts of the existing literature. If you already have experience with platforms, you can skip this part.

- **Chapter 3 in Part One** introduces the Platform Business Navigator, its underlying structure and core logic. It also gives a very concise idea of each pattern so that you can effectively dive into the individual patterns later.

- **Chapters 1 to 5 in Part Two** are the heart of the book and consist of one- to three-page profiles of each of the 88 patterns providing quick reference and inspiration during innovation and strategy work. We take you on a deep dive into each pattern by providing multiple real-world examples, quotes from leaders and actionable questions to help you apply the pattern to your context. This section is not geared towards platform fundamentals anymore. So that you can enjoy reading the patterns independently, we provide a brief introduction with an overview at the beginning of each chapter. This brings you up to speed and gives you the context you need.

While you can jump directly into a single pattern or a whole section of patterns in Part Two, we provide three concrete starting points for you:

1 **You have no platform idea yet** and want to brainstorm ideas: Use the ideate patterns.
2 **You have a viable platform idea** and need to design the underlying business model: Use the design and monetise patterns.
3 **You have one specific platform business model** and want to bring it to life: Use the scale and manage patterns.

Before you start reading, a quick final note: For ease of reading we have placed the references and interview quotes at the end of the book supplemented by suggestions for further reading. Additionally, it is important to acknowledge that the platform industry is constantly evolving. Some of the platform ventures discussed may no longer be active by the time of reading, but this does not necessarily render their concepts irrelevant.

[PART ONE]

Platform business innovation

How platform businesses work

1

Platforms dominate our economy

Platform companies like Amazon, Alibaba, Apple, Microsoft or Google dominate our economy. They are digital intermediaries connecting two or more distinct market sides, creating win–win situations. In fact, seven out of the ten most valuable companies worldwide were built upon a platform business model in 2021[1] – compared with only two out of ten in 2011.[2] Over the last decades, platform companies have been able to outperform traditional businesses as they established themselves as powerful intermediaries. Amazon and Alibaba, for example, facilitate transactions between sellers and buyers. Apple facilitates transactions between app developers and app users. Google facilitates transactions between ordinary web users and advertisers. It is also evident that many more platforms are on the rise and have the potential to disrupt entire industries, from retail, tourism and transportation to regulated industries such as healthcare or law.

The widespread success of platform companies is based on network effects. In essence, network effects describe a situation where more users lead to more value.[3] Messaging platforms like Signal, Telegram or WhatsApp have no value if you are the only person using it. You can only message yourself. With more and more family members, friends or colleagues joining the messenger, network effects kick in and the value of the messenger dramatically increases for the corresponding user. This is in stark contrast to, for example, a weather app. The utility of a weather app does not depend on the number of other users. It does not matter to you if your family and friends use the same weather app as you do. In fact, the value the weather app provides to you does not increase with them adopting the app.

Platforms are also relevant for established companies

Compared with traditional businesses that own and build up their own assets (e.g. real estate in the case of a hotel chain), a significant number of platforms only provide the digital infrastructure for interactions between the respective market sides (e.g. interactions between apartment owners and travellers in the case of Airbnb).[4] Accordingly, a large number of successful platforms are digital in nature and asset-light. But it is not just digital companies that have embarked on a platform journey. Established companies are just as affected by the shift to platform business models. Many companies have tried to extend their traditional business models and have launched their own platform businesses. For instance, the chemical company LANXESS has developed CheMondis, a B2B and manufacturer-independent marketplace for trading chemicals. Similarly, Klöckner & Co has established XOM Materials, a marketplace for trading steel and materials. With 365FarmNet, the agricultural machinery manufacturer CLAAS has developed a farm management platform for automated documentation in the field and in the stable. The platform leverages data from connected machinery and features an app store, somewhat comparable to that of a smartphone, only for a different domain. The success and business opportunities of platforms make it almost inevitable for a manager or entrepreneur to engage in the platform economy, whether by building their own platform business from scratch, participating in an existing platform as a complementor (partner) or by becoming a platform user.

Platforms are a challenging endeavour

Looking at well-known platform giants like Amazon, Google, Microsoft or Airbnb, building and managing a platform business model might not seem to be a challenging endeavour. However, most platform initiatives fail,[5] and even experienced platform companies like Google struggle to make their nascent platform projects a success. For instance, Google has not been able to scale Google+ and Google Health. Apple's operating system for computers, macOS, lagged behind Microsoft Windows for a long time in the 1990s.[6] Even being the first platform in a given market is no guarantee for success. The payment platform Billpoint was overtaken by PayPal despite its first-mover advantage. Examples such as Predix by General Electric (GE) and MindSphere by Siemens also show how difficult it is to build platforms in emerging domains such as the Internet of Things (IoT). In fact, there are many reasons (both internal and external) why platforms have failed. First and foremost, most platforms struggle with the nature of network effects and specifically the challenge of establishing them.[7] Many industries are also confronted by the platform paradox: Everyone wants to create a platform, but nobody wants to join a platform of other ecosystem players.[8] As a result, none of the platform initiatives can build up viable network effects and, consequently, none of the platforms become successful.

What to expect in the next sections

Considering the opportunities and challenges, this book is designed to give guidance on platform ideation, design and management with the help of many real-world cases. However, we begin by demystifying the platform concept about which there is still so much misunderstanding and confusion. By relying on existing literature, we provide you with the fundamentals and knowledge to make the most of our 88 platform patterns that are presented in Part Two of this book.

From pipeline to platform business

Reuse as the essence of early platform thinking

While digitalisation has been a fundamental driver for platformisation, traits of platform thinking have already existed before. For example, car manufacturers like Volkswagen or camera manufacturers like Nikon have utilised product platforms. While each camera model consists of a few unique features, most of these products are based on an underlying product platform that comprises reusable components that can be shared across models. The primary goal was to make production more efficient and enable a broad portfolio of products at competitive cost.[9] However, when we talk about today's leading platforms – the Amazons, Apples or Airbnbs – we usually have a second platform notion in mind that is based on network effects between different market sides and joint value creation.

Platforms facilitate transactions and enable complementary innovation

With the Microsoft Windows platform, Microsoft developed an operating system that enabled other software companies like Adobe or Electronic Arts to build complementary applications on top of Windows (a PDF viewer and computer games, respectively). In comparison with a traditional pipeline business where companies seek to optimise their internal value chain, Microsoft optimised its offering so that other developers could complement Microsoft's own offering. Shifting value creation from the inside to the outside gave Microsoft Windows a competitive advantage in the years to follow as numerous complementary software solutions were developed. The Windows platform was able to scale fast because Microsoft did not have to create all the competitive assets, such as complementary applications, but instead drew value from external resources.[10] This, in turn, benefitted the adoption of Windows in the early years, making it the leading operating system; in turn, Apple's operating system was left behind at that time as Apple only opened up to external developers much later.[11]

Platforms fundamentally differ from pipeline business models

Traditional companies with so-called pipeline business models are characterised by a linear value chain with a well-directed value flow from suppliers to customers.[12] The value accumulates and increases as the good or service moves from the supplier to the (end) customer.[13] For example, the automotive manufacturer Daimler creates value by owning resources and controlling the automotive value chain, from sourcing components to designing, manufacturing and marketing cars. In this way, Daimler and other pipeline companies can capture the value created in the value chain steps that they control.

Platforms are digital intermediaries bringing two or more sides together

Platform companies are intermediaries that bring two or more sides of a market (customer groups) together (see Figure 1.1.1).[15] Airbnb brings hosts and travellers together to facilitate stays, Amazon connects sellers and buyers of products and Kickstarter links investors and entrepreneurs to exchange money and bring ideas to life. WhatsApp brings people together to exchange messages and photos, and Apple brings app developers and smartphone users together through their App Store. This is in stark contrast to pipeline companies where value moves from left to right in the value chain. A platform derives value from both sides of its value chain.[16]

Figure 1.1.1 Platform business models are digital intermediaries

Host	Airbnb	Traveller
Seller	Amazon	Buyer
Investors	Kickstarter	Entrepreneurs
Content provider	WhatsApp	Content consumer
App developer	Apple	Smartphone user

Providers
Market side 1

Consumers
Market side 2

Platform
❯ Rules
❯ Infrastructure

Source: Adapted from Van Alstyne, Parker and Choudary (2016) and Eisenmann, Parker and Van Alstyne (2006)[14]

Platforms provide infrastructure and rules to facilitate interactions

Platforms provide the digital infrastructure as well as rules for the different market sides to interact with each other, to enable transactions (transaction platforms like eBay) and/or to enable innovation (innovation platforms like Microsoft Windows). Amazon, for example, provides digital (e.g. Amazon website) and physical infrastructure (e.g. warehouses) for its buyers and sellers. Moreover, it sets strict rules for how interactions are conducted, e.g. by enforcing well-defined payment and shipping terms and conditions. Platforms often focus on the provision of a digital infrastructure and hence are rather asset-light. This also allows them to scale faster than traditional companies: Think about Airbnb (who owns no real estate) versus traditional hotel chains (who owns real estate), Amazon marketplace (who has no assets on the balance sheet) versus a classic e-commerce company (who puts assets on the balance sheet), or Uber (who owns no cars) versus a taxi company (who owns taxis). But it is not always black and white as today's platforms start to become more asset-heavy. Just think about Amazon, which owns physical warehouses and has built up significant logistics capabilities.

Platforms are based on network effects

While platforms can take many forms, network effects are core to every platform. They refer to the dynamic that the platform's value increases with the number of platform participants: 'the more users who adopt the platform, the more valuable the platform becomes to the owner and to the users because of growing access to the network of users and often to a growing set of complementary innovations'.[17] Due to a lack of network effects, many online stores, such as simple fashion online stores, are often incorrectly portrayed as platform businesses. Similarly, Amazon started as an online merchandiser selling books via an online shop and not as a platform business. No network effects were present in the beginning. It was only by transforming the online store into an open marketplace with third-party vendors that Amazon became the thriving platform business model with network effects we know today.

Shifting the focus from inside to outside

Many traditional companies have a hard time with the platform concept. For years, they have been pursuing a classic value chain approach with the strategic goal of optimising their internal activities. Platform business models are quite the opposite as they primarily focus on external resources and try to coordinate and optimise those instead of internal ones.[18] Think about Airbnb again: While hotel chains would focus on optimising their own assets, i.e. real estate and service capabilities, to increase revenue and decrease costs, Airbnb focuses on increasing external excellence and productivity, e.g. how can apartment owners offer high-quality apartments to guests in ways that are easier, safer, better, faster? Apple has been very rigorous in shifting its strategic focus from the inside to outside. Why did Apple introduce the new programming language Swift in 2014, although there was Objective-C, a well-established programming language in the Apple ecosystem? Was it because they wanted to increase internal developer productivity? Well, maybe, but certainly they had to act in light of competition, i.e. Google Android with its Java programming language. The Objective-C programming language could not compete with faster, safer and more modern programming languages such as Java. It was just too complicated and took too long for the huge app developer ecosystem to develop or update an Objective-C application. Apple has invested hundreds of millions to develop and introduce Swift. Instead of seeing developers simply as suppliers, Apple recognised their value and made their lives easier.

It is a customer and not a supplier

Unlike a pipeline company, where there is usually only one end customer, platforms always have two or more types of customers. Each of the market sides represents a customer and must be treated as such. This is often neglected by managers from established companies who only think of the end customer. Think about Uber – who is the customer in the case of the ride-hailing platform? Is it the tourist ordering a cab on Uber? Or is it the Uber driver? Actually, both sides of the market (Uber drivers and users) must be treated as customers with their individual, and often different, needs. Who is the customer in the case of Android? Manufacturers of devices (e.g. HTC, Samsung), app developers (e.g. Epic Games) and smartphone users are Android's customers. Eisenmann summarises this fundamental difference between pipeline and platform business models very well: 'In traditional value chains, value moves from left to right: To the left of the company is cost; to the right is revenue. In two-sided networks, cost and revenue are both to the left and the right.'[19] Platforms therefore require a change in thinking for managers of established companies. They only work if all market sides of a platform benefit and hence there are only customers, even if the respective parties provide the supply.

The flywheel of network effects

Direct and indirect network effects

Network effects are a key prerequisite for the success of platform companies, and platforms cannot thrive without them.[20] In essence, the more platform users there are, the greater the value of the platform to all users. This is in contrast to traditional products and services, which have a stand-alone value that is independent of the number of users. Hence, to become a successful platform, you have to be able to identify network effects and systematically nurture and manage them. Direct and indirect network effects can be distinguished (see Figure 1.1.2). Indirect (or cross-side) network effects refer to network effects between different market sides of a platform. In the case of Amazon, additional sellers leads to a larger product offering, which attracts more buyers. Vice versa, more buyers leads to an increased demand, which attracts additional sellers to join the platform. In comparison, direct (or same-side) network effects refer to the same side of the platform. For instance, in the case of Amazon, additional buyers leads to more product reviews, which, in turn, fosters trust and attracts additional buyers to the platform.

Figure 1.1.2 Platform success relies on direct and indirect network effects

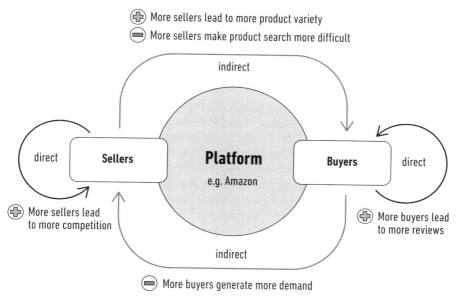

The nature of network effects

Strong network effects can lead to a virtuous circle such that both market sides are positively reinforcing each other. Metcalfe's law describes the nature of network effects and states that the value of a platform grows with the number of its users. More specifically, it states that the value of a platform increases in proportion to the square of the number of its users: $n (n - 1)/2$.[21] If the number of users doubles, the value increases fourfold. Reed's law proposes that the value of a network is even greater than what Metcalfe's law suggests: It posits that the value of a network increases exponentially with its size. Core to this law is the existence of subgroups, which are vital to the overall value of networks. Social media platforms, for instance, offer users the option to join or create various subgroups so that these networks can be more valuable than a larger network with less potential for creating subgroups. However, Metcalfe's law, as well as Reed's law, neglect important aspects of networks such as the level of individual engagement, quality of interaction and the fact that too many users can also overcrowd a network. The reality is much more complex than these helpful, yet oversimplified models.[22]

Network effects can also be negative

The example of Amazon also shows how positive network effects can turn into negative ones. If too many sellers join the platform, at some point buyers might become overwhelmed. Product search becomes cumbersome and leads to dozens of similar results which take significant time to compare. Consequently, negative indirect (cross-side) network effects kick in. If you look at the other side of the platform, additional sellers intensify the competition, making it less attractive for new sellers to join the platform. As a result, negative direct network effects might arise with a negative vicious cycle. Accordingly, successful platform companies are not only good at managing positive network effects, but also at preventing and mitigating negative ones.

Network effects can lead to winner-takes-all platforms

Depending on the platform type as well as the competition situation, network effects can generate so-called 'winner-takes-all platforms'.[23] A winner-takes-all situation emerges when there is only one platform or a very selective number of platforms addressing the entire demand in the market. Once the network has exceeded a certain number of users, it becomes very difficult for competitors to establish a second platform in the same segment. As a seller, why would you want to leverage an Amazon competitor that has far fewer customers on its marketplace? As a customer, why would you want to use an Amazon competitor that has higher prices (because of less seller competition), much smaller product variety and fewer reviews? The same is true for WhatsApp. After privacy concerns became known, many users, specifically in Europe, wanted to turn away from WhatsApp. In the end, however, most of them stayed because their family, friends and colleagues were all on the platform.

At the same time, companies often overestimate their chances of creating a winner-takes-all platform. Some industries, such as the credit card industry, are subject to multi-homing, i.e. the situation when platform users take advantage of competing platforms simultaneously.[24] In essence, multi-homing is characterised by low switching costs and the lack of platform lock-in mechanisms. For instance, people often use multiple credit cards at the same time, thereby relying on different payment platforms. Or they use both the Uber and Lyft apps for ride-hailing. Ultimately, the specific platform context is crucial for a winner-takes-all situation. While people use multiple credit cards and different ride-hailing apps, they often have only one smartphone and thus rely either on the Apple iOS or the Google Android platform. Other industries, specifically in the B2B space, face the platform paradox[25]: Everyone wants to create their own platform. Nobody wants to join the platforms of other ecosystem players. These are just two root causes why network effects often do not unfold. This in turn is the reason why only a few platforms are highly successful and thousands of platform initiatives from corporates and start-ups fail.

Data network effects as the new wave of network effects

In addition, data network effects have recently become an essential ingredient for platform success. They are also referred to as the 'virtuous cycle of AI'.[26] While the value from network effects is derived mainly from the interaction between the different platform users, the value from data network effects stems from user data, learning from it and scaling it across all users on the platform (see Figure 1.1.3).[28] In essence, data network effects are about more users leading to more data, and more data leading to better products and services, which ultimately attract more users.[29]

Figure 1.1.3 Network effects and data network effects

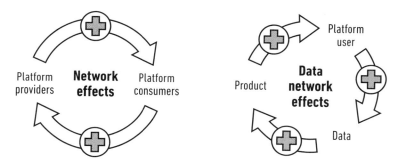

Source: Adapted from Ng (2018), Hagiu and Wright (2020) and Currier (2020)[27]

For instance, Amazon has a lot of user data and can therefore offer good and helpful product recommendations, which in turn attracts new users to Amazon. New users further increase Amazon's ability to provide more helpful recommendations. This creates a self-reinforcing flywheel effect. In essence, the greater the number of users who use Amazon, the better the Amazon product recommendation engine, the more users are attracted. The generative artificial intelligence chatbot ChatGPT also relies on data network effects: The greater the number of users who use ChatGPT, the more feedback ChatGPT receives. Incorporating the feedback, ChatGPT can further increase its performance and attract even more users, leading to a positive virtuous circle.

Product versus platform: It is not either or

While in the past, there was a rather clear distinction between product/pipeline and platform companies, the distinction has now become increasingly blurred. We have learned that network effects are tied to platforms, while stand-alone value is tied to products. But it is not black and white anymore as many companies are trying to play both games simultaneously. In essence, these companies implement and integrate different value propositions that rely on stand-alone value and network effects (see Figure 1.1.4).

Figure 1.1.4 Product versus platform

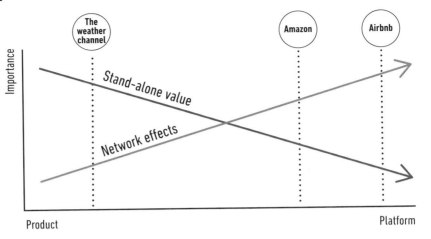

While stand-alone value clearly dominates a weather app like The Weather Channel and network effects clearly dominate in the case of Airbnb, what about Amazon? Many would probably argue that Amazon is an ideal example of a platform business model relying on network effects. However, there is no easy answer. First of all, it depends on which Amazon business you look at. Today, Amazon has a portfolio of business models, ranging from its market-place to Amazon Kindle, Amazon Prime, Amazon Basics, Twitch, Audible and Amazon Alexa.

Let's focus on the Amazon product platform which you can access via amazon.com. This platform started as an online bookshop. There were no indirect network effects and Amazon was *just* an online retailer buying books from suppliers and selling them online. Only after Amazon opened up its online store to third-party sellers did it become a platform based on indirect network effects. Now Amazon was enabling sales between buyers and third-party sellers without being the seller itself. If you look at amazon.com today, it is a mesh between a product and a platform business. If you order products from a third-party supplier (depicted as 'Sold by Company Name'), you leverage Amazon's platform business and often also its logistics backbone. If you order products directly from Amazon (depicted as 'Sold by amazon.com'), you leverage Amazon's e-commerce offering. In the latter, Amazon just acts as an online retailer and the stand-alone value dominates over network effects. Only direct network effects are present as a result of the star ratings and user reviews, i.e. the more users make reviews, the more attractive it is for me to search and buy a product on Amazon. Finally, Amazon also sells its own products on its platform (Amazon Basics) realising a private label approach and making a push towards a direct-to-user model. This example shows that platforms are not static and ultimately it is not about product versus platform, but about unique value propositions based on both network effects and stand-alone value.

Thinking in ecosystems

Ecosystems are about novel value propositions that rely on joint value creation

The term 'ecosystem' has its origins in biology and was first coined in a business context by large corporations such as Apple, Ford and Walmart, who began to build partnerships beyond industry boundaries.[30] These early traits of ecosystem strategy gave them a competitive advantage in comparison with the 'lone wolves' in the same market. In the course of digitisation, more and more ecosystems are currently emerging, e.g. in healthcare, mobility, housing and construction. These ecosystems often revolve around customer journeys and bridge industries that were previously disconnected.[31] Therefore, they break existing industry boundaries and overturn existing structures.[32] In essence, the core aim of ecosystems is to create novel, superior value propositions that rely on a set of partners that complement each other.[33]

There is a fundamental difference between platform and innovation ecosystems

While platforms and ecosystems are closely linked and are often used interchangeably in practice,[34] there are fundamental differences that matter in corporate practice.[35] Ecosystems are all about joint value propositions. However, realising joint value propositions can rely on fundamentally different collaboration modes. Platform ecosystems, or platforms, in short, rely on network effects that require a substantial number of partners and users on both sides of the platform, e.g. sellers and buyers on a marketplace such as Amazon.[36] The objective for a platform owner is always to 'grow the relevant sides of the market in order to increase value through direct and indirect network externalities (effects)'.[37] In the long run, platforms strive to achieve control over their ecosystems. Innovation ecosystems, often just called ecosystems, by contrast, rely on alignment rather than control. The individual partners and the quality of their relationships play an important role. Often, single partners cannot be replaced easily as the number of involved players is rather limited, and each partner brings in unique capabilities to achieve the joint value proposition. However, there are also important commonalities between both types of ecosystem. To kick off, both must create a 'win–win–win' situation.[38] Users, partners and the orchestrator of the platform or ecosystem must profit.

Platforms often start as innovation ecosystems

A platform often starts as an innovation ecosystem with a few (mostly) equal partners. With the ecosystem's growing success and an increasing number of partners, it is common that one platform owner emerges, who ultimately dominates the ecosystem (see Figure 1.1.5). Android, for example, started with only a few partners (including hardware original equipment manufacturers

(OEMs), telcos and software companies such as Google), but as the ecosystem grew bigger, it moved towards a platform ecosystem. The roles of the individual partners diminished, and the individual complementary products became less important – even replaceable, because of the large number of partners and emerging network effects. Ultimately, Google became the dominating orchestrator and the centre of power. Hence, if you are invited to become part of an innovation ecosystem composed of equal partners, keep in mind that your peer partners might have different plans and power can shift over time. Innovation ecosystems can become platform ecosystems and you might end up as an obedient and dependent platform complementor who has to adhere to the rules of a mighty platform owner.

Figure 1.1.5 Ecosystem versus platform

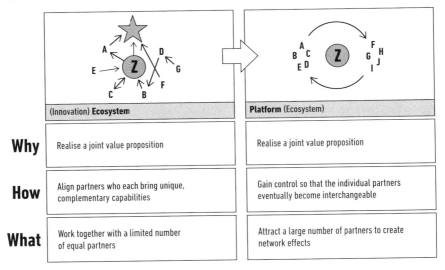

	(Innovation) **Ecosystem**	**Platform** (Ecosystem)
Why	Realise a joint value proposition	Realise a joint value proposition
How	Align partners who each bring unique, complementary capabilities	Gain control so that the individual partners eventually become interchangeable
What	Work together with a limited number of equal partners	Attract a large number of partners to create network effects

Ecosystem strategy

Essential to ecosystem strategy is delivering a novel value proposition that provides unique benefits to customers based on an aligned set of partners. Ecosystem strategy can be defensive to fight an ecosystem disruptor or offensive to drive the success of a company's own ecosystem initiative. As Adner outlines and illustrates on the basis of Amazon Alexa, offensive ecosystem strategies often rely on three fundamental principles[39]: First, they build upon a minimum viable ecosystem (Principle 1). Amazon Alexa, for example, is Amazon's interactive voice assistant, which started with a select feature set and a very limited number of partners such as Philips and Uber. Second, ecosystem strategies develop in staged expansions (Principle 2). After the initial launch of Alexa, Amazon added additional partners such as Spotify. In addition, Amazon launched skills. Alexa Skills are like apps for Alexa. They extend the core functionality of Alexa and, e.g. enable the control of smart home devices or give users the possibility of ordering a ride via voice commands. The Alexa Skills Kit is a software development framework that empowers any third-party developer to develop Alexa Skills. In a next step, Amazon introduced 'Works with Alexa' so that smart home device manufacturers could certify their products to work with Alexa. However, users still needed an Amazon device (Amazon Echo) to interact with the certified device. In a final step, Amazon launched 'Alexa Built-in' so that the manufacturers of third-party devices and products could integrate the Alexa voice service. With Ford's Alexa Built-in, for example, you can control your vehicle through voice commands. To initiate minimum viable ecosystems and to fuel the staged expansion, ecosystem strategies leverage carryover tactics (Principle 3). Amazon, for example, integrated its Amazon Music service into Amazon Alexa to carry its existing user base over to the new offering. Once again, the example of Amazon Alexa illustrates well how companies often begin with a dedicated ecosystem strategy, but can gradually evolve into a platform as more interfaces are standardised and more partners and users join.

2

The types of platform businesses

Although platform business models vary widely, there are two underlying types of platforms that need to be recognised: transaction and innovation platforms.[1] Transaction platforms, like marketplaces, focus on enabling exchanges between two or more sides, while innovation platforms focus on enabling complementary innovation by third parties on top of the platform. Some platforms can be characterised as hybrid as they combine elements of both worlds. It is important to understand the distinction between the two underlying platform types, as the key design decisions are very different.

Transaction platforms

The essence of a transaction platform business model

In essence, transaction platforms connect sellers (supply) and buyers (demand) of products and services. Unlike traditional e-commerce companies that buy and sell products, transaction platforms act solely as intermediaries, thereby connecting the different sides of a market to facilitate a transaction. Platforms can unlock value if market participants want to interact with each other, but a lack of trust and high transaction costs, such as search or opportunity costs, hinder the exchange. Platforms can often create the necessary trust and significantly reduce the mentioned transaction costs. The unit of value being exchanged between the market sides can vary widely, ranging from physical to digital products and services. One of the most prominent transaction platforms is Airbnb (see Figure 1.2.1). It brings apartment owners (supply side) together with people looking for temporary accommodation (demand side). By orchestrating external resources, i.e. (empty) apartments, Airbnb has been able to scale very quickly.

Figure 1.2.1 Airbnb as a typical transaction platform

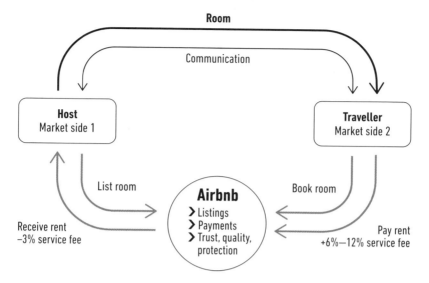

Transaction platforms can be found in almost all industries and niches today. The marketplace AptDeco, for example, connects sellers and buyers of used furniture; Rover matches people who own a dog with people who are willing to walk the dog; the company Outschool is a marketplace for online high school classes where parents can find teachers and classes for their children. While marketplaces seem to flourish in each and every domain, chances to create a successful marketplace are not the same in every industry. More specifically, areas with a high fragmentation of demand and supply, high frequency of purchases or a large addressable market are more likely to be the home of successful and dominant marketplaces.[2]

The development of transaction platforms

In the past, marketplaces were physical gatherings where vendors and customers would meet regularly to trade in items such as fresh produce or second-hand goods, like a flea market. With the advent of the Internet, many companies took this concept and applied it to the Internet, creating a digital marketplace for almost everything. Among the first marketplaces were Craigslist and eBay, both peer-to-peer marketplaces. What all marketplaces have in common is that they aim to bring together supply and demand on a large scale. The purpose of marketplaces is to simplify the process of connecting buyers and sellers, enabling them to communicate with one another and successfully conduct a transaction. Thus, trust in the platform as a secure intermediary plays a pivotal role.[3]

Since the emergence of the first digital marketplaces, there has been a transition from unmanaged to managed marketplaces. The first marketplaces were relatively basic, with platforms like Craigslist, eBay or Etsy serving as prime examples. Such platforms allowed users to list their products or services but did little to promote trust (e.g. by facilitating ratings, reviews or providing insurance) or to make sure offers and transactions were safe. Essentially, Craigslist was an unmanaged marketplace with little gatekeeping and few quality checks. Today, most marketplaces put significant effort into curating their offerings to foster trust and enhance the customer experience, for example, through insurance or other forms of guarantees. Some go as far as managing the entire journey, e.g. Airbnb does a quality check of apartments in the beginning, offers photo services for hosts, provides insurance for both sides of the market and also closely manages payment.

In addition, early marketplaces had a broad scope, spanning multiple categories without a clear focus, thereby addressing very large and heterogenous markets. For instance, Craigslist listed cars, homes, services and other items, while eBay concentrated on second-hand products across various categories. Despite the continued existence of horizontal marketplaces such as Craigslist, eBay, Fiverr, Etsy and Amazon, there has been a shift towards vertical marketplaces that specialise in specific niches. This second wave of marketplaces aims to better serve particular markets by concentrating on individual product and service categories.[4] For example, instead of using eBay to sell watches, cars, shoes or clothing, sellers can now turn to specialised marketplaces like Chronext (a marketplace for second-hand watches), AutoScout24 (a marketplace for second-hand cars), StockX (a marketplace for rare shoes) or ThredUp and Vinted (marketplaces for second-hand clothing). These vertical marketplaces share a commitment to curating their offerings and providing niche-specific services, such as domain-specific quality assurance and authenticity verification.

The two developments – from unmanaged to managed and horizontal to vertical – go along with a shift from asset-light to asset-heavy. Marketplaces started to invest in physical assets to support their operations. For example, Amazon invested in logistics and warehousing to support its marketplace business, while FlixBus has chosen to invest in a physical fleet of buses (FlixBus acquired Greyhound Lines) rather than continuing to just connect bus operators with travellers. In addition, product-focused companies like Withings (a manufacturer of smart watches and scales) have created marketplaces for sharing health data, thereby meshing an asset-heavy product business with an asset-light marketplace.

Finally, there is more and more momentum for business-to-business (B2B) marketplaces, while investment in business-to-consumer (B2C) and peer-to-peer (P2P) marketplaces remains strong. There are many procurement platforms in B2B, such as Ariba and Tradeshift, with the objective of making it easier to find, vet and connect with suppliers and customers. B2B markets are characterised by rather heterogenous needs as well as long and complex sales cycles which are very relationship-driven. Hence, B2B marketplaces stand out in addressing these particular characteristics of B2B markets. Amazon is a prime example of a B2C marketplace, where companies can sell their products to consumers. B2C marketplaces are characterised by high demand, homogeneity and shorter sales cycles. P2P marketplaces, such as Uber, Etsy, eBay, WhatsApp and YouTube, primarily connect private individuals to sell or share content. Although more difficult to monetise, these platforms often rely on advertising and offer the benefit of allowing users to switch roles between provider and consumer.

Transaction platform operating models

Looking at the history of marketplaces and the most successful platform business models of today, it is clear that there are different operating models for transaction platforms. To understand these typical operating models (see Figure 1.2.2), we have consolidated a broad set of insights from consulting firms, research and venture capital (VC) firms, such as a16z, Dealroom, Adevinta Ventures, SpeedInvest and VersionOne.[5] Ultimately, there is no superior or inferior operating model, but six archetypes of operating models that can be observed in practice. The amount of value creation that the platform owner assumes differs significantly between the different archetypes.

Figure 1.2.2 Operating models of transaction platforms

Listing platforms	Light marketplace	Full-stack marketplace	Market maker	E-commerce	Direct to customer
Listings	Listings	Listings	Listings	Listings	Listings
Matchmaking	Matchmaking	Matchmaking	Matchmaking	Discovery	Discovery
Trust	Trust	Trust	Trust	Trust	Trust
Payment	Payment	Payment	Payment	Payment	Payment
Fulfilment	Fulfilment	Fulfilment	Fulfilment	Fulfilment	Fulfilment
Inventory	Inventory	Inventory	Inventory	Inventory	Inventory
Branding	Branding	Branding	Branding	Branding	Branding
Manufacturing	Manufacturing	Manufacturing	Manufacturing	Manufacturing	Manufacturing
Platform business models				**Complementary business models**	

On the left side of the continuum in Figure 1.2.2, there are listing platforms. Listings platforms simply match two or more market sides and provide a digital marketplace for sellers to upload and list their product or services. They also facilitate the necessary trust for the market sides to conduct transactions, e.g. by enabling reviews and ratings. The German B2B marketplace wind-turbine.com is an example of a listings platform. Companies and individuals can list used wind turbines, spare parts and services, such as dismantling and transport, on the platform. Interested buyers can directly contact sellers through a 'contact provider' button. But the marketplace wind-turbine.com does not facilitate payments over the platform. Many platforms in fact start as listings platforms. In the beginning, eBay really was a flea market on the Internet. eBay only provided the platform for sellers and buyers to connect with each other, and the handover of and payment for purchased products often happened offline.

Light marketplaces go beyond listings platforms by handling payments and transactions. In the case of eBay, this meant integrating wire transfer or direct payment services such as PayPal into the platform. Naturally, handling payments gives platforms the opportunity to take a revenue share. Airbnb is one of the most prominent examples of this, as it not only connects homeowners with travellers but also takes care of payment and trust-related services, e.g. insurance and price setting. Light marketplaces have emerged in virtually every sector. HomeAdvisor is a US-based platform that connects local service providers such as plumbing, maintenance fixers, cleaning and tree service contractors with interested customers. HomeAdvisor is actively involved in setting prices by offering a fixed-price guarantee. Interested customers can submit their project details, location and scheduling preferences to receive an offer from the platform. Once a service is booked, a professional will be assigned by HomeAdvisor to complete the service as requested. Another example of a light marketplace is Faire, a B2B marketplace that connects brands from various categories such as home decor, food, beauty and wellness with independent wholesale shops. Faire guarantees 'secure, on-time payments' to sellers and provides them with exposure to independent retailers globally. It also offers a tool for sellers to manage their orders and fulfilment. Sellers can choose between a 'ship on your own' and 'ship with Faire' option that includes discounted carrier fees and online label printing. However, Faire does not manage actual order fulfilment like Amazon, for example, does.

A light marketplace can evolve into a full-stack marketplace by taking on responsibility for the actual fulfilment of transactions. Amazon is a well-known example of a full-stack marketplace, as it allows its supply-side customers to store and ship their products using Amazon's warehouse and logistics infrastructure. However, there are many other instances where various types of fulfilment are realised. For example, Masterclass is an online platform where renowned experts, including celebrities, can upload educational content like video lectures on topics ranging from cooking to public speaking. On the other side of the marketplace, individuals can subscribe to access the content by paying a recurring fee. As it is a digital platform, Masterclass provides a website to manage and show the educational content. Thus, Masterclass is directly responsible for the provisioning of the classes. Another example is Instacart, the US-based marketplace that connects three market sides: customers, grocery stores and so-called shoppers. Customers can browse the offerings of various grocery stores online and place an order, which is then accepted by a shopper who provides 'shopping as a service'. However, there is no direct contact or relationship between the customer and the shopper as Instacart manages (except for drop-off of groceries) almost the entire relationship, for which Instacart takes a substantial mark-up on every order.

Assuming even more value creation, some transaction platforms also put assets on their balance sheet and hold inventory (see right side of the continuum in Figure 1.2.2). So-called iBuyer or market maker platforms such as Auto1 or Opendoor put assets (used cars and real estate, respectively) on their balance sheets temporarily, e.g. to speed up sales transactions for rather complex and costly assets. However, matching sellers with buyers remains their core value proposition. Conversely, e-commerce companies are about buying an assortment of products and selling products at a profit margin. While they enable product discovery on their website, matchmaking is not at the core of their business. You can search for and buy various products on e-commerce websites such as Walmart or BestBuy. However, these companies do not match you with a specific supplier. Instead, you buy directly from the e-commerce company. Hence, e-commerce is a traditional non-platform business model that is, however, often used in conjunction with platform business models.

Finally, companies pursuing a direct-to-customer business model are involved in all value creation steps, from manufacturing and branding a product, to selling it directly to a customer. No matchmaking takes place. Like e-commerce business models, direct-to-customer models are often combined with or complement platform business models. Just recall the earlier example of Amazon. Amazon today combines a light marketplace (i.e. third-party sellers can sell via Amazon but ship themselves) and a full-stack marketplace (i.e. third-party sellers can sell as well as ship via Amazon) with e-commerce (Amazon sells products that it buys from its suppliers), and it now also sells its own private label products (e.g. Amazon Basics), moving towards a direct-to-customer model.

Innovation platforms

The essence of an innovation platform business model

Innovation platforms are platforms that serve as a technological foundation 'upon which a larger number of firms can build further complementary innovations'.[6] One very prominent and hugely successful innovation platform is Google's smartphone operating system Android (see Figure 1.2.3). The operating system forms the basis on which external companies such as Facebook, ByteDance (TikTok) or Zoom can develop complementary applications. Google enables this innovation by offering standardised interfaces (application programming interfaces, (APIs)) and software development kits (SDKs) that support external companies in developing these complementary applications. Moreover, the operating system not only runs on Google hardware but also on a variety of devices from third-party manufacturers, such as Samsung or HTC.

But this does not need to be the case, as seen with Apple's operating system macOS where the respective hardware (i.e. iMac, MacBook) is fully owned and controlled by Apple. The value and network effects on an innovation platform result from the complementary innovation. The more complements there are, the greater the quality and benefit for the users. This increases the willingness of new users to join the platform (i.e. to buy a smartphone with the Android operating system). At the same time, this also makes it attractive for new device manufacturers to join the platform (i.e. make their devices Android-compatible). And vice versa, if more consumers and device manufacturers are joining the platform, more third parties are attracted to develop complements. Ultimately, this leads to a virtuous cycle.

Figure 1.2.3 Android as a typical innovation platform

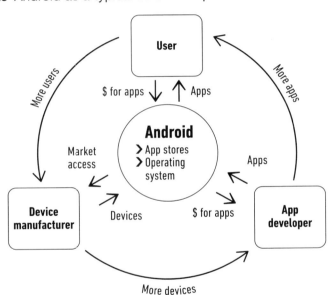

Boundary resources are key to innovation platforms

Managing and incentivising third parties to develop platform complements is crucial for any successful innovation platform. Moreover, complements can be physical (e.g. a new Android-compatible device) or digital in nature (e.g. an Android app). Boundary resources are a core means of enabling the development of complements. In the realm of digital complements, there are a range of platform boundaries at a platform owner's disposal, from technical resources, such as APIs or SDKs, to non-technical resources, such as how-to guidelines or developer support.

Technological interfaces and their documentation are the most fundamental boundary resource for digital innovation platforms. APIs allow for the efficient and autonomous exchange of data and enable complementary applications to interact with and utilise the services of the underlying platform.[7] For instance, features such as 'Pay with PayPal' and 'Login with Facebook' rely on API calls. Ultimately, an API offers access to a set of readily available building blocks that can be used to create a new complementary application. SDKs provide a set of tools that enable developers to create high-quality platform complements in an efficient way. A typical SDK could include code libraries and code samples, as well as integrated development environments. If APIs are about readily available components, an SDK is a fully equipped workshop that you can use to build your digital platform complement (application).[8]

Boundary resources are not limited to technical resources. Social boundary resources are key to transferring knowledge about complement development between third-party complementors and the platform provider.[9] Apple, for example, offers extensive documentation and instructions, as well as require-ments to produce accessories, from cases, speakers and smart home devices to Apple Watch bands, that are compatible with Apple products. Many platforms also explicitly share educational resources. Such resources can comprise how-to guidelines, skill workshops or management best practices.[10] Azena, for instance, provides video tutorials, webinars and white papers to facilitate the development of video analytics applications for its B2B security camera innovation platform.

Scope and quality of boundary resources are key to complement availability and platform success. Key reasons for limited complements are the restricted scope of existing APIs and SDKs. Moreover, these boundary resources can be poorly engineered (e.g. too complex, too abstract or contain errors). In addition, insufficient documentation of APIs and SDKs can significantly hinder platform adoption. Bad documentation is often poorly structured, not specific enough (lack of code examples), incomplete or outdated. Also, there are various ways to design and implement boundary resources. For one, platform owners can impose strict specifications for platform boundaries that third parties must follow. Alternatively, platform owners can actively collaborate with the community (including users, partners and complementors) to design and improve platform boundaries.

Operating models of innovation platforms

Innovation platforms are based on a great variety of operating models. However, based on our in-depth literature and case analysis, we see five fundamental questions that are key to their design. These five questions are organised around two perspectives of the innovation platform: the platform core and the platform complements. The platform core can be thought of as the extensible modular foundation providing the core functionality of the innovation platform. The platform core of Apple smartphones, for example, is iOS. Platform complements refer to the complementary innovation that can be realised on top of the platform. This oftentimes includes applications, e.g. gaming apps for iOS, third-party applications for Shopify or third-party analytic tools to be used on the Amazon Web Services (AWS) infrastructure. The platform core and the platform complements can also be physical. For the platform core and platform complements, we see different operating model design choices (see Figure 1.2.4). Once again, there is no generally superior operating model for innovation platforms, so each platform initiative has to reflect on its unique setting, aims and challenges to make the right choices.

Figure 1.2.4 Five questions for the operating model of innovation platforms

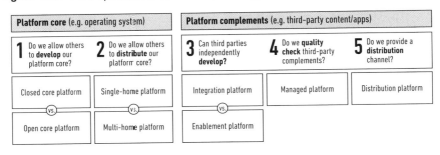

On the platform core level, platform owners must first decide the extent to which third parties are granted access to the platform core.[11] Closed core platforms do not permit third parties to study, customise or alter the platform core.[12] While this gives the platform owner full control over the platform core, sole development might require significant development resources and could discourage third-party developers from contributing complementary applications. For instance, the platform core of the Nevonex platform, an innovation platform to develop digital services for agricultural machinery, can exclusively be modified by the platform owner but not by third parties. On the contrary, the OpenIoT platform, an innovation platform for intelligent, connected products, explicitly allows third parties to modify and extend the platform core making it accessible to anyone. Opening up the platform core enables joint development and sharing the necessary development efforts between different parties, but makes monetisation more difficult.

A second consideration relates to the fundamental basis on which the platform core operates. Smartphone operating systems, for example, can be built exclusively for the devices of one or multiple manufacturers. We call a platform that exclusively has one 'home' a single-home platform. For instance, Apple has its own platform for developing apps (iOS). So far, however, iOS is not available for other device manufacturers. Therefore, apps are exclusively available on Apple devices. Developing a single-home platform requires significant product development resources and a large installed base. By contrast, a multi-home platform allows for integration with various compatible third-party devices. For example, Foxconn's MIH platform for electric vehicles (Project X) designed for autonomous driving applications aims to be manufacturer independent and can be integrated into any suitable electric vehicle regardless of the manufacturer.

Similarly, the Azena operating system can be installed on various video security cameras and is not limited to a single manufacturer. Although multi-homing of the platform core makes it easier to reach a critical mass of connected devices, platform owners may lose touch points with users and potentially cannibalise their own hardware business.

At the platform complements level, the platform owner has to reflect on how independently third-party companies or individuals can develop complements to extend the platform core. On an integration platform, the platform owner and third-party complement providers rely on close collaboration and co-development. For example, on the agricultural platform 365FarmNet, third-party applications must often be deeply integrated into the platform core. This rather high touch integration is necessary to ensure seamless process execution across complements and enable effective data sharing across complements and the platform core. Conversely, high touch integration can limit the platform's ability to scale. Hence, enablement platforms aim to compromise on deep integration and make independent complement development (low touch for the platform provider) as easy and efficient as possible. For example, third-party developers can independently develop applications on iOS without engaging in co-development projects with Apple.

Quality management is inherently connected to platform complement development, and platform owners must decide whether to actively manage the quality of third-party complements and how to do so. This can involve implementing fundamental policies or specific certification processes. Most innovation platforms provide fundamental policies (i.e. programming guidelines and standards) to execute a minimum amount of quality management. Through a strictly defined certification process and enforcement, platforms can promote additional trust and execute tighter control over the provided platform complements.[13] At the same time, it requires considerable investments and resources to implement such a process. On the Bosch Vivalytic platform, for example, biological partners can develop molecular tests using Vivalytic cartridges. However, the platform owner conducts diligent certification processes before making these tests available.

Lastly, platform owners must decide whether to provide a centralised distribution channel for third-party complements, such as an app store. Azena and 365FarmNet are examples of platforms that offer such a channel, which can also serve as a core means for effective monetisation. Alternatively, a decentralised distribution approach allows complements to be downloaded via the Internet, without a managed distribution channel. OpenIoT is an example of a platform that solely uses such a decentralised distribution approach. The ctrlX automation platform offers both centralised and decentralised distribution channels. As a result, ctrlX automation provides a central app store and allows 'sideloading', i.e. provisioning apps without using the official app store.[14] However, in both cases, ctrlX automation performs quality checks that ultimately result in a code certificate that is necessary to execute any ctrlX application.

Hybrid platforms are innovation platforms with a marketplace

Innovation platforms that provide a centralised distribution platform (such as Azena, 365FarmNet and ctrlX) are hybrid platforms. Hence, hybrid platforms are a combination of transaction and innovation platforms.[15] Apple, with its iPhone operating system and the App Store, is another prime example of a hybrid platform in B2C. On the one hand, Apple offers companies and individuals free APIs and SDKs to develop complementary applications (innovation platform). On the other hand, Apple brings app developers and users together via the App Store (transaction platform). With the App Store, users have one single place to buy iOS apps and developers have a readily available sales and distribution channel with millions of customers at hand. This has led to very strong indirect network effects between the two sides (developers and users). With the SaaS industry becoming more and more significant, the app store model is also gaining significance in this domain. In recent years, several B2B software companies such as Shopify, Salesforce, Zendesk or HubSpot have launched app stores, enabling third-party developers to directly extend their SaaS solutions by offering complementary applications via a marketplace.[16]

The platformisation of established businesses

So far, leading platforms have been consumer platforms focusing on digital value exchange. However, the platform economy is shifting more and more towards B2B and product companies. Companies like Bosch, CLAAS, Daimler, Heidelberg, Hilti, LANXESS, Lego, Siemens, Sony and Swisscom have engaged in platform businesses. Indeed, there are several drivers of platformisation for established companies, with the IoT being one of the most important ones.

The IoT as a key opportunity for product companies

The IoT with its smart, connected products opens up completely new business models for product companies.[17] It starts at the product level, where physical devices are equipped with software, sensors and communication technology so that they are able to sense, act and connect to the Internet. However, the value of the IoT does not result from connectivity per se but from the services that build upon the data streams of connected products. Smart, connected products pave the way for smart services, from remote monitoring and control to product optimisation and autonomy.[18] Thereby, the spectrum of smart services spans the whole product lifecycle. Usage data of smart, connected products can be leveraged to improve the products' specification, development and production. Moreover, this data can be used to improve product commissioning (e.g. context-aware training), usage (e.g. remote support) and maintenance (e.g. predictive maintenance), and to facilitate continuous improvement (e.g. updates and upgrades). Platform business models can allow access to the data of smart, connected products so that third parties can develop complementary smart services that go beyond the offering of the product company.

Ultimately, smart, connected products break up traditional industry boundaries and foster collaboration between companies from adjacent industries.[19] Smart farming is a great example where more and more physical products, such as tractors or harvesters, get connected. These smart and connected products enable farmers, for example, to effectively monitor and manage their machine fleets. Initially, smart farming was happening in closed systems. Each and every OEM was creating smart solutions around their machinery. Interoperability between OEMs was just not an important aspect of development. However, the industry took an important step from machine manufacturing to farm equipment optimisation. In a second step, manufacturers learned that the integration of different smart machines into product systems was key to realise smart farming. To facilitate smart planting, for example, tractors and planters have to be connected so that the planter can tell the tractor how fast to go. Hence, manufacturers of different machinery started to align in order to facilitate standardised data exchange between their machines. With the maturation of smart farming, precision farming solutions emerged that leveraged various sources of data to optimise farm performance. These farming solutions are platforms that bring machine manufacturers, external service providers and farmers together in order to integrate and leverage data, such as machinery information, satellite data on plant growth and health, weather data or crop price information. This kind of farming platform becomes more attractive as more value-added services are added, increasing its appeal to farmers and vice versa.[20]

From product to transaction platform

It is no longer a matter of choosing between platforms and products. The lines between product and platform business have become blurry. In some cases, leveraging network effects are even core to product success. Take Bosch Cookit, for example. Bosch Cookit is a flexible cooking machine with the ability to cut, chop, grate, mix, puree and braise, as well as knead dough. Moreover, Cookit users can choose from a selection of pre-stored recipes and are guided through the cooking process with step-by-step instructions displayed on the integrated screen. Although it is primarily sold like a traditional product, network effects are essential to the product's success. Without recipes, the product's appeal is limited, especially compared with competitors who already have a larger inventory of digital recipes that can be accessed via the machine. Therefore, a complementary transaction platform (recipe marketplace) for the provision and exchange of recipes or best practices is vital for the product's success. It is vital that there is a community of Bosch Cookit users willing to create and publish new recipes that can be applied by other users. Even if it is not apparent at first, network effects are central to the success of the product and should be cultivated accordingly. More users, more recipes, more value, more product sales. Ultimately, the success of the Bosch Cookit machine is determined not only by the machine's features but also by the number and quality of available recipes, and for this, an active Bosch Cookit recipe community is key.

ParkingPay is another great example of a product company that went platform. ParkingPay is the PayPal for parking in Switzerland. Initially, the company behind ParkingPay was a traditional midsize product company that provided physical parking solutions (including parking barriers, parking meters) for parking garages and lots. Drivers could pay for their parking at the ticket machine using coins or a card. After a significant number of physical products were installed on-site, ParkingPay introduced a payment platform in addition to the physical infrastructure. They developed an app to connect payment and credit card information, and assigned unique IDs to each parking ticket machine. This allowed users to make payments via the app, thereby creating a two-sided market of parking slots and users of the ParkingPay app. Despite PayPal's dominant position, ParkingPay established itself as the leading parking payment platform in Switzerland by leveraging its extensive base of installed products in the field. Many users were already familiar with the physical product, so convincing them to switch to the transaction platform was relatively straightforward. ParkingPay was originally designed for public parking and cooperated with local authorities, but it has since expanded to include private parking lots. Today, it has grown its footprint way beyond its own physical installations and has become a standard for processing parking payments in Switzerland.

The transaction platform Caruso takes advantage of the rise of the IoT with its connected products and valuable data streams. Founded in 2017 as an industry-wide initiative, Caruso has become a data marketplace for mobility. It primarily connects automotive OEMs such as BMW or Daimler with companies that want to utilise mobility data. This data can range from basic car information, e.g. battery and engine status or user-based data, such as mileage and location, to very specific information such as crash data. Therefore, this type of IoT data exchange platform can enable many business opportunities. Pay-per-mile or pay-as-you-drive insurance, for example, needs mileage and driving data. To offer these innovative insurance products, an insurance company can now find agreements and modes of data exchange with each and every car manufacturer. Or it can install its own tracking hardware in each vehicle. Both approaches are very expensive and significantly cut down the insurance margin. Caruso can ease this pain by bringing all automotive OEMs and all insurance companies together based on one standardised data exchange.

Although Caruso is (so far) limited to mobility data, this type of marketplace for IoT data will play an increasingly important role in the future. In a world where data is becoming a key asset, this kind of marketplace can facilitate new business models for many product-driven companies. In fact, there are various initiatives at the government level and independent from individual companies to build marketplaces for systematically exchanging data. But it is also still in an early stage, and the future success of such marketplaces cannot be taken for granted. It is essential not to overlook how challenging it can be to motivate and coordinate the different parties and companies (often competitors) to exchange and utilise each other's data.

From product to innovation platform

Currently, companies across industries are investing heavily in the platformisation of their connected products. Be it in mobility, healthcare or smart homes, most of the initiatives aim at creating a vital app ecosystem around their products. While the possibilities are almost unlimited when you think of the smartphone app ecosystem, platform initiatives require high upfront investments and include significant risks because even the most promising platform initiatives fail.

A core industry that faces platformisation is mobility. Daimler, for example, has announced MB.OS, an operating system designed specifically for Mercedes-Benz cars. While Daimler controls most of the underlying technology (both hardware and software), the primary goal is to decouple software and hardware and connect core components of the car to the Internet.[21] One fundamental reason for this approach is to provide third-party entities with broad, yet specific access to both the hardware and software of the car. In the entertainment domain, Daimler natively integrates a limited number of apps, such as Apple Music, Spotify or YouTube, but it also integrates the third-party automotive app store faurecia aptoide to leverage the power of an emerging automotive app ecosystem. Daimler also provides access to more critical components for automated driving, charging and in-car comfort. However, this access is only given to a small number of selected partners. Similar initiatives are taking place throughout the industry. Additionally, there are novel players such as Foxconn and LuminarTech who are trying to establish cross-manufacturer platforms with the objective of being integrated by various manufacturers.

Bosch is another example of a company that has embraced platformisation to enhance its existing business through the innovation platform Azena. Although Azena has recently been discontinued, it remains a valuable example of how product companies can platformise their operations. Its vision was to create an app store for IoT-based security camera systems in the B2B segment. Accordingly, Azena developed an operating system (OS), and manufacturers of security cameras could integrate this OS into their smart, connected devices. Azena provided SDKs for its operating system so that external developers could create complementary applications for security systems (innovation platform). Azena offered a marketplace for the developed security camera apps (transaction platform). Users or integrators of security cameras running the respective OS could easily download applications from this marketplace – in an Apple App Store kind of way – and add functionality to their surveillance camera. For instance, by purchasing hardware that runs on Azena's OS, an airport could continuously update or improve the functionalities of its security cameras, e.g. to adapt to changing legal requirements. Concrete examples are AI-based detection of insufficient mask protection in the context of the Covid-19 pandemic or AI-based unattended baggage identification.

Another example is Heidelberg Druckmaschinen (Heidelberg), a German company in the printing industry that is trying to build an innovation and transaction platform with Zaikio. Despite the company's primary business being the production, sale and maintenance of printing machines, Heidelberg aims to enable simple and uniform data exchange between software, hardware and partners involved in the printing industry, creating the basis for end-to-end automated process chains. The platform consists of three essential components: a unified login system enabling access to all connected software systems, a management tool for personal and organisational accounts that connects services and software from various providers and a digital control centre responsible for processing and providing data feedback. The ultimate goal, however, is to develop software to simplify everyday work in the printing industry, e.g. apps for inventory management.

Once again, it must be acknowledged that a large number of IoT-based innovation platforms have encountered difficulties. Several examples, including GE Predix, Adamos and Axoom, to name a few, have failed. Furthermore, many current initiatives such as Siemens Mindsphere are not performing as planned. User growth, number of third-party apps and monetisation are below expectations. Still, with growing experience and more and more lessons learned, many new and ambitious initiatives are evolving.

The Platform Business Navigator in a nutshell

3

This chapter provides an introduction to the Platform Business Navigator and its logic as well as structure. After reading this chapter, you will have a first overview of the 88 strategies and tactics that have made other platforms successful, and you will understand the relationship between the patterns. Thus, this chapter serves as the basis for understanding the essentials. To get even more information on the individual patterns, you can jump to Part Two of this book.

The need for and method behind the Platform Business Navigator

Latest research shows that many companies, especially established pipeline businesses, struggle with the new notion of platform business. Business models are very abstract and, in particular, the logic of platform business models is not very intuitive.[1] There is also still confusion about how platforms differ from traditional businesses. Hence, managers of incumbent firms have a hard time identifying platform opportunities and network effects in their existing business. The lack of platform knowledge also makes it difficult to create a common understanding among employees when setting up a platform venture or communicating platform ideas to stakeholders.[2] Lastly, the external orientation of platforms often collides with existing internal structures.[3] These challenges were the starting point to develop the Platform Business Navigator. Ultimately, the objective of the Platform Business Navigator is to address some of the fundamental challenges in practice.

Building upon the success of *The Business Model Navigator*, we developed a guide for ideating, designing and managing platform business models.

Based on an in-depth literature review and an empirical study of more than 400 platform cases, we derived 88 patterns along five steps (see Figure 1.3.1). Over the course of three years, we analysed a variety of literature, from scientific publications, publicly available interviews with platform CEOs and executives and white papers, to consulting and VC reports. We conducted more than 100 interviews, discussions and workshops with practitioners and researchers. Many of the discussions and workshops were conducted with our research partner Bosch, the German multinational product engineering company. Moreover, our 15+ years of experience in business model teaching and research at University of St Gallen (Switzerland) helped us in developing the Platform Business Navigator. From the beginning, we created several resources (from physical cards depicting each pattern with two insightful examples, to videos, white papers and educational materials). The physical pattern cards (available since 2021) have already been used successfully in numerous workshops, projects and lectures with graduate students and executives (MBAs). This also allowed us to test and refine the patterns early on. In the end, all of these resources have fed into this book.

Figure 1.3.1 The five steps of the Platform Business Navigator

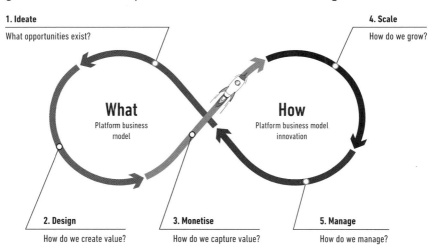

The five steps of the Platform Business Navigator

The five steps of the Platform Business Navigator

The first three steps of the Platform Business Navigator are all about 'what' and the design of a platform business model. The next two steps are about 'how' and the implementation of a platform business model.

Step 1 – Ideate: What opportunities exist?
We often see that companies have started to develop a platform business model but have not fully understood the platform concept – not only from a

conceptual point of view but also from a practical point of view. In essence, they are not aware of the diverse nature and mechanics of existing platforms. Step 1 is about addressing this issue. We present 21 patterns in seven distinct categories that illustrate how diverse the platform phenomenon is. This serves as an inspiration and a starting point to identify opportunities for your own platform business model.

Step 2 – Design: How do we create value?

When you embark on a platform journey, you need to understand that there are two fundamentally different types of platform. On the one side, there are transaction platforms, also known as marketplaces, where you have buyers and sellers (e.g. eBay) or providers and consumers (e.g. Airbnb). On the other side, there are innovation platforms like Microsoft Azure. Microsoft Azure is a cloud platform that serves as a basis for others to develop applications (and innovate) on top. Designing transaction and innovation platforms requires different principles and choices. Step 2 is about these principles and key decisions. We have collected 26 patterns and best practices for designing transaction and innovation platforms.

Step 3 – Monetise: How do we capture value?

In the long run, every business needs a solid monetisation strategy to capture value. Platform businesses often defer monetisation as it can harm network effects. Examples like YouTube or LinkedIn illustrate that it can even take decades until monetisation. Nevertheless, most platforms have a rigid long-term strategy for monetisation from the beginning. The core of monetisation is developing an effective revenue model. It can rely on direct monetisation (e.g. users pay for apps) or indirect monetisation (e.g. users watch videos for free but have to consume advertisements). Step 3 is about addressing the challenge of designing and implementing these revenue models. We compiled 15 patterns that can be leveraged to successfully monetise a platform business.

Step 4 – Scale: How do we grow?

Every platform business faces the famous chicken-and-egg problem. In the case of a new marketplace, for instance, no sellers means no supply and therefore no customer demand. In contrast, no customers means no demand, and hence no seller will engage in such a marketplace. Platforms must overcome this deadlocked situation and Step 4 is exactly about how to tackle this predicament. We compiled 14 patterns that successful platform companies have leveraged to kickstart network effects for their businesses.

Step 5 – Manage: How do we manage?

Once you have your platform running and strong network effects are in place, new challenges will emerge. You must continue to innovate but also defend your platform core as other players will try to copy your successful business model. In addition, you have to manage carefully network effects and quality. We identified 12 guidelines on how to tackle the challenges of a maturing platform business. In addition, we provide insights on how to manage and monitor your platform endeavour. But by no means is it necessary to use all 88 pattern cards or go through all five steps at one time. Our Platform Business Navigator offers three concrete starting points (see Figure 1.3.2).

1 You have no platform idea yet and want to brainstorm ideas: Use the ideate patterns.

2 You have a viable platform idea and need to design the underlying business model: Use the design and monetise patterns.

3 You have one specific platform business model and want to bring it to life: Use the scale and manage patterns.

Figure 1.3.2 Three starting points for the Platform Business Navigator

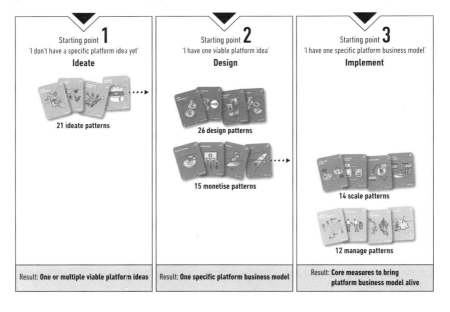

Starting point **1**
'I don't have a specific platform idea yet'
Ideate

21 ideate patterns

Result: **One or multiple viable platform ideas**

Starting point **2**
'I have one viable platform idea'
Design

26 design patterns

15 monetise patterns

Result: **One specific platform business model**

Starting point **3**
'I have one specific platform business model'
Implement

14 scale patterns

12 manage patterns

Result: **Core measures to bring platform business model alive**

Starting Point 1 is all about leveraging inspiring cases for your own platform endeavour and deriving one or multiple platform ideas. Starting Point 2 is all about taking an existing platform idea and deriving a comprehensive yet concise platform business model. While there are no right or wrong decisions, you do have to make some fundamental decisions and choices about what you want your platform business model to look like when you start. Starting Point 3 is about taking a platform business model and deriving core measures to bring the platform business to life.

Ideating platform businesses

How can you ideate and identify viable platform opportunities?

Although a variety of successful platform business models have evolved over the past two decades, most people initially think only of the Amazons, Alibabas or Airbnbs of this world. However, the platform phenomenon is much more diverse. In order to illustrate the variety of platforms and the potential of the platform economy to affect everyone in the enterprise, we have developed a concise structure based on Porter's established concept of the value chain.[4] This structure of the value chain helps moderate the ideation process, if you are thinking about where to start with a platform business. We discovered opportunities to build or use platforms to create and capture value in every part of the value chain. According to Porter, two types of activities can be distinguished in any company. First are primary activities that are needed to run your core business. These activities range from innovation, development and operation of the product and service portfolio (value creation), to sales (value exchange), service and customer interaction. And then there are support activities that relate to cross-functional capabilities. Companies run an HR department to manage their human resources and deal with core topics such as work and education. Finance activities are bundled within the CFO function, and fundamental technology and data infrastructure is orchestrated by a technology department (i.e. office of the CTO or CIO). We leveraged this structure to provide you with easy access to 21 platform business models to use as an inspiration or a starting point for your platform journey – be it as the platform owner, platform user, platform complementor or a partner (see Figure 1.3.3).

Figure 1.3.3 Ideate patterns

	A. Innovation platforms	B. Value creation platforms	C. Value exchange platforms	D. Service and interaction platforms
Primary activities	1 Crowdfunding platforms 2 Open innovation platforms 3 Co-innovation platforms	4 Industrial innovation platforms 5 Data harvesting platforms 6 Asset sharing platforms	7 Product marketplaces 8 Application and data marketplaces 9 Service marketplaces	10 P2P support platforms 11 Social media platforms 12 Content and review platforms
Secondary activities	E. Work and education platforms	13 Collaboration platforms 14 Education platforms 15 Freelance platforms		
	F. Finance platforms	16 Payment platforms 17 Lending platforms 18 Investment platforms		
	G. Technology and data platforms	19 Technology platforms 20 Application platforms 21 Open source platforms		

A. Innovation platforms*

Are you responsible for research and development in your company? What kind of innovation platforms should you know about? First, you should be aware of **crowdfunding platforms (1)**** like Kickstarter. Second, you should be aware of **open innovation platforms (2)** like Innocentive or NineSigma that bring external experts together with companies seeking help with their innovation challenges. There are also **co-innovation platforms (3)** that facilitate the cross-organisational development of innovation. For instance, GitHub has become the go-to platform for open source and software projects.

B. Value creation platforms

If you are responsible for operations, what kind of platforms should you know about? First, you might want to look at **industrial innovation platforms (4)** such as Azena. We all know the app store concept from Apple iOS as well as Google Android, but operating an application platform and marketplace is also prevalent in the B2B industry domain. Azena is an operating system for security cameras with an app store where third-party providers can build and sell applications for security cameras. Second, there are **data harvesting platforms (5)** like Waze, a traffic and navigation app with a social community that serves as a viable data source for Google Maps. Also, **asset sharing platforms (6)** like Airbnb have become indispensable in many areas, especially in the consumer segment. While sharing platforms are popular in the B2C domain, they have also emerged in other, more traditional B2B segments, such as industrial machinery (Burly, YardLink) or healthcare (Cohealo).

C. Value exchange platforms

If we look at the market-related activities of the value chain, such as value exchange, we primarily talk about marketplaces in the platform economy. Most prominent are **product marketplaces (7)** such as Amazon or eBay, but there are also **application and data marketplaces (8)** like Steam, where digital goods (computer games in the case of Steam) are traded. Third, there are **service marketplaces (9)**, ranging from logistics services on InstaFreight to mobility services on Uber to healthcare services on Zeel.

D. Service and interaction platforms

What kind of platforms are emerging in the realm of service and customer interaction? First, we see innovative **P2P support platforms (10)** like Swiss-based Mila that can help increase your service field force by a factor of ten without additional costs. Mila leverages the crowd, for example, to help individual

* In this context, the term 'innovation platform' is not about the distinction between transaction and innovation platforms. In contrast to the rest of the book, it is intended here to refer only to those platforms that relate to a company's innovation activities.

** The numbers following the platform types refer to the platform pattern numbers in Part Two.

consumers with their IT issues – think digital native neighbour helps digital immigrant neighbour. Second, **social media platforms (11)** like Facebook or WhatsApp have become indispensable if you want to communicate with your customers. Third, **content and review platforms (12)** like YouTube are very important, not only for marketing but also for customer interaction, even if you are a traditional manufacturing company. There are many great 'how to' videos on YouTube and first product companies can leverage these ordinary videos by linking to them so that consumers can easily share best practices and learn from other users.

E. Work and education platforms

Are you responsible for HR in your company? What kind of work and education platforms should you be aware of? In COVID-19 times it became very clear that **collaboration platforms (13)** like Zoom are of the highest importance for every company. Second, companies can also leverage **education platforms (14)** like Coursera, Udemy and Udacity, which can bring outstanding educational content in a very affordable way to their staff. There are also **freelance platforms (15)** like Fiverr and Upwork. Instead of committing to long-term contracts, freelance platforms make it easy to hire freelancers for one-time tasks, such as the development or the design of logos and websites.

F. Finance platforms

Looking at the domain of finance, the platform economy has fundamentally changed the way we do finance. First, PayPal as a **payment platform (16)** is now the de facto payment standard worldwide. As of today, manufacturing companies such as automotive manufacturers provide leasing or financing to their customers through organisations like Volkswagen or Mercedes-Benz bank. However, **lending platforms (17)** like LendingClub have emerged that directly connect lenders and borrowers, thereby potentially challenging existing business models. Third, there are **investment platforms (18)** like Republic that are available for consumers and companies to invest money outside the stock market.

G. Technology and data platforms

The last domain of secondary activities, technology and data, is becoming highly important for all companies in light of increasing digitisation. First, there are **technology platforms (19)** like Microsoft Azure or Amazon Web Services. These so-called hyperscalers offer a diverse set of fundamental cloud services for many applications and use cases. In addition, they also host marketplaces where third parties can offer their solutions. Second, there are **application platforms (20)** like iOS and Android. These are operating systems that enable third parties to build applications on top. Today, a lot of software development is now done on the basis of **open source platforms (21)**. A prominent example is Linux, but there are many more open source platforms available for end users, developers or companies.

Ideate in practice

Learning from Amazon: *Amazon* started as an online merchandiser selling books via an online shop and not as a platform business. Only after transforming the online store into an open marketplace where third-party vendors could join, did Amazon become the thriving platform we know today. In fact, it now even runs different successful platform business models in parallel that also complement each other. For instance, Amazon has built a very successful **service marketplace (9)** called MTurk. Companies that want to outsource simple and repetitive tasks can get access to crowd workers via MTurk. As of today, its most profitable business is the **technology platform (19)** Amazon Web Services. The most famous and prominent platform business is the Amazon **product marketplace (7)**. While it started with books and electronics only, it has continuously opened up. Today, third parties can offer a wide range of products, from clothing to food and electronics.

Learning from Android: Android is an OS for smartphones and therefore an **application platform (20)** that hosts an **application and data marketplace (8)**. Based on SDKs and coding guidelines, every developer can build apps on top of the OS. These apps can then be marketed and sold to consumers through the Google Play Store on Android-supported devices.

Designing platform businesses

How can you design transaction and innovation platform business models?

Two fundamental types of platform can be distinguished.[5] First, there are transaction platforms such as marketplaces. Like Amazon, eBay, Airbnb or Uber, they bring two sides of the market together and facilitate transactions between those market sides. Second, there are innovation platforms like Apple iOS and Google Android, but also Microsoft Xbox or Sony PlayStation. Innovation platforms provide the infrastructure and basis for others to develop innovation on top – such as smartphone apps in the case of Apple iOS or video games in the case of Microsoft Xbox. Although there are hybrid forms in practice, acknowledging the differences between transaction and innovation platform business models, we present 26 design choices and norm strategies (see Figure 1.3.4). Essentially, the purpose is to provide an overview of the core decisions when designing a transaction or innovation platform. In a first step, the core value proposition (A) of the platform must be developed. Like in every other business, a meaningful platform value proposition (for each side) is essential for sustainable success. Second, an ownership model needs to be defined (B). Third, an operating model should be determined that outlines the core value creation activities of the platform orchestrator – be it a transaction (C) or innovation (D) platform.

Figure 1.3.4 Design patterns

Design platform fundamentals		Design operating model	
A. Determine core value proposition	B. Define ownership	C. Determine transaction platform model	D. Determine innovation platform model
Enable network effects 22 Aggregate demand and supply 23 Generate trust	31 Single owner 32 Consortium 33 Peer-to-peer community	**Asset-light** 34 Listings platform 35 Light marketplace	**Platform development** 40 Closed core platform 41 Open core platform
Democratise access 24 Unlock latent supply 25 Unlock scarce supply		**Asset-heavy** 36 Full-stack marketplace 37 Market maker	**Platform distribution** 42 Single-home platform 43 Multi-home platform
Establish ecosystems 26 Create a complementor ecosystem 27 Open up the platform core		**Complementary models** 38 E-commerce 39 Direct to customer	**Complement development** 44 Integration platform 45 Enablement platform
Facilitate disruptive interactions 28 Establish a platform vertical 29 Facilitate local interactions 30 Enable an instant experience			**Complement distribution** 46 Managed platform 47 Distribution platform

A. Determine core value proposition

Given the diverse nature of transaction platforms, a variety of value propositions exist. In fact, platforms often combine them. One of the most prominent forms is to **aggregate demand and supply (22)** across multiple domains. For example, a product platform like the Amazon marketplace aggregates supply across multiple areas. Today Amazon's online retail platform's market share in Europe amounts up to 10 per cent, in North America up to 40 per cent (2021).[6] **Generating trust (23)** can be a vital value proposition for a platform to facilitate a new market. Measures such as rating scores and reviews have proven to be effective means of increasing the confidence of providers and buyers. Marketplaces such as eBay would have never been possible without the trust-generating power of ratings and reviews.

Another fundamental value proposition is to **unlock latent supply (24)**. Airbnb did exactly this by focusing on unutilised rooms and apartments. It provided insurance to hosts which took away much of the hosts' fear. This gave them the necessary confidence and security to offer their apartment on Airbnb, thereby opening a new market and unlocking latent supply. **Unlocking scarce supply (25)** can be another core value proposition of transaction platforms. There are certain domains, such as software development, where supply is very low and quality is particularly important. Platforms can democratise access to this scarce supply and provide better quality vetting mechanisms, e.g. with the help of a digital rating system.

By enabling complementors to extend the platform's basic capabilities and 'innovate on top', platforms **create a complementor ecosystem (26)**. Third-party applications expanded WeChat's messaging services by adding flight or hotel bookings or product searches. Today, WeChat is the dominant communication and transaction platform in China. Collaborative and open software development has proven that it can outcompete more proprietary ways of developing software. Thus, platforms **open up the platform core (27)** in order to increase their offering's quality, speed and extent of innovation. Unlike the Microsoft Office Suite, LibreOffice, for example, is based on open source software. This means that anyone can use and modify the core of the platform free of charge.

At the same time, platforms can also focus on **establishing a vertical platform (28)**. Leveraging domain knowledge, such as technical or industry expertise, a vertical platform is active in a very specific niche. For instance, CheMondis has created a marketplace for chemicals building upon the knowledge of its mother company LANXESS, a leader in this industry. Many platforms aim for **facilitating local interactions (29)** such as Uber or Deliveroo. These platforms come with very specific challenges as they have to bring people physically together and create real-time interactions. **Enable an instant experience (30)** is another core value proposition. It is particularly relevant for industries with cumbersome and long transaction processes. On Auto1, consumers can sell cars almost instantly. If you think about the real estate market, selling or buying a house typically takes many weeks. On the platform Opendoor, house owners can sell their homes in five to ten days but at a discounted selling price. Backed by strong financials, the rationale is to speed up a lengthy process to create an instant experience.

B. Define ownership

After developing the core value proposition, you need to think about how to set up platform ownership. While this might seem like an easy task, the right ownership model can heavily influence the future success of a platform. In many industries, platforms are confronted by the challenge that every company wants to build its own industry-leading platform. Instead of joining forces with each other to build one strong platform, every single platform fails in the end due to lack of network effects and acceptance within the industry. The right ownership model, therefore, can be essential to tackling this challenge. Certainly, the most common ownership model is **single owner (31)** like in the case of Amazon or the agricultural platform 365FarmNet, which is fully owned by CLAAS. However, a **consortium (32)** or a **peer-to-peer community (33)** can also own a platform business. A consortium model is particularly relevant in B2B where companies are often hesitant to join a competitor's platform and do not accept a strong marketplace that is owned by only one company. Peer-to-peer communities are very common in the blockchain and Web3 platform space.

C. Determine transaction platform model

As a transaction platform, you must decide on the extent of value creation you want to realise.[7] A platform's extent of value creation can vary substantially from very light to very comprehensive. First, there are asset-light platforms like **listings platforms (34)**. For example, AutoScout24 in its basic version is only a listing of available second-hand cars. Buyers and sellers finalise the transaction offline, and the payment is done outside of the platform, e.g. via cash or bank transfer. This makes the platform very asset-light and the facilitated value creation is rather limited. Going a step further, there are **light marketplaces (35)** such as eBay. On eBay, the entire transaction process is controlled by the platform. In essence, it is a listings platform plus integrated payment.

When assuming more of the value creation, platforms start to become asset-heavy. Amazon, for instance, can be considered a **full-stack marketplace (36)** as it provides a range of additional services that go beyond simple listings or integrated payments. It provides logistics services, has warehouses and manages the entire transaction process for the seller as well as the buyer. Also, the travel company FlixBus did not own any buses for a long time but instead was a well-integrated platform with a strong logistics operation backbone. **Market-maker platforms (37)** like Auto1 and Opendoor even go one step further in value creation: They put assets on their balance sheets for a limited period. Opendoor acquires houses from sellers who want to sell them quickly to achieve a corresponding margin.

In addition to asset-light and asset-heavy platforms, complementary models should also be considered. Although they are not platform business models per se, they are often combined with the aforementioned platform models or result in one. **E-commerce (38)** is in essence an online store where products are commercially traded but without any third-party sellers involved. For instance, Amazon was an online store for books before it became a two-sided marketplace. The second complementary model is **direct to customer (39)**. More and more companies want to own the entire value chain, from producing the product to selling it to the end customer. For instance, companies such as Whirlpool have built up their own online store to sell their products (e.g. a dedicated KitchenAid online store). While they are operating a direct-to-customer approach, they are not facilitating a multi-sided market.

D. Determine innovation platform model

Determining the right operating model for innovation platforms is all about deciding on how much of the value creation you want to control or open up.[8] In essence, you need to define the scope of co-innovation with respect to (a) the platform core (e.g. operating system) and (b) platform complements (e.g. apps). First, on the platform core level, you must decide whether you will be the only one allowed to modify the core. There are **closed core platforms (40)** such as Apple: Nobody other than Apple is allowed to change or modify the operating system of the iPhone. Conversely, there are **open core platforms (41)** such as Linux. These platforms are typically open source and open to any kind of modification by third parties.

In addition to modifying the core, you must think about the distribution of your platform core. There are **single-home platforms (42)** such as Apple macOS. The operating system only runs on Apple hardware and Apple is the only company distributing it. In contrast, there are also **multi-home platforms (43)** such as Microsoft Windows, which is open for distribution as a lot of different companies can sell and integrate Windows into their hardware offerings. Similarly, Android is not coupled to one manufacturer. A lot of hardware manufacturers (e.g. LG, Motorola, ZTE, Huawei, HTC) distribute the Android system. Further, you must decide how you enable others to innovate on top of your platform (complements such as apps). Companies can also become an **integration platform (44)**. For instance, on the agricultural platform 365FarmNet, third-party applications are partially required to be deeply integrated into the platform to create value, i.e. they are not stand-alone. Therefore, codevelopment and close collaboration between the platform owner and third-party application providers is necessary. In contrast, on an **enablement platform (45)** such as Android, everybody can independently develop applications without the need for codevelopment. Only in very exceptional cases is there integration work done by Google. At the heart of enablement platforms is autonomous co-innovation, for example providing boundary resources such as SDKs and APIs, as well as 'how-to' instructions. Finally, as an innovation platform, you need to decide if the quality of platform complements is validated by the platform owner (managed platform) and if the platform owner provides a distribution channel for the complements (distribution platform). For example, the Apple iPhone platform consisting of iOS and the App Store can be considered both a **managed platform (46)** and a **distribution platform (47)**. In fact, developers cannot just develop any kind of app as there are strict rules that are enforced by Apple. For instance, pornography and scams are strictly forbidden. Every app developed for iOS and in compliance with Apple's rules can leverage the Apple App Store distribution channel.

Design in practice

Learning from Amazon: The example of Amazon, a **single owner (31)** platform company, illustrates how platforms continuously need to reinvent themselves and restart the (platform) business model innovation cycle. In 1994, Amazon started as an **e-commerce (38)** company selling books via its online store. Its slogan was, 'Welcome to Earth's biggest bookstore'. Four years later, it became a marketplace and changed its value proposition to **aggregate demand and supply (22)** across various categories. This was the start of the Amazon marketplace as we know it today. When it opened in 1998 to third-party sellers, it was only a **light marketplace (35)**. After introducing adjacent services, such as logistics and warehousing, it integrated more of the value chain and became a **full-stack marketplace (36)**. Today, it has moved even further to a **direct-to-customer (39)** model selling Amazon Basics products, in particular everyday electronics.

Learning from Android: Starting as a **consortium (32)**, the objective of the Android operating system was to establish a common standard for handsets. Looking at its operating model, it can be considered an **open core platform (41)** as its core is open source and others can use and modify it. Exempt from this is the Play Store which is fully controlled by Google. As a **multi-home platform (43)**, and in contrast to Apple iOS, Android runs on various manufacturers' hardware offerings. The development of complements (apps) can be performed independently without interacting with other Android stakeholders so Android can be considered an **enablement platform (45)**. Although there is less quality control than in the Apple ecosystem, distribution is enabled by Google via its Play Store. Therefore, while having an open core, Google can capture much value as a **distribution platform (47)**.

How can you monetise platform businesses?

Once a platform and its network effects have been established, the focus must shift towards capturing value. Even though platform businesses often defer monetisation as it can harm network effects, every business needs a solid monetisation strategy to generate healthy income and profits. Examples like YouTube or LinkedIn illustrate that it can even take decades until actual monetisation happens. However, developing a monetisation strategy early on is very important to determine the business potential of a platform. In fact, carefully thought-out pricing can even become a strategic tool. We therefore present 15 monetisation strategies in three fundamental areas (see Figure 1.3.5). As a very first step, platforms need to determine their core revenue model. They can build upon direct (A) and indirect (B) monetisation strategies. Furthermore, to foster monetisation, platforms can leverage a set of well-established monetisation tactics (C).

Figure 1.3.5 Monetise patterns

Determine revenue model				Foster monetisation
A. Monetise directly			**B. Monetise indirectly**	**C. Apply monetisation tactics**
Transaction-based 48 Revenue sharing 49 Pay per use	**Access-based** 50 Pay once 51 Pay what you want 52 Subscription 53 Membership	**Product-based** 54 Boost your own sales 55 Buy low, sell high	56 Advertisement 57 Pay for visibility 58 Data monetisation	59 Freemium 60 Free trial 61 Add-on 62 Dynamic pricing

Determine the revenue model

Existing management practice distinguishes between direct and indirect revenue models.[9] In the case of direct monetisation, revenue is generated by directly charging the customer who benefits from the service or product. In the Apple App Store, for instance, buyers are directly charged when purchasing a product. In an indirect monetisation strategy, revenue is generated by charging third parties and not the customer who benefits from the service or product. Many platforms leverage an indirect monetisation strategy to keep user fees at a minimum and to prevent harm to network effects. Facebook revenue, for instance, comes mainly from advertisements, but users do not pay anything to use the platform. Since platform businesses build upon two or more market sides, e.g. sellers and buyers in the case of eBay, the appropriate revenue model must be evaluated for each of the sides. After all, one side might be more sensitive to paying money than the other, or one side might be more important for building up strong network effects.

A. Monetise directly

Companies often monetise transactions conducted on their platform. Most often, they rely on **revenue sharing (48)**. For instance, in the Apple App Store, developers have to pay a certain percentage of their app sales to Apple. In this case, the revenue share is a percentage-based commission and can range from 15 per cent to 30 per cent depending on the overall revenue of the app provider. Other platforms monetise transactions through **pay per use (49)**. On the Swiss marketplace for cars, autoscout24.ch, for instance, sellers need to pay a certain fee for every car they offer on the platform (ranging from USD 62 to USD 416). Direct monetisation can also be access based so that users pay a fee independent of the number of transactions conducted on the platform. This can be, for example, **pay once (50)** or **pay what you want (51)** in rare cases. For instance, until 2016, WhatsApp charged a small fee of EUR 0.89 for downloading the app and using the platform. In contrast, in the case of Wikipedia users can just pay what they want. The most common access-based pattern, however, is a **subscription (52)**. On LinkedIn, for example, users can pay a recurring fee to access a certain set of premium capabilities such as enhanced messaging to third-degree connections. In the end, regardless of how often the platform is used, the same monthly or yearly fee must be paid to LinkedIn. Similar to subscriptions, marketplaces often use a **membership (53)** fee to directly monetise their users. For instance, as a member of Amazon Prime, you receive exclusive access to features and services, such as faster and cheaper delivery. Payment can be made on a monthly or yearly basis. In addition to a transaction- and access-based monetisation, the platform revenue model can also be based on product sales. Although this might seem counter-intuitive given that most platforms are only intermediaries, there are examples of platforms that leverage product-based monetisation. Marketplaces like Amazon discovered that it is very profitable to expand their scope and offer their own products on their platform. Today a lot of products offered on Amazon are produced and sold by Amazon itself rather than from third-party suppliers. Thereby, Amazon exploits the existing marketplace as a sales channel for its Amazon Basics products. We call this strategy **boost your own sales (54)**. Other platforms serve as an intermediary between buyers and sellers; however, they do not enable direct buyer–seller interaction. For instance, Auto1, Europe's largest online wholesale platform for used cars, buys and sells cars on its platform. Auto1 tries to **buy low and sell high (55)** to achieve a significant margin.

B. Monetise indirectly

A significant proportion of today's platforms apply indirect monetisation. In an indirect revenue model, revenue is generated by charging third parties rather than end customers or users. The most common form of indirect monetisation is **advertisement (56)**. For instance, users on YouTube do not have to pay to watch videos. Instead, companies that want to advertise on YouTube pay for the placement of advertisements. Another indirect monetisation strategy, similar to advertisement, is **pay for visibility (57)**. On Amazon or eBay Kleinanzeigen, for example, product offerings can be promoted via placement in a prominent position that is advantageous for the sale of the product. Finally, **data monetisation (58)** can be an effective indirect monetisation strategy. For instance, Oikotie, a Finnish job search platform, systematically collects recruiting data, such as search enquiries, on its platform. This data is used for benchmark studies and, ultimately, monetised by selling it to third parties as a service or product.

C. Apply monetisation tactics

If you have decided on your core revenue model, you should think about monetisation tactics. In fact, there are well-established approaches which can help accelerate revenue growth. The first monetisation tactic is **freemium (59)**. In the freemium model, a platform can be accessed either via a free version or via a premium version. For instance, 365FarmNet, a leading innovation platform for the digitised farm, leverages this strategy. It offers a free version with basic functions, such as a field catalogue, cross-compliance documentation and a graphical farm map, while the premium version provides farmers access to an extended set of features, ranging from crop planning and fertiliser optimisation to a profit manager. As a farmer, you might explore the offering with the free version and then pay to migrate to the premium version.

A **free trial (60)** can also help foster monetisation and is an established tool for many platform types. Users on LinkedIn, for example, are offered a free trial of its Premium subscription that provides access to additional features, such as unlimited people browsing or online video courses. A free trial is always limited to a certain period before one has to pay, e.g. in the case of LinkedIn, the trial period runs for one month only. The **add-on strategy (61)** is another very common tool to foster monetisation. For example, a seller on eBay can upload products on eBay for free, but to improve the chances of a successful auction, add-ons, such as larger product photos and extended titles, can be purchased for a fee. Finally, **dynamic pricing (62)** can help to keep an equilibrium between platform demand and supply while fostering monetisation. In this tactic, prices on the platform are adjusted based on actual demand and supply. In particular, mobility platforms such as Uber, Lyft, Blacklane or Getaround have mastered this strategy to balance fluctuating demand and supply.

Monetise in practice

Learning from Amazon: Amazon's marketplace revenue model is primarily based on direct monetisation. In particular, Amazon relies on **revenue sharing (48)** as it receives a part of every merchant's sale on its platform. This monetisation strategy has been implemented right from the start of the marketplace. Today, Amazon also leverages the **membership (53)** strategy and buyers can **subscribe (52)** to Amazon Prime for a monthly fee of EUR 7.99. They receive benefits such as free and faster shipping as well as access to Amazon video and music streaming. In addition, Amazon offers **free trials (60)** of seven days (in some cases one month) with full access to this membership. Typically, consumers get so used to the service that they continue using it after the trial ends. Last but not the least, in its direct-to-customer operating model, Amazon also heavily promotes and highlights its own products, thereby applying the **boost your own sales (54)** strategy. This includes Amazon Basics products (e.g. electronic accessories) as well as Amazon Alexa products.

Learning from Android: Google monetises the Android platform in two fundamental ways. It leverages direct monetisation in the form of **revenue sharing (48)**. It receives a cut of every developer's sale on the Google Play Store. Starting July 2021, Google started charging 15 per cent with some deviation depending on the size of the developer. Google followed the example of Apple, which had previously announced that it would reduce its percentage cut from 30 per cent to 15 per cent on app sales. Conversely, it leverages indirect monetisation. With its Google search, which is set as the default for every Android-supported smartphone, Google generates substantial **advertisement (56)** revenues.

Implementing platform businesses

How can you scale platform businesses?

Every platform business must overcome the well-known chicken-and-egg problem. For many of the failed platform initiatives we have analysed, companies have not been fully aware of the chicken-and-egg problem. In the case of a product marketplace like Amazon, for example, you cannot attract sellers without buyers, and you cannot attract buyers without sellers. Scaling a platform is all about overcoming this deadlocked situation and establishing strong network effects.[10] Once network effects kick in, the different market sides on the platform naturally attract each other. So how can a platform be started and network effects established? In the following, we present 14 scaling strategies in five domains (see Figure 1.3.6) that help you systematically overcome the chicken-and-egg challenge. This includes traditional strategies focusing on one side only (A), attracting key users (B), leveraging existing assets (C), focusing on both sides simultaneously (D) and exploiting opportunistic opportunities (E).

Figure 1.3.6 Scale patterns

Apply traditional strategies				Apply opportunistic strategies
A. Focus on one side	**B. Attract key users**	**C. Leverage existing assets**	**D. Focus on both sides**	**E. Exploit opportunistic opportunities**
63 Single-side product 64 Munchausen bootstrap 65 Boost early supply	66 Subsidise the sensitive them in 67 Get the big shots 68 Get the gang together	69 Let your users bring them in 70 Follow the rabbit 71 Piggyback	72 Micro-market 73 Big bang	74 Platform injection 75 Platform exploitation 76 Platform pacing

A. Focus on one side

One way of systematically scaling your platform is to focus on one of the market sides first before building up a two-sided market. This can be done by providing a **single-side product (63)**. OpenTable, for example, developed management software for restaurants first. The software helped restaurants run their business, from taking reservations to invoicing customers. Only after they had a huge number of restaurants as a customer base did they open up a marketplace where consumers can book a table via the OpenTable platform. They moved from a single-side product to a marketplace. As a critical mass of restaurants was already available through their restaurant software business, OpenTable was capable of establishing a marketplace and attracting the other side of the market, namely the consumers.

The second strategy in this domain is the **Munchausen bootstrap (64)**. In the famous fairy tale, Baron Munchausen got stuck in a swamp but was able to free himself – without external help – by grabbing the straps of his boots and pulling them up. Similarly, Quora, the question-and-answer platform, was experiencing difficulties getting its platform business started; hardly anyone was interested in answering questions and therefore platform uptake was poor. To overcome this challenge, Quora started by answering questions themselves. With a growing customer base, more and more people started answering questions and Quora could back off from this task. Munchausen bootstrap is all about focusing on the supply side first and providing the initial supply on your own.

Another strategy that focuses on the supply side first is **boost early supply (65)**. In this strategy, third parties are incentivised and motivated to provide the very first supply. It is about creating a high-quality supply early on that has the power to attract customers and consumers from the other side. A famous example of this strategy is the Android Developer Challenge in 2008 and 2009. Compared with the Apple iPhone, which already had an app store with interesting apps at the time, Google was late to the game to create the Android Play Store. Developers were hesitant to move over to Android or develop apps for both the Apple App Store and the Play Store. The Apple App Store was just much more established and successful. To overcome this barrier, Google started the Android Developer Challenge, distributing a total prize money of USD 10 million to the best apps. The incentive for developers was clear: If you provided an app, you had a chance to win a substantial amount if ranked as one of the top apps. This strong monetary incentive, together with a gamification aspect, led to many high-quality Android apps. In turn, this attracted many users to purchase an Android smartphone and join or switch over to the new platform.

B. Attract key users

A second way of systematically scaling your platform is to attract key users to your platform. This can be done by **subsidising the sensitive (66)**. Facebook, for instance, is free for consumers but advertisers are charged. Facebook realised that the average user is very sensitive to paying for access to its platform. Therefore, from the start of the platform, they systematically subsidised this user group. In turn, enterprises must pay for placing advertisements on the social media platform.

Attracting key users can also be achieved by applying **get the big shots (67)**. The objective of this approach is to sign up a powerful user or supplier that brings its own network to the platform. For instance, the gaming platform Microsoft Xbox signed deals with large development studios to get premium games, such as Halo, early or exclusively on Xbox. These games, in turn, brought a lot of consumers with them.

The third strategy in this domain is **get the gang together (68)**. This scaling strategy is about getting critical players together to get the platform started. The Android platform, for instance, kicked off as an alliance of 34 companies that included software and hardware, as well as telecommunication companies.[11] Led by Google, the objective of the Open Handset Alliance (OHA) was to create a common standard for (smart)phones. It served as a basis to develop and market Android and the Play Store.

C. Leverage existing assets

A third way of systematically scaling your platform is to leverage existing assets. First, you can leverage your own platform assets. The strategy **let your users bring them in (69)** is about encouraging and incentivising your own users to bring additional users. The fundraising platform Kickstarter, for instance, is inherently designed to leverage its own users to accelerate network effects. If you want your Kickstarter campaign to be a success, you will do everything possible to ensure that your network is aware of your campaign and helps fund your project – it is in your own interest to bring more users onto the Kickstarter platform.

Second, you can leverage existing, non-platform assets from your own company. The **follow-the-rabbit (70)** strategy builds upon a famous analogy from *Alice in Wonderland*.[12] In the well-known novel, sparked by her curiosity, the main character Alice runs after a white rabbit in search of a new and exciting endeavour. In the end, by following the rabbit down a hole into the ground, she discovers a new world and ultimately finds her true destiny. Similarly, companies can explore and go beyond what they originally intended (established business model). For instance, Amazon started as an online bookstore, i.e. an e-commerce business. After they built up a critical mass of customers for their bookstore, they opened up into a marketplace allowing third parties to sell their products on Amazon. The core idea of this strategy is to start with a non-platform business (like the online bookstore in Amazon's case), build up a strong customer base and then turn the business into something bigger (platform business).

With the **piggyback (71)** strategy, you leverage another platform's assets in a collaborative and symbiotic way. Most often, you connect with another platform's user base. For instance, PayPal piggybacked on the eBay platform. At the time that PayPal was getting started with its P2P payment platform, eBay had already built up a flourishing second-hand marketplace. In 2002, PayPal got integrated into eBay and it was about getting the best payment experience for the users. PayPal quickly gained new users from eBay while eBay benefited from the fact that its users enjoyed an outstanding payment experience.

D. Focus on both sides

A fourth way of systematically scaling your platform is focusing on both sides of the platform simultaneously. One of the respective strategies is **micro-market (72)**. Facebook, for example, started at Harvard University. Only after it had traction at Harvard University was it rolled out to other Ivy League universities. After a critical mass of interactions was reached in the second stage, the social media platform expanded further to other universities, and then to high schools and that's when it became a global platform. In this strategy, platforms focus on small and defined markets (e.g. with respect to geography or product) and then try to drive them forward – market by market.

A second strategy that focuses on both sides is the **big bang (73)** approach, which most often can be considered a capital-intensive push marketing strategy. More specifically, platforms can invest in advertisement campaigns that try to penetrate both sides of the market. The objective is to create strong momentum in a very short time frame. In Germany, for example, Auto1, Europe's largest wholesale platform for used cars, invested heavily in advertising to attract sellers (ordinary car owners) and buyers (professional dealers).

E. Exploit opportunistic opportunities

In addition to traditional scaling strategies, there are also opportunistic strategies that try to leverage existing platforms.[13] The first of these strategies is **platform injection (74)**. Certainly, platforms are very sensitive to competing platforms that compromise their business model. For instance, Apple does not want third parties to bypass their revenue sharing–based app, music, games or bookstores and directly sell to customers. However, Amazon does exactly this with its Kindle platform, which brings book providers and book readers together. Today, everyone can download the Kindle app from the Apple App Store and be directly linked to an external marketplace controlled by Amazon. In contrast to the Apple App Store, if you buy a book on Amazon and read it on your iPhone, Apple gets no commission or revenue share. In essence, Amazon injected Amazon Kindle into the iPhone ecosystem. Amazon leverages the App Store community while simultaneously and successfully cutting Apple out of Amazon's value capturing.

Platform exploitation (75) is about copying the core of an open source platform for the benefit of your own platform. Amazon, for instance, has developed an operating system for their Fire tablet. However, instead of developing the platform from scratch, Amazon just copied the open source operating system Android from Google. This saved development costs and allowed Amazon to catch up with the competition very quickly.

A third opportunistic strategy is **platform pacing (76)**. As with platform exploitation, this strategy is about using the assets of another platform to one's own advantage. In contrast to platform exploitation, platform pacing is about copying boundary resources (such as interfaces) of well-established platforms. The goal is to make it as easy as possible for customers and complementors to switch to your company's platform. Imagine keeping the same power socket but replacing the energy supply system behind it. The strategy is most often applied in the domain of open source software platforms. MongoDB, for example, is the most popular NoSQL database as of today. To grow its cloud platform Azure, Microsoft decided to offer a database service (Cosmos DB) that has the same interface as MongoDB. Hence, while communication and control 'feels' like it's MongoDB, Cosmos DB is actually a Microsoft Azure product. This means that, with just a few parameters changed, developers can switch their MongoDB-based applications to Cosmos DB.

Scale in practice

Learning from Amazon: One can identify two fundamental scaling strategies that were of particular importance for Amazon. By opening up its bookstore to third-party sellers, Amazon transformed itself into a two-sided platform. In line with the **follow-the-rabbit (70)** strategy, it systematically leveraged its non-platform assets to quickly realise strong network effects. More specifically, Amazon leveraged its existing user base and also the expertise and knowledge of how to run a digital business. With its marketplace and e-commerce offering, Amazon also relied on the **micro-market strategy (72)**. It stepwise expanded its product categories, from books to electronics and clothing and even to food.

Learning from Android: In 2007, Google joined forces with 34 key partners. The objective was to develop a standard for smartphone operating systems, and this was not possible without key partners from software and hardware, as well as telecommunications. Each of them had vested interests in the mobile industry and there was little incentive to work together. Thus, **getting the gang together (68)** was a means to kick off this platform with few partners and bilateral contracts. It slowly convinced additional partners to join and really transformed Google into a strong innovation platform. To **boost early supply (65)** and to catch up with Apple iOS – which was far ahead at the time – Google launched a competition with USD 10 million of prize money to be distributed to the Top 10 apps.

How can you manage platform businesses?

After successfully scaling the platform and gaining a critical mass of users, the focus must shift to establishing the platform as a sustainable business. Although viable network effects are present, the growth momentum must be maintained as positive network effects can easily turn into negative ones, and competitive pressure in the platform economy is very high. Even being the first provider does not guarantee long-term success, as examples like Sidecar (platform for ridesharing overtaken by Uber) and Billpoint (money transfer platform overtaken by PayPal) show. Because of its immediate access to eBay's huge customer base, Billpoint (purchased in 1999 by eBay) should have won the race against PayPal (founded in 1998). Nevertheless, eBay users preferred PayPal because the payment transaction was smoother and more convenient. Therefore, PayPal overtook Billpoint and was later even acquired by eBay. Similarly, Facebook is now considered the largest social media platform in the world. Yet, at the end of 2004, it had only about 1 million users, while Myspace already had 5 million.[14] Although Myspace was by far the biggest social network at that time, it lost the battle against Facebook. We, therefore, present 12 guidelines and best practices on how to stay competitive and become a sustainable platform business (see Figure 1.3.7). On the one hand, platforms must further grow their platform business through continuous innovation (A) while protecting the platform (B). On the other hand, platforms must maintain network effects (C) and monitor platform performance (D), which requires different approaches and tools compared with traditional pipeline businesses.

Figure 1.3.7 Manage patterns

Innovate and defend the platform		Maintain network effects and manage performance	
A. Innovate the platform	B. Defend the platform	C. Maintain network effects	D. Monitor performance
77 Improve the customer journey 78 Imitate to innovate 79 Open for co-innovation	80 Weaken rivals 81 Acquire early 82 Manage regulator	83 Prevent fraud 84 Manage friction 85 Protect data	86 Track network effects 87 From inside to outside 88 Grow first, monetise second

A. Innovate the platform

Even though a large and active user base may already exist, platforms need to keep innovating. The first opportunity lies in **improving the customer journey (77)**. Platforms like Airbnb have been very successful in this endeavour as they added services like insurance or cleaning services to their portfolio to satisfy adjacent customer needs across the customer journey. The second possibility is to **imitate to innovate (78)**. By closely observing platforms with a similar user base, one can identify successful features that should also be implemented at your end. While this may seem trivial, many established companies in traditional industries struggle with the idea of imitation.

After an initial phase of growth, platforms, in particular transaction platforms, often **open for co-innovation (79)**. A prominent example is Facebook which opened up to external developers after building a strong network of users in order to continue growing. Today, third-party companies can leverage Facebook APIs to build applications and games. Also, Airbnb opened up for developers as well as content producers so that they can enrich the service offering of their core marketplace.

B. Defend the platform

Following the pattern **weaken rivals (80)**, many platforms fight their existing or rising competitors to protect their own core. For instance, by integrating features of emerging competitors into its platform, Amazon Web Services made niche players obsolete and defended its position.[15] To **acquire early (81)** is another pattern that can be recognised when looking at today's most successful platforms like Facebook or Google. Facebook was very successful in acquiring Instagram and WhatsApp very early. Early mergers and acquisitions play an important role in the development of platforms, especially if the acquired platform has a similar user base. By their very nature, platforms have the potential to develop into monopolies or oligopolies. As this may lead authorities to intervene, it is important to **manage the regulator (82)**. By engaging early in discussions with regulators and local authorities, platforms can mitigate potential future conflicts.[16]

C. Maintain network effects

To maintain positive network effects, it is essential to **prevent fraud (83)**. As a platform becomes successful, fraud can become a real problem that must be dealt with. Whether it is PayPal, eBay or Amazon, there is hardly any successful platform that has not had to deal with fraud. With more than 430 million active users (in 2023),[17] PayPal, for instance, has been a popular target for fraud attacks. PayPal users frequently receive fake emails asking for their user credentials to log in. Therefore, PayPal invested significantly in fraud prevention and improved the security of its transactions. Mature platforms must also carefully **manage friction (84)**. While the Amazon marketplace benefits from the ever-growing number of products and sellers, it can become increasingly difficult for users to find the desired product. Too much choice and growing opaqueness can make users switch to other platforms. Amazon has invested heavily to ensure consistent product labelling and enable easy product comparisons. Platforms also need to continuously **protect data (85)**. This may seem trivial at first glance, but the Cambridge Analytica scandal surrounding Facebook shows that trust can be very fragile and user data must be protected.

D. Monitor performance

When developing a platform business, many companies struggle with establishing the right KPIs. Platform businesses are different from pipeline businesses and hence need specific KPIs. First, platforms need to **track network effects (86)**, for example by looking at the number and the quality of successful transactions. The platform's user growth and the ratio of producers to customers are further important indicators of platform performance. Second, platforms work **from inside to outside (87)**. Platform's value creation heavily depends on external resources. The strategic focus must, therefore, be on orchestrating these external resources in the most effective and efficient way. In the case of Apple and its iOS ecosystem, for example, core questions are: How quickly and easily can external developers (complementors) develop and update apps? How much time do they need to learn the necessary programming language (Swift)? How long do they need to make an app available through the app store? Instead of measuring internal productivity, platforms focus on the productivity of their complementors. As network effects are essential, platforms most often follow the credo **grow first, monetise second (88)**. While you should think about monetisation opportunities early on, the priority at the very beginning is to kick off network effects successfully. Companies that try to monetise too early typically do not succeed in scaling their platforms successfully. Therefore, it is critical for traditional companies entering the platform business to rethink how to measure success at early stages. A CEO once told us, 'Tell me how the project started, and I'll tell you how it ended.'

Manage in practice

Learning from Amazon: It took almost 20 years for Amazon to make profits, but this was not because they did not have a profitable business per se, but rather because they focused on **growth first, monetise second (88)**. For example, they accepted losses when they introduced one-day delivery to increase customer satisfaction. Amazon has also made numerous strategic acquisitions. Many of these acquisitions have contributed significantly to today's success. For instance, Amazon **acquired (81)** Audible to build an audiobook platform, LoveFilm to grow its video streaming platform, Ring to complement its Alexa smart home platform and Twitch to establish its own live video streaming platform. At the same time, Amazon's rapid growth made it vulnerable to fraud and quality problems. Today, the large number of products and suppliers make

▶

it increasingly difficult for users to find the right product, and many reviews are faked. Amazon, therefore, has heavily invested in **managing friction (84)** on its marketplace. For one, it introduced the Amazon Standard Identification Number (ASIN) for categorising products, thereby reducing duplicates and making it easier to find products. And then it created a sophisticated prevention system to reduce scam.

Learning from Android: To complement and expand its platform, Google also made various key acquisitions. For instance, they **acquired (81)** Motorola Mobility in 2011, Nest in 2014 and Waze in 2013. Although both Google and Apple have a similar set of rules on its app marketplace, Google was not as strict as Apple. This practice made Android vulnerable to fraud, e.g. fake apps. **Preventing fraud (83)** has, therefore, become a strategic priority. To manage its platform ecosystem and foster growth, Google pays close attention to the productivity of external producers, **from inside to outside (87)**. This is also the reason it decided to build upon the existing programming language Java. Google wanted to make it as easy as possible for developers to join the Android platform ecosystem.

[PART TWO]

88 patterns of the Platform Business Navigator

Ideate: patterns to identify a platform opportunity

1

In order to illustrate that the platform economy affects everyone in the enterprise and to facilitate broad ideation, we have developed a concise structure based on Michael Porter's established concept of the value chain.[1] Two types of activities can be distinguished in any company according to Porter. First are primary activities that are needed to run your core business, e.g. innovation, development and operations of the product and/or service portfolio, as well as sales, service and customer interaction. Second are support activities that relate to cross-functional capabilities, e.g. an HR department to manage human resources and deal with core topics such as work and education. This structure of the value chain helps moderate the ideation process, if you are thinking about where to start with a platform business. Leveraging this structure, we provide you with 21 platform business model patterns as an inspiration or starting point for your platform journey – be it as the platform owner, platform user, platform complementor or partner (see Figure 2.1.1). We discovered opportunities in every part of the value chain to build or use platforms to create and capture value. For instance, if you are responsible for research and development in your company, what kind of innovation platforms (A) should you know about? If you are responsible for operations, what kind of value creation (B) and value exchange (C) platforms should you know about? If you are responsible for sales and service delivery, what kind of service and interaction platforms (D) should you know about? If you are responsible for human resources (HR) at your company, what work and education platform (E) should you know about? If you are responsible for the finance or IT department, what finance platforms (F) or technology and data platforms (G), respectively, should you be familiar with? Previous workshops have shown that the examples on the cards are particularly valuable for ideation. Moreover, these examples often help

Figure 2.1.1 Ideating a platform business (Patterns #1–21)

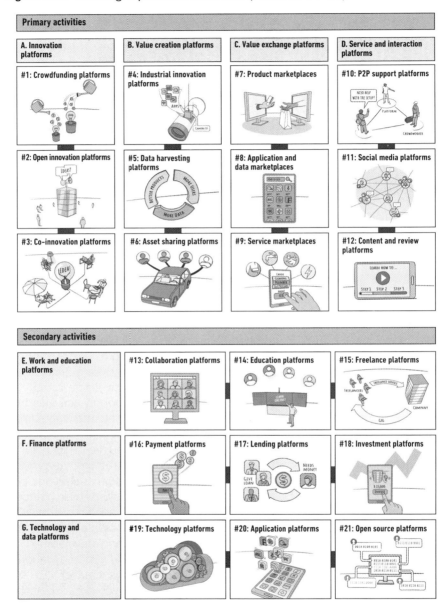

Primary activities

A. Innovation platforms	B. Value creation platforms	C. Value exchange platforms	D. Service and interaction platforms
#1: Crowdfunding platforms	#4: Industrial innovation platforms	#7: Product marketplaces	#10: P2P support platforms
#2: Open innovation platforms	#5: Data harvesting platforms	#8: Application and data marketplaces	#11: Social media platforms
#3: Co-innovation platforms	#6: Asset sharing platforms	#9: Service marketplaces	#12: Content and review platforms

Secondary activities

E. Work and education platforms	#13: Collaboration platforms	#14: Education platforms	#15: Freelance platforms
F. Finance platforms	#16: Payment platforms	#17: Lending platforms	#18: Investment platforms
G. Technology and data platforms	#19: Technology platforms	#20: Application platforms	#21: Open source platforms

communicate your platform ideas effectively to stakeholders within your company. Looking at the specific examples mentioned on the pattern cards, you could ask yourself: How would platform X conduct our business? Can we transfer the business model of platform X into our industry? Should we build our own platform X or is it more feasible to become a complementor or user in an existing platform? How can we benefit from platform X in our department Y?

> Jeff Bezos, founder of Amazon, on platform success: 'Large-scale platforms are not zero sum – they create win–win situations and create significant value for developers, entrepreneurs, customers, authors, and readers.'(n.d.)[2]

Although we provide a structured approach to ideation, every platform journey must start with an analysis of your industry and adjacent industries. Certainly, the collection of patterns is also not mutually exclusive nor collectively exhaustive. Existing platforms can be mapped using more than one pattern card, and when designing a new platform idea, different pattern cards can be combined. Nevertheless, we believe it is a good starting point and provides a structure that many are familiar with and that has so far proven successful in business model workshops, strategy discussions and in the classroom.

Innovation platforms

1 Crowdfunding platforms

Crowdfunding platforms bring people with innovative projects together with backers who are willing to invest in such projects. Usually, backers are private individuals who believe in the project and are less return driven. In general, the concept of crowdsourcing is not new, and early traits go back more than a hundred years. Owing to a funding gap, the completion of the Statue of Liberty was in jeopardy in the 1880s. The deficit of USD 100,000 was finally raised by 180,000 donors in a crowdfunding campaign by the *New York World*. However, today's platforms have opened up many new possibilities for crowdfunding campaigns and make it much easier and more efficient to start one.[3] By pooling financial resources from the crowd, many projects or efforts have been funded on platforms such as Kickstarter, Indiegogo, Patreon or GoFundMe – projects that probably would not have received funding elsewhere. Different variations of return for backers exist, e.g. they get early access to the product, receive a certain percentage of the return or, perhaps, no return at all.

Kickstarter is one of the most prominent platforms where innovative ideas meet private financiers. In fact, 10 years after its launch, Kickstarter has raised more than USD 5 billion and funded over 200,000 projects.[4] Startnext also brings projects and backers together. However, it focuses not only on innovative ideas but also on social, sustainable projects as well as artists and creative professionals. For instance, local stores or projects that have suffered through COVID-19 could promote themselves and collect money. Patreon is a crowdfunding platform dedicated to creatives, e.g. podcasters, bloggers or 'YouTubers'. Creators can set up a profile to connect with their fans, who can support them financially through the platform. For example, fans of the famous podcast *True Crime Obsessed* can search for the podcasters behind it on Patreon and sign up for a subscription to support them financially. Since its launch in 2013, more than 250,000 creators and eight million monthly active patrons (donators) worldwide have used Patreon.[5] Recently, many niche crowdfunding platforms have evolved, such as Fundable (focus on small businesses), mightycause (focus on nonprofit fundraising) and StartEngine (focus on start-ups). Also, blockchain technology promises to further democratise access to finance and decentralise the existing funding processes via digital shares.

Tino Kressner, cofounder of Startnext, on the relevance of staying innovative as a platform: 'With mechanisms such as the start-up phase, our crowdfunding and our Pay-What-You-Want (PWYW), we were always the first in Europe to set bold accents in the crowdfunding process. Our courage and constant willingness to experiment have paid off over ten years. We have discarded many things, but have also strongly developed principles cofunding and PWYW as a unique selling point.'(2020)[6]

Some questions to ask
- If you seek to establish a crowdfunding platform, how do you position yourself against competition?
- As a project that seeks funding, which crowdfunding platforms have the best fit for your project?
- Why do you want to crowdfund a project and not leverage other funding opportunities?

2 Open innovation platforms

Open innovation acknowledges that innovation includes the open exchange of ideas with creative individuals as well as user communities. Hence, open innovation platforms connect external individuals with companies facing a business innovation need, thereby allowing companies to leverage the crowd's collective knowledge and creative potential.[7] On Innocentive and NineSigma for instance, companies can describe and upload a business challenge. Any individual can submit ideas and provide solutions to given challenges for a monetary incentive. The set-up as a competition among participants enhances the engagement and quality of ideas. But Innocentive started very differently as it began as an internal start-up of the American pharmaceutical company Eli Lilly & Co. The goal was to gather community ideas and feedback on select research and development challenges. Ultimately, this innovation ecosystem was opened to other companies to participate and upload their challenges. Only then did it become a platform business model. From then on, it has grown into one of the most successful open innovation platforms.

Similarly, the open innovation platform Ekipa connects companies with students, start-ups and universities. Companies can post challenges based on concrete innovation problems, set a deadline and award prize money to the top teams.

> Darren Carroll, founder of Innocentive, on the differentiation of Innocentive: 'Our approach is revolutionary in a number of ways. First, we've asked for solutions to research that until now has been done only in secret. [. . .] Second, we have found ways to post those problems to people around the world. Third, we have found ways to convince scientists around the world that there is integrity in this new marketplace.' (2004)[8]

A slightly different approach to open innovation is being pursued by Jovoto as well as Lego as they focus heavily on the ideation part of innovation. For instance, on the platform Lego Ideas, engaged fans can connect with each other. They can enter into competitions to share and propose their own Lego creations to their fellow fans. If a proposal reaches more than 10,000 supporters among the platform's community, Lego will start a review process to decide whether it will be actually offered as an official kit and go on sale. To incentivise its community, Lego promises that a 1 per cent revenue share of the total net sales of the new kit will go to the creator (fan). This has enabled Lego to work more closely with its customers, receiving feedback while harnessing their creativity and innovation to develop new product ideas. Ultimately, opening up your innovation efforts to the public can accelerate innovation and even increase your success rate, owing to its collaborative nature.[9]

Some questions to ask

- How and where can you benefit from open innovation platforms?
- How can you seamlessly embed such a platform into your digital offerings, like Lego has?
- How can you leverage an external innovation platform to innovate your business?
- Is your intellectual property protected?
- Are you ready to disclose internal challenges for the benefit of potentially innovative ideas?

3 Co-innovation platforms

Co-innovation platforms enable the collaborative, cross-organisational reali-sation of joint projects. They bring together professionals and private individuals who work together to create innovation. Because of the intangible nature of software, co-innovation is particularly well known in the field of software devel-opment. GitHub is an example of a co-innovation platform that focuses on collaborative software development. Companies and individuals can leverage GitHub to share and manage source code to realise joint software innovations. Founded in 2008 and acquired in 2018 by Microsoft, GitHub has become the de facto standard and go-to platform for open source projects. At the core of GitHub is distributed version control and source code management. Companies as well as individuals can deposit software source code and collaborate with others to improve, extend or test the code.

> Chris Wanstrath, founder of GitHub, on the purpose of GitHub: 'We want to enable people who don't know each other to collaborate on the same thing towards the same goal. This is all I want to do – forever.' (2014)[10]

Similarly, Synapse enables co-innovation in the field of digital health data. Participants can exchange ideas and work together on research projects. The Hugging Face platform consists of a community that develops, trains and deploys machine learning (ML) models. In an open source format, the network of scientists and researchers can share their models and solutions and work together on it. A more unusual co-innovation platform is PlaytestCloud, a platform for gamers but also ordinary people to test unreleased mobile games, help find bugs or increase their usability. Test players are rewarded with around USD 10 per game tested or survey participated in (15 minutes' time effort), and they can play the games on their own devices from home.[11] Participating game studios benefit from authentic feedback and can improve their games in a cost-efficient and effective way. Another example is Thingiverse which is a platform to work jointly on 3D designs for physical objects (e.g. for a 3D printer) as well as to share those user-created design files on its open marketplace.

> Clément Delangue, cofounder of Hugging Face on the goals of Hugging Face: 'The mission of Hugging Face is to democratise good machine learning. We're striving to help every developer and organisation build high-quality, ML-powered applications that have a positive impact on society and businesses.' (2023)[12]

Some questions to ask
- Where is the specific co-innovation need that you want to address?
- How can you convince the different co-innovation stakeholders to collaborate?
- How can you enable effective and efficient co-innovation by means of a platform?
- How can you create a mindset of open innovation and overcome the 'not-invented-here' syndrome?
- How can you offer management frameworks for collaborative innovation?

Value creation platforms

4 Industrial innovation platforms

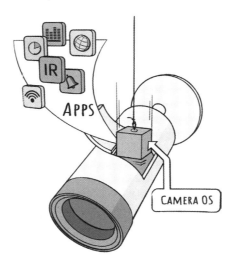

Industrial innovation platforms bring well-established platform concepts like the app store to the industrial space. One of the key enablers of this development is the Internet of Things, which, in essence, aims to connect the physical and digital world. For instance, manufacturers who connect their products to the Internet can give external companies access to their product data to enable third-party analysis or digital services. Ultimately, so-called smart, connected products open up many new possibilities for companies from the same industries, as well as adjacent industries, to collaborate and create new value.[13] A prominent example is the industrial innovation platform Azena, which is all about security cameras and corresponding applications.

Azena developed an OS for security cameras – just like Android or iOS, but for security cameras. Security camera manufacturers can integrate this OS into devices to make them smart and connected. At the same time, Azena provides software interfaces (SDKs) on the basis of its OS to external developers so they can unleash their imagination and create complementary applications for security systems. On the Azena marketplace, these third-party providers can then distribute and sell their applications. When camera manufacturers install the Azena OS, their customers gain access to a wide range of third-party security applications, such as baggage tracking for airports, shelf monitoring for retailers or tracking proper mask usage in the context of COVID-19. In fact, users or integrators of security cameras working on Azena OS can download applications from this marketplace as easily as from the *Apple App Store*, adding functionality to their surveillance camera. Only a year after launch, the app store already featured more than 72 applications to realise various camera use cases in the B2B context. However, for its vision to work, Azena must convince three sides: (1) hardware manufacturers to implement their OS, (2) application developers to build complementary applications and (3) customers to purchase and deploy Azena-based security solutions. The ability to connect devices to the Internet has created many opportunities for businesses to participate in the platform economy. The example of Azena has already briefly illustrated this, but many other examples of industrial innovation platforms can also be found in other sectors, especially in the context of Industry 4.0, agriculture and automotive.

> Nikolas Mangold-Takao, cofounder of Azena, on the idea behind Azena: 'The goal of Azena is to develop an open ecosystem for the security industry. We start with video security cameras and together with partners, we develop video cameras compatible with this ecosystem.' (2018)[14]

For instance, 365FarmNet is an agriculture platform that facilitates the entire farm management process and allows for the integration of partner apps. By offering interfaces, 365FarmNet promotes innovation and accessibility on its platform. Today, 365FarmNet develops applications together with more than 20 partners and integrates them as modules into their software.[15] Among others, the integrated services include crop planning, harvesting and farm analysis. In the end, such farm management platforms bring (1) machine manufacturers together with (2) external service providers and (3) farmers. The more value-added services there are on the platform, the more attractive it is for farmers to join the platform, and vice versa. In fact, the agricultural industry seems quite advanced as various start-ups and projects like Nevonex, ClimateFieldView, Agricircle, Farmobile and DataConnect are emerging. But many challenges exist, and the question remains of how many platforms can coexist and which of them will become the dominant one.

> Maximilian von Löbbecke, CEO of 365FarmNet, on the challenge of achieving a critical mass of connected devices: 'A software like this only makes sense if I can digitally map my entire machine fleet. But most of the machines I have are not thalew [. . .]. I think the average age of tractors or equipment in Germany is over 20 years. That's why we have sensors, the ActiveBox, as we call it, so that we can digitally equip every machine – for little money and very simply. I just attach a box to it and link it to an application on my smartphone so that the whole process is mapped and I know who has actually been in the tractor, with an ancient injection pump from 1982, for how long, in which field [. . .]. And only then it makes sense. It doesn't make sense if I only track the data of 2x2 tractors but not the rest, because then my record is so full of gaps that it doesn't bring me any added value in the end.' (2020)[16]

Another example, but from a very different industry, is Tapio. It is an app platform for carpenters, furniture manufacturers and panel processors to collaborate and work together. Machine, material or tool manufacturers for the wood industry can extend their existing offerings with digital services, such as condition monitoring or materials management, that are provided by third parties. Additional examples of industrial innovation platforms are Bosch ctrlX (an innovation platform for automation applications), Uhlmann Pexcite (a platform for software solutions across the value chain of pharmaceuticals) and relayr (a platform combining hardware and software to monitor, maintain and analyse machinery to enable OPEX operating models).

Some questions to ask
- Can you decouple hardware from software in your industry?
- What kind of complements (apps) can or could be built upon your platform?
- Who will use the complements and who will provide them?
- Are customers and providers really willing to join or do they fear a monopolistic platform?
- Have you considered the business models of your competitors and potential partners (create value, capture value)?

5 Data harvesting platforms

Adapted from Ng (2018)[17]

The goal of data harvesting platforms is to harness the power of data network effects.[18] Data harvesting platforms such as Amazon or Waze collect data from their users (e.g. shopping data, traffic incidents). As a result, they are able to offer better products and services (e.g. product recommendations, real-time traffic routing), which in turn leads to more users and data. Users either actively enter data or the platform passively collects user data. On the navigation platform Waze (acquired by Google in 2013) users can enter traffic-related incidents (e.g. speed limits, traffic jams or hazardous locations) and modify map data (e.g. add new roads). This creates strong network effects, and the data can be used for additional value creation by the platform. Today, this data is especially leveraged to improve the navigation accuracy of Waze as well as Google Maps, but it is also sold to third parties. Waze is increasingly partnering with authorities (e.g. Waze for Cities) and TV stations (e.g. Waze for Broadcasters) to further leverage the collected data. In addition, advances have been made in collecting more sustainability-relevant data, for example on charging stations that are relevant to electric vehicle owners (e.g. location and power levels, current waiting times and tariffs). In the end, the success of Waze heavily depends on building a strong community (which counts more than 100 million users today and more than 500,000 map editor volunteers) that contributes data and spends a lot of time to keep it up to date.[19]

Noam Bardin, former CEO of Waze, on the misperception of data: 'Data is one of the most misused terms today in the start-up world. People have this idea that data is valuable. Data is only worth what you sold it for! That's it. I see so many companies telling me, "Oh, we're collecting all this data, and it's so valuable." [. . .] Data is not valuable. What you do with the data is valuable. So if you can sell the data, package it in a way that someone will pay for it – that's valuable. If you can take that data and create a product that provides value to the consumers, then that's value. [. . .] Just to say that because you have a lot of data that it's valuable, no. You can have a lot of data, but who cares?' (2021)[20]

One widely employed method of passive data collection relies on location data from smartphone devices. Two examples are the COVID-19 contact tracing apps and Apple's platform business built around the AirTag. The Apple device for tracking everyday objects (from your keys and bags to even your car or bike) relies on the existing community of iPhone users. The more iPhones there are physically around your AirTag, the more accurately you can track down your objects. While being very closed in the beginning, Apple slowly opened the platform up to third parties. Hardware manufacturers such as VanMoof (e-bikes) or Belkin (wireless earbuds) were the first ones to integrate the tracking technology into their products. iPhone users can now track these devices via the Find My app.

Data harvesting is also at the heart of Google's smart home platform Nest which is all about the collection and analysis of data with the aim of providing smart heating services to users. The higher the number of devices that collect data and send it to Nest, the more powerful the knowledge base is to develop heating-related smart services, and the better the customer experience will be. Another example is reCAPTCHA – the Google tool for differentiating real versus fake users (bots) and, ultimately, protecting websites from malicious attacks. If you want to access a website, you are first asked to decrypt difficult-to-read text or match images. In addition to this protective function, reCAPTCHA leverages this user input for the benefit of others, i.e. the second side of the platform consists of companies that benefit from the data input. For instance, in 2009, by transcribing words and numbers from millions of users, reCAPTCHA helped to digitise the archives of *The New York Times*. Nowadays, when users are asked by reCAPTCHA to classify pictures or objects (typically from a situation on the street, e.g. traffic lights, mountains, busses), it can help train algorithms for autonomous driving.[21] One more example of data harvesting platforms are dacadoo (a Swiss platform to harmonise individual health data into a health score that can be leveraged by third parties).

Some questions to ask

- Which data is at the core of your platform idea?
- Is there information that is of interest to you that could potentially be crowdsourced?
- Can you rely on data network effects, i.e. more data, better products, more users, more data, . . .?
- How can you start data network effects and create initial momentum?
- How do you make sure that privacy principles are protected?

6 Asset sharing platforms

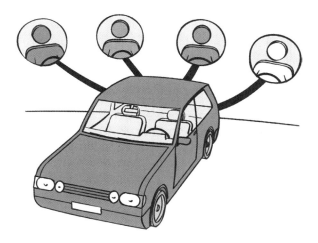

The objective of asset sharing platforms is to enable asset sharing among individuals or companies.[22] With the rise of the 'sharing economy', many successful platforms have emerged in the consumer space. However, sharing platforms are not limited to this domain. More and more B2B platforms for sharing assets such as industrial machinery are being established. In general, asset sharing platforms can serve several purposes: They can increase asset utilisation, they can spread the cost of use (including acquisition and maintenance costs), they can democratise access to expensive assets or they can unlock latent supply. The most prominent example of an asset sharing platform is probably Airbnb which came into being because one of its founders, Brian Chesky, could not afford his rent in San Francisco. To earn some extra money, he and his roommates had the idea of renting out air beds to participants at the International Design Conference that was held in San Francisco.[23] Today, millions of individuals can share their homes with others for short-term or vacation rentals on Airbnb. Starting as a local asset sharing platform, Airbnb is now active in almost every country and city in the world. They also offer insurance to the homeowners so that they will entrust their house to complete strangers.[24] Ultimately, by providing a trustworthy and reliable go-to place, it was able to unlock new supply. The sharing economy also has a large footprint in the mobility sector. However, not all companies in this economy can be considered a platform business model. Zipcar is often mentioned in this context, as it was already founded in 2002, but it operates more like a car rental company or landlord rather than a true platform business. Nevertheless, there are real platforms out there – the 'Airbnbs' of mobility. For instance, Turo and Getaround can be considered genuine platforms. They offer P2P car sharing as they match owners of idle cars with strangers looking for short-term and spontaneous car rentals.

Nicolas Ferrary, country manager AirBnB France, on the difficulty to scale a sharing platform: 'In the sharing economy, one of the challenges is how you grow international and adopt to different cultures around the world. We often build one product which is a feat for one market, in [. . .] the US and Europe for instance, and when you go to Asia, to Africa, to Latin America, for instance, then you have challenges.' (2015)[25]

BlaBlaCar is a P2P platform for ridesharing, the digital version of hitchhiking. It matches people looking for a ride from A to B with drivers who have that exact destination or route and would like to give someone a lift in return for a fee. Beyond mobility, asset sharing platforms have emerged in all kinds of niches, such as MyCamper or Hipcamp (P2P marketplaces for sharing a campervan, campsites or RV space) and Wardrobe (P2P marketplace for sharing luxury or vintage clothing). As mentioned earlier, asset sharing platforms are not limited to the consumer segment but can also be established in B2B. However, many of them are still in the early stage and have very limited traction. On the early-stage marketplace, Burly, for instance, companies or individuals can rent or share construction equipment. While owners can earn additional money by renting idle equipment, renters can get the equipment fast and inexpensively. The offerings range from forklifts and excavators to trailers and chainsaws, and all are covered by property insurance. In essence, Burly is an Airbnb of construction equipment. Many other B2B marketplaces for asset sharing exist, for example, Kreatize (a marketplace for sharing manufacturing capacities), FLOOW2 (a marketplace for sharing equipment, services and even personnel internally and across organisations), Cohealo (a sharing marketplace for healthcare equipment between facilities), Xometry (a marketplace that matches unutilised manufacturing capacity with on-demand manufacturing services, thereby sharing production capacity) and Klarx (similar to Burly, but a more integrated marketplace to share and rent out machines as well as construction equipment).

Some questions to ask

- Which assets are at the core of your platform, and is there a willingness to share these assets?
- How can you facilitate trust that assets are shared and treated carefully (e.g. insurance, reviews)?
- How can you facilitate the effective sharing of assets?
- What time horizon do you and your partners take as the base for the business cases?
- Are there potentially unutilised or very costly assets in your industry that could be shared?

Value exchange platforms

7 Product marketplaces

Product marketplaces bring sellers and buyers of physical products together. These marketplaces have to pay specific attention to the very unique characteristics of physical products. You cannot just produce and ship a physical product like a digital product in zero time with marginal costs close to zero. Hence, product marketplaces have to ensure that they balance demand and supply carefully to avoid buyer or seller dissatisfaction. Product marketplaces are probably one of the most well-known types of platforms, but also often the most misunderstood. Due to a lack of network effects, many e-commerce businesses, such as simple fashion online stores, are often incorrectly portrayed as platform businesses. In contrast to an ordinary retail online store, product marketplaces match and facilitate transactions. Although Amazon is probably the best-known product marketplace today – next to Alibaba – it did not start as a platform business. Amazon started as an online merchandiser buying and selling books via an online shop. It was only by transforming the online store into an open marketplace with third-party vendors that Amazon became the thriving platform we know today. Now it has a diversified portfolio of platforms but also acts as a classic retailer on its own platforms by offering products itself ('sold by Amazon') and even selling its own products (Amazon Basics).

Given their economic benefits when aggregating demand and supply, product marketplaces have emerged in almost every industry. A distinction can be made between horizontal and vertical (niche) product marketplaces. Horizontal product marketplaces like Amazon, Alibaba, eBay, JD.com or Craigslist try to aggregate a very broad category of products, while vertical platforms, like Pinduoduo (agricultural products), Etsy (handmade items), Chronext (watches), CarOnSale (used cars) or Vinted (second-hand clothes), try to focus on primarily one product category. Owing to the diversity and heterogeneity, many niche marketplaces have developed, especially in the B2B sector. For instance, the chemical company LANXESS has launched the B2B marketplace CheMondis. It is one of the first marketplaces to connect suppliers and buyers of chemical products and is open to all manufacturers in the industry, including competitors of LANXESS. With regard to the circular economy, product marketplaces offer great opportunities, especially for used products, and can give them a second life as platforms and can unlock hidden demand. Founded in 2016, wind-turbine.com is a marketplace for used wind turbines and spare parts. The founder had no experience in the industry but had successfully set up a marketplace before and saw great potential in bringing together owners of used wind turbines (especially owners in Germany, who would soon be buying new turbines given the government subsidies) with interested buyers who do not have the resources to build a new wind turbine from scratch (especially in Eastern Europe). It has since outgrown the original vision and become the global marketplace for wind turbines that now orchestrates supply and demand across the entire wind energy industry, connecting over 9,500 companies.[26] Looking back, the founder is convinced that it was exactly his lack of experience and footprint in the industry that made him successful: Being completely neutral can be an important success factor in the B2B sector. Other examples of niche platforms in B2B include equippo.com (marketplace for used construction equipment), traktorpool (marketplace for agricultural machinery and equipment), MoBase (marketplace for rail products and spare parts), CaeliWind (marketplace for acquiring land suitable for the operation of wind turbines), Toolplace (marketplace connecting tool suppliers with plastic processors) and Wucato (marketplace for supplies and C-parts).

> Bernd Weidmann, founder of wind-turbine.com, on how he came up with the idea: 'I was incredibly keen to start another platform in the B2B area and it was clear to me that renewable energies are really starting now. Then I dealt with the topics around renewable energies like wind, solar, hydro power, bio. These wind turbines have in fact always excited me and I planned to start there. At this time, there were no real solutions and I decided to build a marketplace for the wind industry, especially with the aim of targeting the secondary market.' (2022)[27]

Despite the many successful examples, building a successful product marketplace can be challenging and is not always reasonable. Africa's first unicorn, Jumia, operated an e-commerce business in Nigeria, but thought about transforming into a marketplace by onboarding third-party sellers – just like Amazon and Alibaba. Management recognised the many advantages of a platform business (e.g. low asset investment, better choice for users, greater scalability), but eventually had to discard the new strategy. They faced major challenges in transforming into a multi-sided business, e.g. Jumia no longer had control over quality, many counterfeit products were sold and many suppliers even refused to sell on their own and take the risk (instead of selling directly to Jumia as before). Therefore, they refocused on improving their existing e-commerce (reseller) business instead.[28]

Some questions to ask

● What products are at the heart of your platform and is there a need for yet another marketplace?

● How can you differentiate yourself from existing product marketplaces?

● Should you have a different brand name or have competitors on board to get wide acceptance?

● Can you succeed as a platform, or will providers fear your potential market power?

8 Application and data marketplaces

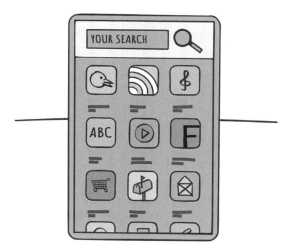

Application and data marketplaces bring together providers and users of digital goods. As of today, a wide range of digital products is sold through application and data marketplaces. Oftentimes, they complement innovation platforms like Apple iOS or Android. Through the Apple App Store, for example, developers can distribute their apps and offer them to iOS users for download or purchase. At the same time, the App Store helps Apple capture a greater share of value creation. In the domain of B2B, companies like Microsoft sell products such as Microsoft Office 365 through an application marketplace. But there are also more independent marketplaces such as Steam. It is essentially a digital sales and distribution platform for game developers. For gamers, it is the go-to place for buying games, logging into their games and accessing their gaming community. By creating a comprehensive marketplace, Steam has become a strong gatekeeper in the industry. Developers can also use Steam's capabilities to integrate microtransactions or user-generated content. Similar to Apple, Bosch Rexroth is complementing its industrial innovation platform ctrlX with an app marketplace. Third-party developers can sell and distribute their automation applications (which are compatible with ctrlX) through this marketplace. Customers, by contrast, can purchase apps developed by Bosch Rexroth and third-party suppliers via the ctrlX app store and manage their software licenses. Since the apps are provided digitally via an online update or download directly, ctrlX users can independently set up a customised software system for their production and automation system without external help. As data is becoming a core resource for value creation in many industries,[29] data marketplaces – in addition to app marketplaces – become more and more important.[30] The IoT contributes to this development by increasing the number of connected products and, thereby, giving access to valuable data. For instance, Caruso provides a marketplace for IoT-based mobility data. It connects automotive manufacturers with companies that want to utilise mobility data. This data can encompass a wide range of information, from basic car details such as battery and engine status, to more specific information like crash data and user-based data, including mileage and location. By facilitating access to a diverse range of data sources, data marketplaces like Caruso are instrumental in reducing transaction costs and enabling use cases that depend on data from various sources. For example, insurance providers could directly access mobility data on Caruso from all major OEMs, e.g. Daimler and BMW, rather than engaging in bilateral agreements. Data marketplaces are currently emerging in many (niche) industries. Agrimetrics, for instance, is a marketplace for agri-food data. On the one hand, companies can sell data such as weather or field data via Agrimetrics as data providers. On the other hand, companies can easily search and purchase data packages on Agrimetrics. Ultimately, however, data marketplaces are very difficult to scale because incumbents are often reluctant to share data with others, especially in the B2B space when competitors are present on the same marketplace. Also, harmonising data to be used across organisations as well as overcoming data protection barriers are challenging tasks.

Pedro Reboredo, director at Bosch Rexroth, on how its ctrlX marketplace works: 'Our ctrlX Store is part of the ecosystem surrounding our automation platform. The related ctrlX World for partners and the ctrlX AUTOMATION community are continuing to grow. The aim of the ctrlX Store is to make functionalities and apps easy for users to access, in a way that is familiar to them from the world of smartphones. We want to make users' day-to-day work easier, literally at the press of a button.' (2021)[31]

9 Service marketplaces

Service marketplaces bring service providers together with service seekers. These marketplaces help service consumers identify the right provider, they assure that the service has the desired quality and they ease the coordination with the provider. Although Craigslist was not intended to be a services-only marketplace, by the early 2000s there was already a separate service listings section where anyone from wedding photographers to painters could offer their services. Out of this confusing jungle of service providers and seekers, smaller service platforms emerged. They focused on only one category, but with a higher degree of curation. Today, service platforms are available in various domains, from mobility and logistics to healthcare, with Uber being one of the most prominent ones. Essentially, it is a service marketplace that matches drivers with riders. Users particularly appreciate the convenience of on-demand matching and the high level of trust. Uber has served as a blueprint for many companies trying to build their own 'Uber for X'. Ultimately, the concept is based on the idea, 'What if you could request a ride from your phone?'.[32]

Similarly, InstaFreight seeks to digitise the analogue road freight industry. On its marketplace, it brings shippers and carriers together to match the demand and supply of road freight. By offering a fully managed and digital transport process, both sides of the market benefit from increased transparency as well as efficiency gains (better capacity utilisation). Service platforms can also exist in small niches. Leadnow, for instance, matches influencers with companies that want to organise marketing campaigns on social media. Companies can compare the most relevant performance indicators (number and type of followers) to find and book the best-suited influencer. While Sixt is not a platform business per se, they recently integrated third-party ride-hailing services like TIER Mobility (a scooter company) and taxi services into their smartphone app. This transformed Sixt into a multi-sided service platform that was able to increase customer loyalty, and also started competing with existing platforms such as Google and Apple.

> Philipp Ortwein, cofounder of InstaFreight, on the benefits of a service market-place: 'Our platform business model has the advantage that we can consolidate both sides: The demand for transport from shippers and the supply of transport capacity from trucking companies. On the one hand, we can combine several part loads that go in the same direction, and on the other hand, we can offer haulers targeted return loads.' (2019)[33]

In general, the lines between product and service marketplace can be blurry. For instance, pferde.de is primarily a marketplace for selling and buying horses, but includes components of a service marketplace. Individuals or companies can also offer services on the marketplace, e.g. training and horse care, and it matches people looking to share horse ownership. In the B2B segment, Schüttflix, the marketplace for bulk material procurement and disposal, is also such an example. While it connects different service providers (e.g. contractors, bulk materials sellers, carriers and disposers) with service seekers, in the end, it is about buying and selling bulk materials. To deliver value, it depends on a long-term network of more than 20,000 vehicles from independent suppliers.[34] In addition to Schüttflix, many service platforms have emerged in the area of supply chain and procurement, for example, Maistro, Lumi and SupplyOn to name a few. Their goal is to eliminate potential trust and contract fulfilment issues by bringing together the sourcing, comparison and management of supplier interactions on one platform. Another emerging area for service marketplaces is healthcare, where, for instance, several telemedicine market-places, like OnlineDoctor, WeDoctor, Babylon or kry are currently developing. They connect medical service providers, such as doctors, with patients who can make appointments digitally and remotely.

Ultimately, all service marketplaces, from Uber, Helpling and Leadnow to booking.com, Tripadvisor or WeDoctor, try to aggregate a defined group of service providers and curate the different offers on their marketplace, e.g. through a vetting or review mechanism. Lately, these platforms are increasingly investing in machine learning to make the matching process more efficient and effective.

Some questions to ask
- Which service marketplaces are potentially relevant to your business – as a consumer, provider?
- Can you bring service providers together with service seekers in a yet underserved market?
- What is the value proposition for the service provider to participate on the platform?
- How can you help identify the right provider, assure desired quality and ease coordination?
- How can you ensure recurrent business on the platform after the contact has been established?

Service and interaction platforms

10 P2P support platforms

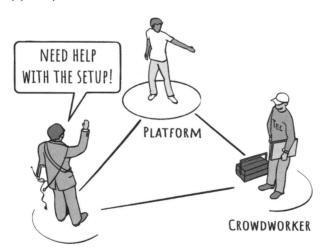

P2P support platforms bring individuals together to help each other. Individuals can put their skills or knowledge to use and most often monetise them, while others can conveniently and easily receive help. But established companies can also leverage P2P support platforms to increase and extend their service offering. The Swiss-based platform Mila, for instance, can help increase a company's service field force by a factor of ten without any additional costs. For years, the platform operated as a Swisscom subsidiary with the aim of allowing customers to book a private tech enthusiast with some free time, a Mila 'Friend', to install a WLAN router, for example, instead of a professional Swsscom technician. Thereby, Swisscom leveraged the crowd to help individual consumers with their IT issues – think digital native neighbour helps digital immigrant neighbour. This has boosted the Swisscom service fleet significantly and increased customer satisfaction due to the personal interaction. While it was initially limited to the Swisscom product sphere, many product manufacturers (e.g. Sonos, Logitech) and retail and e-commerce companies (e.g. Microspot, Conrad) have since joined the platform as corporate partners. To better balance the supply, Mila also started allowing professionals to help out, but in doing so moved more and more towards a traditional service marketplace. Today, it therefore connects individuals with either private tech enthusiasts (Mila 'Friend') or professional tech experts (Mila 'Pro') to solve their tech problems. Moreover, in contrast to the past, these technical problems can now be independent of a specific product brand, e.g. the installation of a barbecue or a washing machine. Similarly, Experify is trying to transform the whole customer interaction and experience of product companies. It connects individuals who are interested in buying a product with neighbours who already own that product. In times of anonymous and fake reviews, this is a way to get an honest opinion and test a product in real life.

> Manuel Grenacher, former CEO of Mila, on the two sides of the platform: 'When a customer rings us up and wants to know how to record something on the TV it can sometimes take a long time to just explain where the right button is on the remote control [. . .]. We want to be able to offer our customers a "geek next door" that can come round.' (2014)[35]

Stack Overflow is a question-and-answer (Q&A) website for programmers and can also be considered a P2P support platform. Developers help each other to solve coding issues and to improve their skills. So far, it has received over 20 million questions and 30 million answers.[36] In fact, programmers, or software users, often prefer to go directly to Stack Overflow to discuss their programming problems or get help, rather than going down a formal route and asking a large corporation. An alternative example that follows the credo of 'bringing peers together to help each other' is mydealz, a community of people who share discount codes and deals. The independent platform PiggyBee also uses the power of the crowd, namely for the delivery of shipments. Similar to car sharing, when you drive from A to B, you can post this route and other people can ask you to pick up and deliver a parcel along the route in return for a small fee. While P2P support platforms hold great potential for both individuals and companies, labour laws will strongly influence the future of all types of platforms that rely on services provided by individuals – as Uber has already shown several times in the case of service platforms.

11 Social media platforms

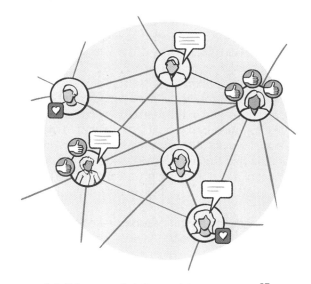

With an average of 2.5 hours of daily social media use,[37] platforms such as Facebook, WeChat, Reddit and Instagram have become an established means of communication with family, friends and beyond.[38] Essentially, it is about building virtual networks and communities. At the same time, they have become indispensable for many companies to communicate with their customers. For instance, product companies leverage social media platforms for marketing, customer service or to build a community around their product offerings. While the social media platform WhatsApp focuses on messaging, companies also use it for communicating or interacting with customers. In fact, in 2018, WhatsApp started offering dedicated APIs for businesses to integrate. KLM or Sixt, for example, have their own WhatsApp hotlines where responsiveness and customer satisfaction are significantly higher than with the traditional hotline. Also, the World Health Organization used WhatsApp to distribute timely and verified information in the context of COVID-19.

Social media platforms typically benefit from, but are not limited to, one-sided (direct) network effects: The greater the number of users who join, the more interesting it is for others to join. Recently, the online store for sportswear Keller Sports complemented its core business with sMiles. Individuals can use the sMiles app to collect points for completing sports challenges that can be exchanged for rewards from partners. Moreover, they can share their results and interact with family and friends. The story of Strava is very similar. While essentially being an app to track riding and running activities via GPS, they have built a community around their products, thereby transforming Strava into a social media platform. On one side of the platform, corporate partners, such as LeCol (a brand for bike clothing), can upload challenges on Strava where users can win real prizes. On the other side of the platform, users not only can track their sporting activities, but can also share their experiences with their community, move up the rankings and win sporting challenges. Indirect network effects, therefore, result from the fact that the larger the number of sports users who join the platform, the more interested corporate partners are in offering sports challenges with benefits, and vice versa. The German network nebenan.de is a place where you can find and offer support in your neighbourhood. The exclusively local platform is used to connect with like-minded people, explore local activities or use its market-place. This could include borrowing an item or finding a babysitter. In addition to neighbours, local businesses or the municipality can also join the community to offer services or information, making it a two-sided marketplace. Moreover, domain-specific social media platforms exist, such as LinkedIn, Twitter or TikTok. SocialDiabetes and PatientsLikeMe are two examples of social media platforms in the healthcare domain. On PatientsLikeMe, for instance, more than 850,000 individuals can share their experiences and treatment results with others.[39]

In the end, social media platforms provide great potential for companies to 'build a community around their product' – either by integrating into an existing platform or by developing their own platform.

Some questions to ask

- How can you best build a community around your products and services?
- Which social media platforms can you leverage to build such a community?
- Is there a specific opportunity for a novel community or social exchange platform?
- How can you utilise data and keep up with privacy principles?

12 Content and review platforms

Content and review platforms provide an infrastructure for others to create, share and review content, such as music, videos or text. Wikipedia and YouTube, for example, fully rely on the crowd to create content, encyclopaedic knowledge in the case of Wikipedia and videos in the case of YouTube. Since essentially 'everyone can become a creator' on YouTube, thousands of videos are uploaded daily, ranging from educational and inspirational to funny. Content and review platforms are important not only for marketing, but also for customer interaction, even if you are a traditional manufacturing company. For example, there are many great 'how to' videos on YouTube and first product companies have leveraged these ordinary videos by linking to them so that consumers can easily share best practices and learn from other users. Galaxus, a Swiss product marketplace, for example, links 'product unboxing videos' or 'product reviews' on YouTube directly to the respective products on the market-place. Created in 2014, the platform Little Red Book (Xiaohongshu) has become the most influential product review platform in China. People share and comment on their product purchases, in particular in the fashion and luxury sector. Today, it is the go-to website and often the first point of contact for product information – with a direct link to online stores and product marketplaces. Similar examples are Trustpilot, Tripadvisor or Yelp, which have created platforms for crowdsourced reviews.

Medium has revolutionised the publishing industry by eliminating interme-diaries. Everybody, from amateurs to professionals, can write down his or her ideas and share them. Over the last few years, it has become one of the leading platforms for sharing and consuming readable content. For companies, it can be a source for strategic insights, lessons learned or case studies from others. Similarly, Inkitt started a platform with the objective of democratising the publishing industry and discovering hidden talent. Unknown authors can upload any story to the platform, finished as well as unfinished book content. This text can then be read by a community that provides feedback. In addition, an algorithm tries to analyse users' reading behaviour as they read the unfinished texts. On the basis of this, Inkitt aims to identify those stories and books that have the potential to become bestsellers. They can even provide authors with data-driven feedback on where in the text readers are particularly captivated by the content or when they stop reading. Books that receive good ratings from readers may receive a publisher's offer to release the book on Inkitt's corresponding reading app. As a result, Inkitt manages to publish more than 300 books every year.[40] Another example is Thatch, a nascent platform for travellers to create, share and monetise travel tips.

> Ali Albazaz, founder of Inkitt, on the idea behind it: 'We have an online platform on inkitt.com where authors can upload their manuscripts. We have about 50,000 authors writing actively on the platform and over a million readers who can read these books completely for free. While the readers are reading, we analyse their reading behaviour. [. . .] Based on this feedback or data points that we get, we can predict if a book has the potential to become a best-seller.' (2017)[41]

Some questions to ask
- How can you leverage existing content and review platforms to promote your offerings?
- How can you encourage your users to become creators and, e.g., share best practices?
- How can you keep up the quality level and prevent selfish or ugly comments?
- Can you gather and enable a community to create and share content on a novel platform?
- How can you use generative artificial intelligence, like ChatGPT, to create initial reviews to overcome the chicken-and-egg problem?

Work and education platforms

13 Collaboration platforms

Remote work has become commonplace, and collaboration platforms can empower individuals to work together from anywhere. They facilitate communication, knowledge management, teamwork and project management across distributed teams and individuals. However, winner-takes-all dynamics are often not as pronounced compared with other platform business models because users can easily switch between or use different collaboration platforms simultaneously. With the rise of home offices during the COVID-19 crisis, the collaboration platform Zoom became very popular. Essentially, it is a platform for virtual meetings, distance education and socialising. Similarly, Microsoft Teams is a collaboration platform that aims to bring work colleagues together virtually. In addition to video conferencing, it is tightly embedded in the Microsoft Office Suite, but third-party vendors can also integrate their software or collaboration tools.

RefinemySite from Bosch Power Tools is a cloud-based tool for more effective and efficient collaboration on construction projects. While people used to collaborate using sticky notes on large walls, Bosch is trying to digitise this industry through a collaboration platform. It enables everyone involved in such projects, from the client to the craftsman and the project manager, to plan together and communicate with each other digitally, with the objective of creating a lean construction site. Another example is Confluence, a platform for knowledge sharing and collaboration on joint projects, no matter whether it is a software, innovation or strategy project. Like Microsoft Teams, Confluence also offers software interfaces for the integration of third-party services and thus enables complementary innovations. Other examples of collaboration platforms are Slack, Focusmate, Asana or Trello.

Some questions to ask

- Can you facilitate new collaboration modes, e.g. based on novel technology such as augmented reality (AR)?
- Can you offer a platform that addresses a unique opportunity, e.g. AR-enabled service?
- How can you improve social presence and social richness of the platform to make a great user experience (UX)?
- Which platforms could you use to improve your customer and supplier collaboration?

14 Education platforms

The objective of education platforms is to facilitate online learning and provide teaching marketplaces. Anyone can be a student. Anyone can offer a course and act as an instructor. Ultimately, education platforms take the YouTube idea that everybody can be a creator to the education space and make education more affordable and accessible. MasterClass is an online learning platform where individuals can access lectures from renowned experts. Unlike most education platforms, MasterClass does not focus on hard skills such as coding. Instead, MasterClass focuses on private hobbies and domains such as writing, cooking or acting. Coursera focuses on hard skills instead and goes a step further by offering a variety of online courses and even degrees, with subjects ranging from history to mathematics to law. The teachers are not only private individuals, but also professors as the platform cooperates with more than 150 universities.[42]

> David Rogier, cofounder of MasterClass, on their goals: 'A lot of it was thinking about how to bring back the joy of learning. If you talk to most people about whether they like school, the answer is, "no". If you ask people if they like learning, the answer is, "Of course".' (2021)[43]

Udemy and Udacity follow a similar business model, often also referred to as massive open online courses (MOOCs). CoachHub is a platform for digital coaching for employees at all career levels and consists of a large pool of certified business coaches. Among others, the platform provides different coaching solutions in the field of leadership, employee wellbeing and diversity. By connecting coaches with employees, CoachHub aims at developing inspiring leaders, increasing team performance or helping employees grow personally and professionally. Junto is a platform similar to CoachHub but it has a stronger focus on live training and interactive sessions. Ultimately, all education platforms are expected to grow in popularity over the next few years, as much of the existing workforce will need to be retrained or reskilled in the face of technological advances.

It is important for these platforms that they are not only a cost-effective mass communication platform, but that they can also reach new levels qualitatively. While lecturing in traditional university or company education rooms is synchronous and therefore can be too slow for some students and too fast for others, online education platforms enable asynchronous, personalised learning. The speed can be personally adapted, but so can the sequence, content, style, etc., depending on personal goals. The future of education will allow for automated learning in a very entertaining way, but complemented by in-person learning.

Some questions to ask

- Would your employees, customers or partners appreciate special training or education?
- Can you match these stakeholders with offerings on existing education platforms?
- Can you build up your own education platform for your customers or a dedicated industry niche?
- How do you attract the opinion leaders and stars to your platform?
- What are the verticals where you should start with quick wins and high acceptance?
- How do you create quality checks, both for teaching materials and student progress?

---

15 Freelance platforms

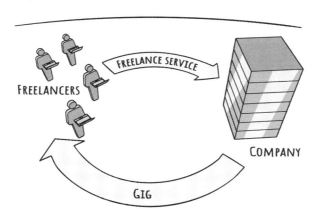

Freelance platforms connect businesses with freelancers. Photographers, designers or software developers, for example, can use freelance platforms to list their services or bid on listed service requests. Freelance platforms are also known as gig platforms, as freelancers fall into the category of gig workers who are not employees but work on a non-permanent, temporary basis. Rather than hiring employees who commit to long-term contracts, freelance platforms make it easy to hire freelancers for one-time tasks, such as the development or the design of logos and websites.

Today, a wide variety of freelance platforms have been developed in terms of duration, type, scope and remuneration of tasks. Fiverr has become one of the most popular marketplaces for freelance services. Dominant service categories on Fiverr are graphics and design, digital marketing, writing and translation and video and animation, as well as programming and tech. From the start, they did not see themselves as a recruitment company, but as a marketplace. Hence, their aim was to increase the number of freelancers as fast as possible and kickstart the supply side. Upwork is very similar to Fiverr, but with a broader scope and focused on the needs of businesses, e.g. it also features longer-term service assignments on its marketplace and provides support services for overcoming recruitment challenges.

> Micha Kaufman, founder of Fiverr, on the idea behind Fiverr: 'Fiverr is redefining the way people work online. It allows anyone to turn their skills, talents and resources into income in a matter of minutes. Think of it as the eBay for the services economy.' (n.d.)[44]

MTurk is an on-demand marketplace for so-called micro-tasks. In contrast to Fiverr and Upwork, it is a marketplace for companies to hire remotely located crowdworkers to perform simple and rather repetitive tasks such as manually labelling pictures for the development of AI algorithms. The freelancing platform TaskRabbit is even integrated directly into other companies: When purchasing furniture online at IKEA Germany, for instance, at the check-out, customers are offered help from a 'Tasker' from TaskRabbit in assembling their furniture. There are many other examples of freelance platforms, Jobandtalent, Thumbtack, Cornerjob, Guru, uTest or Maypal, to name a few, some of which have a very niche focus. For instance, uTest is a freelance platform that unites the world's largest community of digital software testers. More than 700,000 testers test and provide feedback for global brands that want to improve their digital customer experiences.[45] While testers may earn money, on the other side companies can receive more authentic feedback and real-world insights within hours, which they can use to improve their digital experience.

Some questions to ask

- Is there already a freelance platform in your industry or are there freelance opportunities?
- What kind of services could be at the core of a freelance platform in your industry?
- What is the kind of work that is difficult to automate (AI) and easy to evaluate (progress, quality)?
- How and where could you leverage existing freelance platforms in your company?

Finance platforms

16 Payment platforms

Payment platforms enable sellers to offer their customers easy and safe payments. Payment platforms heavily depend on network effects as a payment transaction can only occur if sellers and buyers leverage the same payment channel. PayPal started with the aim of making exchanging money between friends as easy and fast as possible. Today, it is one of the most dominant payment providers – not only for peer-to-peer transactions but also to pay money to online or offline merchants. In essence, credit card companies such as Mastercard or Visa are also all about network effects. One side of the platform comprises the merchants and the other side is made up of the customers. The more merchants accept Mastercard, the greater the value for a customer to own a Mastercard – and vice versa. The increasing global adoption of smartphones had led to the emergence of many mobile-based payment platforms, often local platforms, such as Twint (Switzerland), MobilePay (Scandinavia), AliPay (China), Paytm (India) or Wise (international). The Kenyan company M-Pesa has become Africa's largest payment platform and has successfully expanded across multiple African countries. Established in 2007 by Vodafone's Kenyan unit Safaricom, it now enables more than 50 million users to pay for goods and services, make transfers and access their bank accounts.[46] On the other side of the platform, more than 600,000 businesses use the M-Pesa payment platform to process transactions (up to 61 million transactions every day).[47] Sometimes platform business models can only be recognised at a second glance. For instance, ParkingPay not only provides the physical infrastructure for (public) parking spaces or car parks in Switzerland (such as a parking machine to get a ticket) but can also be considered a payment platform. Complementing its installed base of parking machines, it digitally connects the driver with the car park operator to process payments directly through its smartphone app – just like PayPal, but for parking.

> Nick Read, former CEO of Vodafone, on the achievements of M-Pesa: 'M-Pesa has helped millions of people access financial services for the first time and millions more improve their lives, start businesses and gain control of their finances. We are still in the early stages of M-Pesa's development and will continue to invest to capture this significant opportunity – building value for shareholders.' (2021)[48]

Some questions to ask
- Do you see potential to integrate an additional digital payment platform into your business?
- Can you become a payment platform in a specific niche, just like ParkingPay?
- What is your base platform, for transactions, e.g. PayPal?
- Can you prevent multi-homing and address the threat of becoming disintermediated?

---

17 Lending platforms

Bypassing traditional financial institutions, lending platforms connect borrowers directly to lenders, also known as peer-to-peer lending. Investors can simply search for a loan project they want to invest in – just like searching for and buying a new jacket in an online store. In fact, both private individuals as well as businesses can conduct transactions on lending platforms. Eliminating the oftentimes costly and untransparent intermediary, platforms can democratise access to capital and the credit market. The necessary transparency is typically created either by providing risk profiles to investors or by using incentives to motivate loan seekers to provide comprehensive information. However, it has to be acknowledged that many of the companies that started out as P2P lending platforms have since evolved into real (online) banks and have ceased their P2P business – often because it became economically unviable, or the legal conditions and regulations changed for the worse.[49] For instance, on one of the pioneering lending platforms LendingClub, borrowers were able to apply for a loan and investors could directly finance such loans. A risk profile for each loan seeker was created so that investors could screen the different projects and selectively invest in them. At the end of 2020, however, it stopped its P2P business and began focusing on institutional lending for investors. Similarly, Zopa was one of the first companies to launch a pure P2P lending platform, and since its launch in 2005 more than GBP 5 billion have been raised. But also in 2020, Zopa announced it would become a full bank closing down its P2P loan business. Funding Societies is Southeast Asia's largest digital financing and debt investment platform for small- and medium-sized enterprises. While not directly connecting individual investors and credit seekers, it does bring them together on one platform, but in a more integrated manner. On one side of the platform, the financial capital is provided by individual and institutional investors. This money is then disbursed within 24 hours to businesses on the other side. Since 2015, Funding Societies has financed over USD 1.8 billion through more than 4.8 million loans to nearly 100,000 micro, small- and medium-sized enterprises in Southeast Asia.[50] Other lending platforms include Funding Circle, Roostify, Lendify and Lendbiz. However, in the end, only very few genuine P2P lending platforms are still active.

Kelvin Teo, cofounder and CEO of Funding Societies on the idea behind Funding Societies: 'My cofounder, Reynold, and I started Funding Societies to make a positive difference in Southeast Asia and we're heartened to see the huge impact to SMEs over the past 6 years. We are looking to empower SMEs not just in digital financing but also solving their other pain points over time.' (2021)[51]

Some questions to ask
- Do your customers seek financing in addition to buying products and requesting services?
- Can you help your customers find the right financial offering through a marketplace?
- Can you support the risk evaluation process for the lenders?
- Do you have the chance to connect borrowers and lenders on a (industry-specific) marketplace?

18 Investment platforms

Investment platforms are all about democratising investments. While similar to crowdfunding platforms, investment platforms are about receiving a share of the company at the end. They aim to make investment opportunities that were previously reserved for professional investors accessible to everyone. As of today, a variety of investment platforms have emerged that allow individuals to invest directly in a broad variety of private companies. Online stockbrokers can also be considered platforms to some extent, but they are strong gatekeepers and are, both, very integrated and closed.

Meanwhile, more open investment platforms have emerged that allow individuals to invest directly in a variety of private companies or other assets outside of the stock market. For instance, on the investment platform Republic, private individuals can invest as little as USD 10 directly in unlisted start-ups, real estate projects or video games in exchange for equity shares. Comparable platforms are Crowdcube or Seedmatch, where private individuals can invest directly in start-ups or growth companies, starting from very small amounts such as EUR 250 on Seedmatch. With Seedmatch Crowdbonds, individuals can also invest in fixed-interest debt securities.

> Johannes Ranscht, CEO of Seedmatch, on the background of Seedmatch: 'We launched in 2011 as the first crowdinvesting platform in Germany and paved the way for this then still new form of financing in this country with a great deal of pioneering spirit and passion. As a result, we can look back on a particularly rich wealth of experience and have been able to build up extensive expertise that benefits both our users and the companies financed through us.' (2022)[52]

In addition, there are sector-specific investment platforms, in the energy or real estate sectors, for instance. RippleEnergy is in the start-up phase and seeks to make investments in wind farms accessible to private individuals. One can make an upfront investment in a share of a future wind farm. As soon as the plant is built and in operation, the investor's return is credited directly to the electricity bill in the form of a rebate. Ultimately, RippleEnergy manages and operates the entire wind farm on behalf of the numerous owners. Very similar to RippleEnergy, but in the real estate sector, is Crowdhouse, which is at its core a marketplace for buying and selling real estate. However, compared to traditional real estate marketplaces, individual investors can also invest in small shares of real estate assets. Therefore, individual houses are then owned by several owners, while the Swiss platform manages and operates the buildings. An even more open approach is being taken by the nascent Tailwind project, which aims to tokenise wind turbines. Private individuals or companies can invest in (existing) wind turbine projects for starting with as little as EUR 50. Conversely, the operators of such projects are given the opportunity to receive funding and accelerate the roll out of wind power systems. In the end, both wind energy projects are still in their infancy and need to prove themselves.

Some questions to ask

- Does your industry offer an opportunity to democratise investing?
- Can you tokenise assets in your industry to make investing possible for a broader audience?
- Can you serve as an intermediary that brings together investors and investment opportunities?

Technology and data platforms

19 Technology platforms

Technology platforms focus on providing fundamental technologies and services, such as cloud storage, computing or networking. Infrastructure-as-a-Service (IaaS) platforms are a prominent type of technology platform that provide fundamental infrastructure on a pay-per-use basis for others to deploy software applications on top of. IaaS platforms enable users to remain flexible and always have access to the latest technology without having to upgrade their internal server constantly and expensively.[53] The virtualisation of computing power over the last years has been driven largely by a select number of companies, the so-called hyperscalers, including Amazon, Google and Microsoft. In its early days, Amazon struggled with infrastructure problems due to its swift growth. To keep up with IT demands, they developed an internal cloud solution and later started selling it to external customers as a technology platform. In their press release, Amazon described the first version as 'a simple storage service that offers software developers a highly scalable, reliable and low-latency data storage infrastructure at very low costs'.[54]

> Jeff Barr, chief evangelist of AWS, on the launch of AWS in 2006: 'Storage for the Internet was – I don't want to say obvious – but so clear that if we had it, customers would find it useful.' (2021)[55]

While the infrastructure services are today sold as a product that provides stand-alone value, they also form a proprietary innovation platform that third parties can develop complements for. In fact, complementors can develop applications for various domains and use cases based on the cloud infrastructure. Therefore, Amazon employees often call AWS the 'Lego of the IT World'.[56] In addition, IaaS platforms often host marketplaces where third parties can offer their solutions. In the case of Amazon, they can sell them via the AWS marketplace. Similarly, Microsoft operates its own cloud computing platform Azure. Azure customers can build and run their applications on top of Azure. Through Azure IaaS, customers can access the computing resources they need from an external provider via the Internet.

Some questions to ask

- What are the technology platforms that are relevant for you – beyond Amazon and Microsoft?
- Do you have fundamental technology that you can provide as a platform offering?
- How can you build an ecosystem around the technology platform?
- What are complementary products and services for your platform and who can provide them?

20 Application platforms

Application platforms provide a foundation on which third parties and developers can create and run applications without worrying about computing infrastructure and application runtime environments.[57] By providing SDKs and APIs, hardware development kits or graphical user interfaces (GUI), the objective is to 'unleash complementary innovation'. Apple iOS, the operating system for the iPhone and iPad, is a prominent example in the domain of smartphones. Apple offers a rich set of SDKs and interfaces that make it as easy as possible for external developers to create apps for iOS users. Today, the operating system serves as a basis for over 4 million apps, which is one reason why the iOS platform is so attractive to users. Acquired by Salesforce in 2010, Heroku is another example of an application platform enabling third parties to develop as well as run applications in the cloud.

> Sasha Reminnyi, general manager at UiPath Marketplace, on the importance of recognising both sides of the platform as being your customers: 'We're focusing on delivering more business value to both, our consumers who are downloading Marketplace content and our publishers who are creating that content.' (2021)[58]

With its Alexa Skills Kit, Amazon offers external developers the opportunity to expand the capabilities of its voice assistant Alexa. Third-party applications can range from controlling a light bulb to a skill called 'Good Night' which provides custom-made good night messages. End users who own an Alexa-enabled device can download and install skills from the Alexa Skills Store. UiPath has developed an application platform that enables others to develop, operate and manage software robots that mimic human actions in a digital environment. In 2018, the company launched a marketplace for reusable robotic process automation (RPA) software. This allowed partners, community members and other vendors to expand their reach and monetise reusable RPA components that were built upon the UiPath application platform. Since then, it has evolved into the largest marketplace for RPA. Many application platforms are proprietary with the aim of binding developers and making it difficult to switch or multi-home (i.e. develop for two platforms at the same time). There is also the trend to simplify the development environments for applications as much as possible. Low- or no-code platforms are arising that require less programming knowledge and thus unlock a large number of new developers. Overall, a wide variety of application platforms have emerged across the board, from gaming (PlayStation, Xbox), computers (macOS, Windows) and smartphones/tablets (Apple iOS, Google Android, Amazon Fire) to software (Salesforce, Firefox, UiPath). Application platforms are also emerging owing to advances in distributed ledger technologies (e.g. blockchain) and in other sectors such as virtual reality (e.g. Oculus) or automotive (e.g. Calponia, Android Automotive OS).

> James Lindenbaum, cofounder of Heroku, on the hosting of applications: 'We follow a very different model from hosting. The end point that we are after is that you can come and say "Hey, I need to build something" and then just have it run.' (2008)[59]

Some questions to ask
- What types of third-party applications could add value to your product/platform?
- How can you enable third parties to develop complementary applications on your offerings?
- How can you create an attractive development environment for both the tech and business communities?
- What existing and emerging application platforms are relevant to your business?

21 Open source platforms

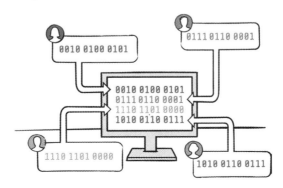

Today, a lot of software development is done on the basis of open source platforms. A prominent example is Linux, but there are many more open source platforms available for end users, developers or companies. Open source platforms allow anyone to use, change or distribute the platform and its source code for free.[60] The goal of open source platforms is to ensure universal platform access and to foster open collaboration between platform developers. Open collaboration serves as a basis to develop an active developer community that continuously extends the scope and quality of the platform so that more and more users and developers are convinced to join the community. Linux is one of the most prominent open source operating systems. As one of the only alternatives to Windows and MacOS, and in contrast to those platforms, Linux can be used, changed or distributed by anyone. Linux has become a very successful and robust platform thanks to its unique and very active developer community. Similarly, Android is an open source operating system for mobile devices. In fact, it is based on a version of Linux. The development of Android is led by the Open Handset Alliance, and basically anyone can contribute code to the corresponding Android open source project (AOSP). However, most Android smartphones come with additional proprietary software, such as Google Mobile Services (including apps like Play Store, YouTube or Chrome), and one of Google's core aims is to monetise app sales via its Play Store. Robot operating system (ROS) is a software development platform for robotics applications that is based on a global community that contributes and improves the underlying open source software. The network consists of developers and users from different industries who develop individual applications from research and prototyping towards actual productive deployment. On both sides of the platform, contributors and users benefit from an active community. While the idea of open source seems to contradict the concept of a profit-seeking enterprise, there are successful open source companies that collaboratively build their products and platforms with the community. However, these open source platform companies can only become successful with very broad adoption, i.e. a large user base and an active community. Since a significant number of users will not pay for the open source platform, these companies can typically only capture a small amount of the created value. However, even with open source projects there must be someone to turn to for service and support. Moreover, while core features are often provided for free, commercial versions of the software can provide premium features and be sold as proprietary software (open core business model).[61]

Linus Torvalds, initiator of Linux, on the advantages of open source: 'For complex technical issues you really need open source simply because the problem space ends up being too complex to manage inside one single company. Even a big and competent tech company.' (2021)[62]

Some questions to ask

- Do you face technical issues that are too complex to manage inside one single company?
- Can an active community of developers be established that addresses these technical issues?
- What is the core of the open source platform and how do you set up strategic guidelines and decision-making processes (like Linus Torvalds with the kernel of Linux)?
- Will an open source approach still allow you to create and capture value?
- What are the potential business models and offerings which can be created around the open source platform to create and capture value?

Design: patterns to create and deliver value as a platform

2

The purpose of the design patterns is to provide an overview of the core strategic choices when designing a platform business model. To make use of the design patterns, two fundamental types of platform business model need to be distinguished.[1] First, there are transaction platforms and marketplaces. Like Amazon, eBay, Airbnb or Uber, they bring two sides of the market together and facilitate transactions between those market sides. Second, there are innovation platforms like Apple iOS, Google Android, but also Microsoft Xbox or Sony PlayStation. Innovation platforms provide the infrastructure and basis for others to develop innovation on top, such as smartphone apps in the case of Apple iOS or video games in the case of Microsoft Xbox. Although, in practice, there are hybrid forms that incorporate features of both types, the core design choices of transaction and innovation platforms are fundamentally different. Acknowledging the differences, we present 26 patterns (see Figure 2.2.1). In the first step, the core value proposition (A) of the platform must be developed. Like in every other business, an effective value proposition is a prerequisite for sustainable success. In particular, the multi-sidedness of platforms must be considered so that a compelling value proposition is offered for each side (user type) of the platform. Given the diversity of platforms, we can only provide fundamental archetypal value propositions that are common in practice. Second, an appropriate ownership model needs to be defined (B). Lastly, the operating model must be determined. The operating model outlines the core value creation activities of the platform orchestrator, e.g. from asset-light to asset-heavy, from open to closed innovation and from loosely to closely coupled third-party complements. If your platform idea mainly incorporates features of a transaction platform (C), you can leverage the pattern cards #34 to #39. If your platform idea mainly incorporates features of an innovation platform (D), you can focus on the pattern cards #40 to #47.

Figure 2.2.1 Designing a platform business (Patterns #22–47)

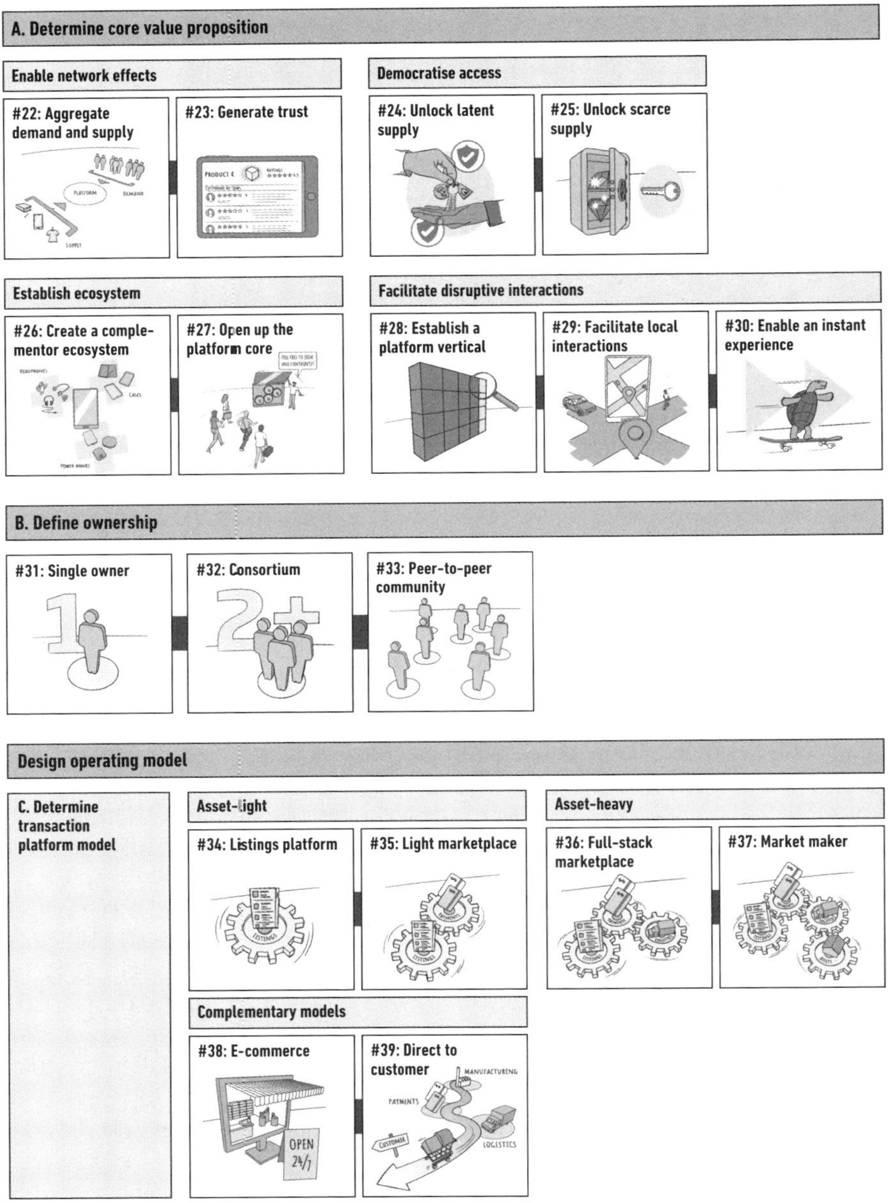
A. Determine core value proposition
Enable network effects
#22: Aggregate demand and supply
#23: Generate trust
Democratise access
#24: Unlock latent supply
#25: Unlock scarce supply
Establish ecosystem
#26: Create a complementor ecosystem
#27: Open up the platform core
Facilitate disruptive interactions
#28: Establish a platform vertical
#29: Facilitate local interactions
#30: Enable an instant experience
B. Define ownership
#31: Single owner
#32: Consortium
#33: Peer-to-peer community
Design operating model
C. Determine transaction platform model
Asset-light
#34: Listings platform
#35: Light marketplace
Asset-heavy
#36: Full-stack marketplace
#37: Market maker
Complementary models
#38: E-commerce
OPEN 24/7
#39: Direct to customer
MANUFACTURING
PAYMENTS
CUSTOMER
LOGISTICS

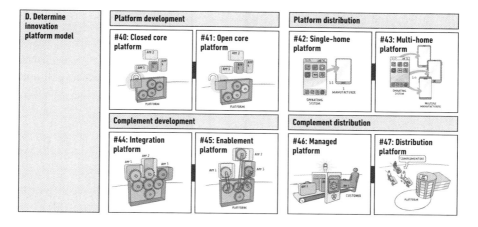

D. Determine innovation platform model	Platform development		Platform distribution	
	#40: Closed core platform	#41: Open core platform	#42: Single-home platform	#43: Multi-home platform
	Complement development		Complement distribution	
	#44: Integration platform	#45: Enablement platform	#46: Managed platform	#47: Distribution platform

Marc Andreessen, general partner of Andreessen Horowitz (U.S. venture capital firm), on the power of innovation platforms: '[A platform is] a system that can be programmed and therefore customised by outside developers – users – and in that way, adapted to countless needs and niches that the platform's original developers could not have possibly contemplated, much less had time to accommodate.' (2013)[2]

Determine the core value proposition

22 Aggregate demand and supply

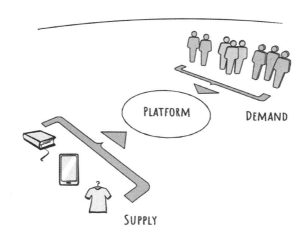

Certainly, all platforms have in common that they enable network effects. They often do this by aggregating supply and demand across multiple domains. A product platform, for example, can span different product categories. In addition, it can be present in various regions or even operate globally.

This allows platforms to reduce transaction costs on both the supply and the demand sides. This creates a strong value proposition for all platform participants and can also help to capture the 'long tail' in a specific market.[3] For instance, aggregating supply is at the core of Alibaba. When Jack Ma started the product marketplace, he wanted to enable suppliers to sell and compete more effectively in the domestic and global markets. Similarly, Tripadvisor has become the one-stop shop for travel bookings. On its global marketplace, it bundles offers and user reviews across various categories, from hotels, restaurants and flights to local activities. Thereby, it has made the rather inefficient market for travelling more transparent and accessible for all market sides.

> Jack Ma, founder of Alibaba, on the importance of a big vision for platforms: 'By the year 2036, we aim to serve 2 billion global consumers, empower 10 million profitable businesses and create 100 million jobs.' (2018)[4]

In essence, all marketplaces aggregate demand and/or supply, from Amazon and Pinduoduo (product marketplaces) to booking.com and Airbnb (marketplaces for travel and vacation), and Mila (P2P support platform), as well as Fiverr (freelance platform) and emerging data marketplaces like Caruso. More specifically, Caruso provides neutral access to in-vehicle data and aligns the interests of vehicle manufacturers and third-party service providers such as insurers to enable novel products, like pay-as-you-drive insurance.

When and how to apply

To aggregate demand and supply, at least two market sides that can be brought together must be identified.[5] This works particularly if market participants want to interact with each other but cannot because existing transaction costs, such as search or opportunity costs, are high and the intended platform can reduce these costs significantly. Ease of use and seamless user journeys are key to aggregating supply and demand, especially if you need to change the behaviour of two or more market sides. For example, unlike numerous other market entrants, the Square payment platform was successful because it only changed the way merchants work, not the way end users work: While merchants had to install and use a new device at their point of sale, users could continue using their classic payment instrument, credit cards.[6]

> Philip Ortwein, cofounder of InstaFreight (a marketplace for road freight), on its value proposition: 'Land transportation is still highly inefficient and we at InstaFreight are taking a technological approach to make it more sustainable and efficient, thereby doing our part to secure global supply chains.' (2022)[7]

23 Generate trust

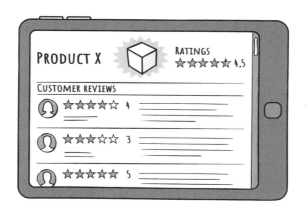

A key prerequisite for viable markets is trust, as American economist George Akerlof has shown in his Nobel Prize-winning work.[8] Platforms create new markets, and sustain established markets by leveraging powerful trust-building mechanisms.[9] Rating scores and text reviews, for example, help to evaluate products and services as well as providers and buyers. Hence, in markets where trust is often missing, e.g. second-hand products, platforms can generate trust and provide neutrality as a core value proposition to the different market sides. For instance, buyers on eBay are only willing to send money to unknown sellers before they receive the product because peer-to-peer reviews indicate the seller's trustworthiness. eBay also introduced quality labels such as 'Top Rated Seller' to complement its rating system. The same is true for the second-hand car market. Marketplaces such as Auto1 can create value for both market sides by providing the necessary trust and transparency.

> Frédéric Mazzella, CEO at BlaBlaCar in France (a marketplace for hitchhiking), on the opportunity to create value by generating trust: 'The building block of society – interpersonal trust – has been transformed from a scarce to an abundant one. Our potential to create value is also transformed.' (2019)[10]

On Auto1, buyers can even buy cars without a test drive as they benefit from a 14-day return option and have access to a wide range of photos and videos before the car sale.[1] Similarly, hitchhiking is considered dangerous, but on the ridesharing platform BlaBlaCar, drivers must verify their identity and provide meaningful profile descriptions. Compared with traditional hitchhiking, this creates the necessary trust to create a substantial ridesharing market. In the U.S., Lyft is the second largest ride-hailing service platform after Uber. After its foundation in 2012, Lyft needed to create trust in order to convince riders to get into a stranger's car. Hence, Lyft started to implement certain features that created the needed trust. One key element was that they tried to eliminate the anonymity of a ride. Therefore, they required drivers to upload a photo of themselves. Moreover, Lyft introduced a rating system and asked riders and drivers to rate each other after every trip. These features helped boost the required transparency as well as the accountability of the platform. Similarly, Uber allows users to send their location automatically during every ride to their closest friends to monitor their safety.

> Doron Reuveni, CEO of uTest (a marketplace for freelance testers and companies seeking feedback on their software), on how monetisation can also lead to trust and high quality: 'We knew what is important to the buyer. Keeping a large QA [Quality Assurance] team in-house is expensive, so we offered a pay-per-performance model. The community of testers was built as a pyramid scheme. As a new tester, one has to prove himself through online tests (created by uTest) as well as small projects, that build his initial ranking. Payment to the testers was also offered for performance (pay-per-bug).' (2009)[12]

When and how to apply

Both transaction and innovation platforms can create trust in markets as a core value proposition. This value proposition pattern is particularly relevant for markets with little transparency and significant information asymmetry. Several trust-building mechanisms are at a platform's disposal, from rating scores, written reviews and personal profiles (e.g. pictures and descriptions), to identity verifications and other information (e.g. badges, membership duration, average response time or previous behaviour on the platform).[13]

Some questions to ask

- What are the risks of buying and selling products and services in a given market?
- Which platform features are vital to address these risks, and can they ultimately create trust?
- Can you mitigate risks from trust misuse?
- How can you establish a brand that fosters trust in your platform as a reliable market facilitator?

24 Unlock latent supply

Many platforms try to match existing demand and supply more efficiently. However, platforms can also create additional supply. In the realm of the sharing economy, platforms can unlock latent supply as they build upon assets that are already in use, for example, unutilised apartments or private cars. Whereas marketplaces such as booking.com and Tripadvisor focus on aggregating supply (e.g. hotel offerings) and demand (e.g. travel guests), Airbnb unlocks latent supply by focusing on underutilised apartments. By providing insurance to hosts, Airbnb mitigates the hosts' potential fears and provides them with the necessary confidence and security to rent their apartment to strangers. Thereby, Airbnb unlocked latent supply and opened a new market. While Airbnb created additional supply by leveraging private accommodations, ByHours leverages unutilised hotel rooms. They provide a platform for short-term stays on short notice, mainly during the day when a hotel room is free or in between bookings. Customers may decide between packages of 3, 6 or 12 hours in hotels around the world. Vinted is one of the largest marketplaces for second-hand clothing. The platform encourages individuals to clean and sort out their closets by providing an efficient and trustworthy channel to sell used clothes, thereby creating additional supply on the market.

> Pierre Omidyar, founder of eBay, on unlocking latent supply: 'What eBay did was really to create a new market of one that wasn't really there before and that was a global market for the kind of goods that were usually traded at flea markets and garage sales and this kind of thing. [. . .] And that was the start of it and it hadn't existed before and now it's progressed past that into consumer electronics, computers [. . .].' (2013)[14]

When and how to apply
To unlock latent supply, companies need to first identify assets that are in demand but underutilised. These assets can come from inside or outside of

the company or platform, or even from an adjacent industry. If identified, one needs to analyse the possibility of making these assets available for others on a platform. The unlock latent supply value proposition often goes hand in hand with the circular economy (e.g. reusing second-hand assets) as well as the sharing economy (e.g. sharing assets with each other). It is not limited to the consumer sector, and is increasingly seen in the B2B sector, e.g. sharing of machinery, or marketplaces for used equipment. Most often the assets are rather expensive (e.g. apartments in the case of Airbnb or cars in the case of Uber). Hence, platforms can create value by increasing asset utilisation. This strategy also works particularly well when the market sides involved can satisfy both supply and demand, e.g. an Airbnb host can also be a guest and vice versa.

Some questions to ask

- Are there assets that are in high demand on the one hand, but underutilised on the other?
- What does it take to unlock underutilised assets and make them available to others?
- Can you create a sustainable baseline supply that is key to establish a viable market?

---

25 Unlock scarce supply

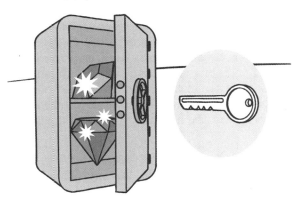

In addition to unlocking latent supply, transaction platforms can also unlock scarce supply as a core value proposition. Domains such as healthcare, education, law or software development are still highly regulated or opaque. Platforms can democratise access to scarce resources and services by building trust or verifying the quality of supply, as well as through other sorts of guarantees. As a result, platforms can tap into the scarce supply of these regulated markets.

For example, supply in the domain of software development is very low, but high quality is particularly important. Hence, for many companies finding highly skilled developers is a major challenge. The marketplace Arc addresses this problem by creating an exclusive marketplace with developers that have already been vetted. By bringing developers onto one marketplace and vetting them, it unlocks scarce supply. Similarly in the healthcare domain, the marketplace Zeel brings together customers and health instructors, such as massage therapists. The individual providers are vetted by Zeel and high quality is ensured via customer reviews and a rigorous application process. Another emerging domain in healthcare is live-in care, which is also highly regulated. Up to six intermediaries are involved in the process of arranging live-in care for elderly relatives, and oftentimes no suitable caregiver is found. Hence, supply is very scarce. The European marketplace Marta has set itself the goal of changing this by making the process more transparent and easier. It connects potential caregivers directly with those who seek care for themselves or relatives.

> Jan Hoffmann, cofounder of Marta, on the need to unlock scarce supply in the live-in care domain: 'There are hundreds of examples of how elderly care can go wrong and it's almost impossible for humans to accurately predict placement success because it's just so many data points. We have seen how difficult it was to organise care with our grandparents. Ageing is a normal process and it should not pose a major problem. We believe that we can leverage technology significantly to help elderly people and their families as well as the caregivers.' (2022)[15]

Examples of unlocking scarce supply also exist in the B2B domain. Supported by the International Finance Corporation (IFC), a member of the World Bank Group, the company Achilles Information, which conducts risk and performance management analyses for supply chains, has developed a marketplace to connect Western Balkan companies with regional and global suppliers. A particular challenge in this market is ensuring quality and trustworthy suppliers. In addition, companies often do not have the resources to vet suppliers themselves. Hence, the key value proposition of the marketplace is to unlock scarce high-quality supply. In addition to matchmaking, it achieves this by screening and certifying every supplier before registration. It provides the demand side with a detailed risk profile of each potential supplier.[16]

When and how to apply

Whereas the central value proposition of unlocking latent supply lies in the creation of additional supply, unlocking scarce supply is about improving the discovery and vetting of high-quality supply in regulated markets, for example in healthcare, engineering, accounting, teaching and law, to mention a few. Think about any industry where supply is licensed by a government agency or a professional or industry organisation. In essence, platforms can reduce the need for traditional forms of (external) regulation and licensing, as they can create trust in other ways.[17]

> **Some questions to ask**
> - Which scarce resources are at the heart of your platform?
> - How can you democratise access to these resources, e.g. by vetting or giving guarantees?
> - How do you address associated risks such as liability?

26 Create a complementor ecosystem

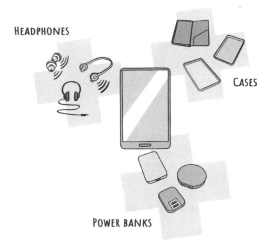

HEADPHONES

CASES

POWER BANKS

Platforms enable complementors to develop solutions that extend the platform core and its basic capabilities. Complements can be as simple as physical additions to your smartphone. Think, for example, of Apple-certified headphones, external batteries or cases. Apps available through the App Store extend the basic capabilities of the innovation platform Apple iOS. Complements such as apps can be loosely coupled to a platform if interfaces are standardised. However, complementors and their complements might also be tightly integrated into the platform based on strategic partnerships, as it is often the case in the B2B domain.

The Chinese social media platform WeChat benefits from a rich complementor ecosystem. In addition to simple messaging, users can leverage a variety of third-party services directly in the WeChat app. Third parties offer, for example, flight or hotel booking, product search or access to banking information. Another example is Airbnb. While most people are only aware of

Airbnb's core features, there are a variety of complementary third-party applications. For example, third-party pricing tools for Airbnb hosts connect directly to the Airbnb platform via standard interfaces (APIs). They dynamically optimise prices to increase revenue for professional or private hosts. The same is true for Facebook where a large ecosystem of applications and tools has been developed on top of the social media platform.

> Chuck Robbins, CEO of Cisco, on the relevance of complementors in 2016: 'Now we're transitioning all of our platforms. [. . .] We're opening up programmability on everything we build, so that you can then develop on top of it, add value [and] build business.' (2016)[18]

Creating a complementor ecosystem is also a core aim of Fitbit. In essence, Fitbit is a physical product (smartwatch) and most revenue comes from classic product sales, i.e. one-time purchases. However, already at the founding of the company, the vision was to open up and allow others to innovate on top through hardware and software interfaces, in particular by sharing health data with third parties. Imagine a research institute that harnesses health data from thousands of users for analytics and value-added health services. After acquisition by Google, continuous investments have been made to make it easier for others to complement Fitbit. In 2022, Google announced it would connect Fitbit to its cloud to complement data collection with the data processing power of the cloud.[19] Even traditionally closed industries like finance are opening up to complementors. In the context of 'open banking', retail banks such as Commerzbank offer APIs that enable start-ups and other companies to offer innovative services and product value to their customers.[20]

> James Park, CEO of Fitbit, on the potential of Fitbit beyond just a product back in 2016: 'While Fitbit is known as a consumer brand, the real potential of our brand and technology is to become a digital health platform that improves people's health and integrates into the healthcare ecosystem.' (2016)[21]

When and how to apply

Many companies try to build a complementor ecosystem around their platform or product, usually by creating and offering interfaces (APIs) to external parties.[22] This strategy is at the heart of innovation platforms but is not limited to them, as the cases of transaction platforms like Airbnb and Facebook illustrate. From a timing perspective, a complementor ecosystem can already be important right from the initiation of a platform (e.g. Apple iOS, Microsoft Xbox), or it can become important in a later stage of platform development (e.g. Airbnb, Facebook, Fitbit).

27 Open up the platform core

Well-managed, liberally licensed, collaborative software development has been proven to outcompete more proprietary ways of developing and maintaining software with respect to quality, speed and extent of innovation, as well as development economics (individual risk and costs).[23] Hence, platforms such as Linux rely on open ecosystems that develop and maintain the core of a platform in a collaborative way. In contrast to Microsoft Office, LibreOffice, which also includes word processing, spreadsheet and presentation software, is free and can be modified and used by anyone. However, there are varying degrees of openness when comparing platforms that use an open platform core strategy. The operating system Android, for instance, is also based on an open source project but, in the end, is more closed than the operating system Linux. In essence, Google leads the AOSP that develops a free and open source mobile operating system. However, most devices rely on a proprietary Android version developed by Google that also includes closed source components. Opening the core is also popular in the AI domain. For example, the core of TensorFlow is open source. The innovation platform provides the foundation for others to develop and deploy machine learning models.

When and how to apply

Certainly, opening up the platform core is particularly relevant for innovation platforms. First and foremost, companies have to decide how much of their platform they want to open up. Even if at first glance it might seem advantageous to open up (e.g. need for fewer resources, lower costs, better quality), this strategy comes with challenges. Because of its open nature, it can be difficult to capture value and monetise the platform. Most often, to capitalise on open source, broad adoption, both among developers and paying users, is needed to become economically successful. In addition, managing an open source community is not easy, and does require time and money.

> John Mertic, director at Linux, on how to start with an open source project: 'I think it is a crucial thing for a company to be thinking about what they're hoping to achieve with a new open source project. They must think about the value of it to the community and developers out there and what outcomes they're hoping to get out of it. And then they must understand all the pieces they must have in place to do this the right way, including legal, governance, infrastructure and a starting community. Those are the things I always stress the most when you're putting an open source project out there.' (n.d.)[24]

Some questions to ask
- Is there enough external interest to create and grow an active open source community?
- How can you capitalise on your open source engagement?
- What are the fundamental legal implications of going open source?

28 Establish a platform vertical

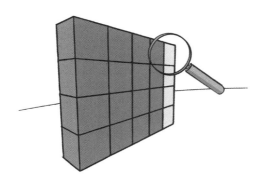

Companies can leverage their domain knowledge, such as technical or industry expertise, to establish a platform vertical and focus on a niche. This works particularly well if the niche requires deep expertise and relies on niche-specific interactions. As horizontal platforms like Amazon and Alibaba become larger and more diverse, opportunities for differentiated platforms emerge. They are typically more carefully managed and curated so they can cater better to the needs of the specific niche. For instance, many platform verticals have developed in the B2B domain.

The German company LANXESS is a producer of chemicals and was looking for digital business opportunities. They realised that they – and the entire chemical industry – lacked a digital distribution channel. Therefore, an industry-wide but independent B2B marketplace for buying and selling chemicals was established in 2018. From the very beginning, LANXESS leveraged its deep domain knowledge to establish CheMondis. The platform has grown successfully in recent years and now has more than 3,500 registered buyers and 1,200 sellers.[25] A similar example is XOM Materials, a marketplace for industrial materials. It was developed by Klöckner & Co, a steel and metal distributor, which had been under pressure because of decreasing margins in the industry. They used their existing resources and expertise to develop the marketplace for the very specific needs of buyers and sellers of materials.

Many other niche platforms have developed across domains. For instance, the innovation platform Bragi is an operating system just for wireless headphones. Wind-turbine.com is a marketplace for selling and buying used wind turbines. TREEO is a marketplace that brings small-holder farmers from developing countries (e.g. Africa, South America) together with companies worldwide that seek high-quality carbon removal, and Schüttflix is a marketplace for products and services revolving around bulk material handling. In the B2C sector, the Zeel marketplace is geared towards the particular needs of providers and consumers of healthcare services.

When and how to apply

Both niche innovation and transaction platforms are emerging, and they can be found in the P2P, B2C and B2B segments. However, to establish a vertical platform, companies need to have deep domain expertise, i.e. industry and/ or technical knowledge. Essentially, you have to provide a value proposition that is superior to existing horizontal platforms such as Amazon, Upwork or Android. While deep industry experience and unique resources can provide a sustainable advantage, vertical platforms run the risk of being enveloped, i.e. a larger, horizontal platform absorbs the functionalities of the vertical platform.[26] This, in turn, can lead to users switching to the more comprehensive platform.

Some questions to ask

- In which niche do you have distinct knowledge to differentiate yourself from others?
- What niche-specific platform services can you offer that no other platform provides?
- How sustainable is the vertical platform opportunity? Can you defend the niche?

29 Facilitate local interactions

Many platforms are digital-only but known as 'Uber for X'. They bring people together physically to enable real-time interactions. With Uber, drivers and riders must meet at a very specific place and time. Unlike simple product marketplaces, where buyers and sellers do not have to meet in person, this requires a significant amount of coordination. At the same time, facilitating local interactions can create great value for both sides of the market and is not limited to mobility or delivery platforms.

Over the last six years, Rappi has become one of the leading mobility platforms in South America. It provides ride-sharing services as well as delivery services for restaurants or other merchants. The platform Delivery Hero connects consumers with restaurants and manages food delivery through its network of delivery riders. The goal is to provide a seamless delivery experience based on an outstanding logistics capability. Rappi, Uber and Delivery Hero show that facilitating local interactions is often about 'on-demand' services, e.g. food or grocery delivery, that are about instant service fulfilment. But there are also platforms with local interactions that do not rely on an 'on-demand' experience, such as marketplaces for household (e.g. Helpling, Mila) or healthcare services (e.g. Treatwell, Zeel, Marta). Also, travel-related marketplaces like FlixBus and Airbnb rely on facilitating local interactions. On Airbnb, providing seamless access to the apartment or house is of paramount importance.

Two companies that take this value proposition to the next level are the platforms Nextdoor in the United States and its German counterpart nebenan.de. While Facebook or LinkedIn only offer a digital social network for private or business contacts, nebenan.de focuses on developing a social media platform for your neighbourhood. The core objective is to promote physical interactions and help neighbours connect in real life. Another example is the Urban Sports Club. Although at first glance it looks like a simple membership programme with access to different gyms, it relies heavily on network effects. Urban Sports Club offers its end customers not just access to one gym, but access to a large number of gyms with just one subscription. Hence, the second side of the market consists of various gym chains or local gyms (e.g. in a hotel) that want to increase their utilisation. The more gyms join the platform, the more attractive it is to join as a user and vice versa.

> Christian Vollmann, Founder of nebenan.de, on the initial idea: 'Our network makes it possible to exchange ideas with people in the immediate vicinity. People underestimate how lonely many people are. They want to make social contacts and find like-minded people, for example, for board games or a reading circle. But most are inhibited about approaching their neighbours in person. Our users are 43 years old on average. We observe that interest in the immediate neighbourhood increases with age. However, nebenan.de is most frequently used for everyday problems; if you want to borrow or lend an item, or are looking for a babysitter or removal man, for example.' (2019)[27]

When and how to apply
A particular challenge in facilitating local interactions is to achieve viable network effects. Reaching a critical mass of interactions in a local area is typically much harder to achieve than in a global market. Moreover, creating a 'winner-takes-all' platform is also less likely under these conditions.[28] Furthermore, platforms that facilitate local interactions are very likely to face strong competitive dynamics. Uber and Lyft, for instance, coexist in the same local areas but are very vulnerable to multi-homing, i.e. users take advantage of two or more platforms simultaneously as the cost of switching between platforms is low.[29]

Some questions to ask
- How do you address the specific challenges of enabling local interactions for your market?
- What characteristics must a local market have to facilitate a viable platform business?
- How can you defend your local interaction platform against multi-homing?

30 Enable an instant experience

Platforms can take advantage of industries where transactions are lengthy and cumbersome. Backed by strong financials, iBuyer (Instant Buyer) platforms, for example, make instant offers for assets such as houses or cars. Sellers benefit from a quick and easy sale, while the iBuyer platform aims to resell the product through its large network. For example, if you think about the real estate market, selling or buying a house usually takes many weeks. However, on the Opendoor platform, owners can sell their homes in only a few days. Its core value proposition is to significantly speed up the lengthy selling process by paying the house owner a discounted price. Opendoor uses its economies of scale and network to then resell these houses on the open market. But this model requires Opendoor to put the assets on its balance sheet before reselling them again.

Europe's largest wholesale platform for used cars Auto1 follows the same principle. It provides consumers with an easy and fast way to sell their used cars, but at a discount. It shortened the sales process from an average of around 90 days to only 10 days.[30] In addition, it offers a digital wholesale platform for dealers to buy cars. PayPal is a different type of platform that pioneered instant experiences with its payment platform. In a matter of seconds, you can send money to your peers, and PayPal is working on further simplifying and speeding up this process. This has led to many users preferring PayPal to traditional bank transfers.

Dan Schulman, CEO of PayPal, on their efforts towards an instant experience: 'We need to modernise so we can get a payment instantaneously. If I send a digital wallet to digital wallet transaction, you get that money instantaneously. I could send you a PayPal transaction, and you will get it in less than two seconds. You have it in your wallet to spend. It's remarkable. The other thing is, if we can do away with some of the intermediaries in the system, we can probably lower the cost as well. And so the promise of this new technology is that it can be more inclusive, it can lower the costs of basic transactions, it could speed the time to get your money, make the system more efficient and bring in more people. That is why we established a full business unit around blockchain technology and digital currencies.' (2022)[31]

When and how to apply

Providing an instant experience is highly valued specifically in markets with complex and expensive assets, such as real estate or cars.[32] Such markets are typically also characterised by cumbersome and lengthy transaction processes. However, compared with simply matching supply and demand on a digital platform, enabling an instant experience can be capital intensive and hence require strong financial backing. Thereby, iBuyer platforms that put assets on their balance sheet expose themselves to additional risk. In order to effectively resell assets, they have to have access to a large customer base to ensure timely asset turnaround.

Some questions to ask

- Is your industry characterised by lengthy and cumbersome sales processes or transactions?
- How can you significantly shorten and simplify these sales processes and transactions?
- Is putting assets on your balance sheet a strategy to disrupt customer experiences while maintaining an acceptable risk exposure?

Define ownership

31 Single owner

The right platform ownership model heavily influences the future success of a platform. Certainly, most platforms are run by a single company rather than a consortium or peer-to-peer community. Single ownership gives the owner maximum freedom in designing and managing the platform. However, if the ownership and power is centred around just one company it can be very difficult to establish a viable platform that includes all relevant players in an industry. Take CheMondis as an example. The marketplace for chemical products is owned by the German chemicals company LANXESS but formally acts as an independent enterprise. As a result, the CheMondis management has made a conscious decision in its communications and branding not to highlight LANXESS.

The same is true for Tapio, an industry-wide and independent B2B innovation platform for the wood industry. Although originally initiated by HOMAG,[33] a major company in the industry, the Tapio brand is at the forefront and HOMAG is only mentioned as one of the platform's many partners. Single-owner examples go way beyond these B2B examples. Ownership of YouTube has always been centred around a small set of cofounders, including Steve Chen, Chad Hurley and Jawed Karim. Since it was bought by Google in 2006, it has been fully controlled by Google as a single owner. Apple is another prominent case where power is highly centralised and concentrated in a single owner. Apple fully controls its ecosystem with the different innovation platforms (e.g. iOS, macOS). It does not allow others to participate in decisions related to governance and it also provides the hardware for its platforms, i.e. MacBook, iPhone, iPad and Apple Watch. This offers Apple the advantage of easily expanding its product and service portfolios based on a large installed base, as was seen in the case of 'Sign in with Apple' and Apple AirTags. However, Apple's image was tarnished when the company was accused of exploiting its market power as a single owner. Unfair revenue sharing practices on its App Store (e.g. the Fortnite lawsuit) and new terms and conditions for data collection and usage that heavily limit third-party providers' monetisation opportunities were at the heart of these accusations.

> Jörg Hellwig, former chief digital officer (CDO) of LANXESS, on the independence of their platform venture: 'Use your domain knowledge and make sure your platform is independent from your [parent] company. Independence is very important, otherwise you are just pushing the platform to optimise your own business and not to bring value to the industry.' (2020)[34]

When and how to apply

The decision to use a single-owner strategy strongly depends on the specific situation and must therefore be determined on an individual basis. It certainly comes with the advantage of speed, a higher degree of control and easier decision making. For established companies, however, it also has disadvantages such as the increased difficulty of onboarding third parties, in particular competitors, as they prefer an independent and neutral platform. To address this challenge, platform ventures are often set up as independent companies despite being owned by one single parent company. Some enterprises even go so far as to establish a Chinese wall between the start-up and the parent company to emphasise their neutrality towards any third-party partners and users.

32 Consortium

In contrast to single ownership, platforms can also be owned by a consortium. In many industries, platforms are confronted by the challenge that every company wants to build its own industry-leading platform. Instead of joining forces with each other to build one strong platform, every single platform fails in the end owing to the lack of network effects and acceptance within the industry. A consortium ownership model can therefore be essential to tackle this challenge and can be a viable solution to align interests and realise a multi-owner platform business model.[35]

The marketplace Caruso for mobility data, for example, started as an industry initiative of the Independent Automotive Aftermarket (IAM) association and is now owned by a consortium of companies, including Bosch, Continental, Valeo and Schaeffler, all of which are competitors active in the automotive industry. The nature of a data marketplace, i.e. aggregating data from different companies, requires a high degree of independence and trust among data providers, which would be difficult to achieve if it were owned and controlled by a single company. Ultimately, the establishment of Caruso as a consortium has created the necessary neutrality so that each individual company is more comfortable sharing data for the benefit of all. Hence, Caruso emphasises its neutrality very clearly in public. The HERE platform that used to belong to Nokia, as another example, struggled with being too closed in the beginning. HERE's business is similar to Caruso's, only with a focus on location data and navigation services. Today it is owned by a consortium that includes automotive OEMs such as Audi, BMW and Daimler.

The e-commerce platform for luxury clothing Yoox Net-A-Porter (YNAP) was long owned by Richemont only. But in August 2020, 47.5 per cent was sold to Farfetch (a longstanding competitor) and a 3.2 per cent stake was sold to Allabar (an independent investor), so YNAP became a more neutral platform with no dominating shareholder.[36] Another example is Cloud Foundry. While it is now an open source platform that is orchestrated by the Cloud Foundry Foundation, it began in 2009 as a proprietary solution owned by VMware, a Palo Alto–based company. Four years later, VMware, EMC (now Dell EMC) and General Electric formed a consortium, to which the software was transferred.[37] Later, the governance was opened up further and today's foundation was initially established with nine members. The number of members continued to grow. Today, the Cloud Foundry Foundation has more than 65 members, including companies such as Google, IBM, Microsoft, Cisco, Dell EMC, IBM, Pivotal, VMware or SAP.[38] While all intellectual property is owned by the foundation, the members jointly manage and promote the platform.[39]

> Johann Rupert, chairman of Richemont, on the rationale for giving away ownership to competitors: 'Today's announcement is a significant step towards the realisation of a dream I first voiced in 2015 of building an independent, neutral online platform for the luxury industry that would be highly attractive to both luxury brands and their discerning clientele. We knew back then that if we wished to control our own destiny and protect the uniqueness of the luxury industry as it was digitalised, we would need to collaborate as the task was too big to undertake on our own.' (2022)[40]

When and how to apply

A consortium model is particularly relevant in B2B domains where companies are often hesitant to join a competitor's platform and do not accept a strong marketplace that is owned by only one company. One reason is that the number of companies is smaller than in the consumer sector, where you will likely have a quite homogeneous group of millions of potential users. A serious challenge for a consortium, however, can be the slow speed of decision making and agreeing on core strategic decisions, especially if the vested interests differ significantly and if too many parties become involved.

33 Peer-to-peer community

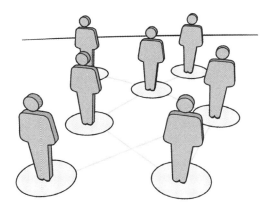

A platform can also be managed, developed and operated by a peer-to-peer community. A peer-to-peer community is about individuals rather than a consortium of enterprises. The concept of a peer-to-peer community first became well known in connection with open source software.[41] For instance, Linux is an open source operating system that is developed by a peer-to-peer community. However, the Linux Foundation guards the interest as a non-profit consortium and supports Linux's further growth. The Linux Foundation serves as the neutral body for organisations to develop and organise open source projects, but the peer-to-peer community provides direction and develops the core of the platform.[42] The numerous individual authors of Linux have the copyright for its source code, but due to its open source licensing, Linux is accessible to everyone for free.

Currently, peer-to-peer communities are heavily discussed in the context of web3 and blockchain.[43] Platforms in the realm of web3 and blockchain are often managed by a decentralised autonomous organisation (DAO), a collective management not relying on centralised leadership. Decisions are made bottom-up by a community that relies on a set of rules which are encoded on a blockchain. DAOs are collectively owned and managed by their users based on governance tokens. This contrasts with web2 platforms, where single companies often have sole control over governance decisions.

For instance, the 2017-founded District0x is a web3 platform that others can build applications on. It allows users to create new decentralised marketplaces on top of District0x and provides the infrastructure to manage one. To facilitate open governance, i.e. participation and coordination, network tokens were introduced.[44]

When and how to apply

Opinions on the future of peer-to-peer platforms vary widely. Certainly, decentralised platforms can enable radical and powerful innovations and neutrality is rooted in their core, but their development and operation bring unique challenges, such as aligning interests of diverse stakeholders in a non-hierarchical manner. Furthermore, DAO legislation is still in an early stage and hence DAOs still face significant uncertainty.

Some questions to ask

- Why does your platform need a peer-to-peer rather than a traditional ownership approach?
- Can you attract enough individuals to participate in the platform's governance activities?
- Do you have the resources and know-how to kick off a web3 project?
- How can you capitalise your platform investments if there is peer-to-peer ownership?
- Can you generate sustainable income streams if you invest in a platform available to the public?

Determine transaction platform model

34 Listings platform

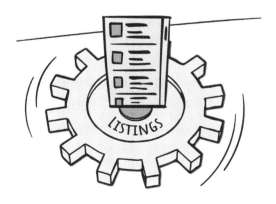

As a transaction platform – a marketplace for digital or non-digital products and services – you must decide on the extent of your value creation. A platform's extent of value creation can vary substantially from very light to very comprehensive. A listings platform is a platform where the degree of value creation is rather low and almost no assets are needed to operate the platform. Providers can simply list a product or service on the platform. However, activities such as payments or logistics are not enabled by the platform. One of the very first listing marketplaces was Craigslist. Everybody could list a product or service on the marketplace, but the platform did not put a lot of effort into clustering or curating the offerings. This also meant that buyers of services or products had limited assurance of the quality. While Craigslist is a marketplace across various product and service categories, vertical platforms with a niche focus can also leverage an asset-light strategy. For instance, the European marketplace AutoScout24 is a listings platform for buying and selling second-hand cars. While there is more curation compared with Craigslist, buyers and sellers ultimately finalise the transaction offline. The payment and vehicle logistics are not managed by the platform. Therefore, AutoScout24 is still asset-light and the value creation at its core is matching buyers and sellers rather than end-to-end transaction processing. AutoScout24 has recently expanded further by integrating third-party services such as car insurance, quality and price checks.

Another example of a listings platform is Stack Overflow, the Q&A website for professional and private programmers. Programmers can ask questions on the platform to receive feedback from other programmers. Stack Overflow's operating model is asset-light as it simply provides a platform where programmers can pose questions. Even the curation is done mainly by Stack Overflow users themselves who can rank a question and its answers up or down. Although Stack Overflow only has a very small share of the platform's value creation, the platform is now one of the most well-known websites in the software developer community and serves around 100 million users every month. On StepStone, companies can simply post job vacancies on the marketplace. The job marketplace's value creation is rather focused. Only the very first step of the hiring process is supported by the website, and for subsequent steps applicants must directly contact the job advertiser. Many other examples of listings platforms exist, also in B2B. For instance, wind-turbine.com is an asset-light marketplace for second-hand wind turbines, components, spare parts and related services such as logistics.

When and how to apply

Implementing a listings platform usually requires fewer resources, but the revenue per user is also lower compared to other platform operating models.[45] In general, many companies start as a listings platform but add new services along the customer journey over time to increase user loyalty.[46] Therefore, they gradually become a more asset-heavy marketplace which puts them in a better position to capture value. At times, listings platforms can appear to be unstructured and unorganised, especially if they are not focused on a specific niche, and, therefore, platform managers need to put special attention on reducing friction and ensuring a convenient matching of supply and demand.[47]

35 Light marketplace

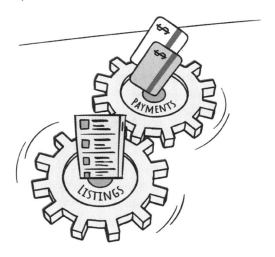

Light marketplaces go beyond simple listings. They are still asset-light but offer an extended set of services. For example, payment is deeply integrated into light marketplaces. Moreover, the entire transaction process between suppliers and buyers is more standardised, curated and controlled, e.g. by predefining prices. On eBay, the entire transaction process is controlled by the platform. In essence, it is a listings platform plus integrated payment. But this was not always the case as eBay did not facilitate payments on its platform in the beginning. Airbnb, the marketplace for short-term accommodation, also goes beyond simple listings. It curates its offering closely, offers insurance and payment is settled via the Airbnb platform. Hence, it remains the first point of contact for both travellers and apartment owners. This is comparable to booking.com, the marketplace for hotels and travellers. The platform tries to retain customers with various additional services, including loyalty points, so that they do not book directly with the hotel. In contrast to StepStone, the job marketplace Indeed not only allows listings of job vacancies but also aggregates job offers from other platforms. Also, applicants cannot contact recruiters directly but must go through the platform's portal. This distinguishes Indeed from a job market-place with a listings operating model.

> Nathan Blecharczyk, cofounder of Airbnb, on platforms as facilitators: 'In a sense, we've built a platform to facilitate payments, reviews, search, but we're actually not the provider of the ultimate service, which is the accommodation [. . .]. We've really made sure that the facilitation we do speaks to the specific customer needs.' (2016)[48]

In general, the services you offer in addition to the simple listing depend heavily on your niche and user needs. On the freelance platform Upwork, for instance, each freelancer is assigned a category based on their skills and previous employment history. Upwork provides a list of the top freelancers for a task once a business or organisation needs to hire a freelancer for one of their projects. The business can then select the top freelancer from Upwork's list. As the project develops, conversations and file sharing can be run over the Upwork platform. Finally, payments are also managed via Upwork. Through all these means, Upwork tries to prevent freelancers from starting to work directly with organisations. As part of its value creation, Chronext, the marketplace for luxury watches, checks originality, assures quality and even gives guarantees. In doing so, it creates the necessary trust and goes far beyond a simple matching of supply and demand.

When and how to apply

Similar to a listings marketplace, a light marketplace is still asset-light and therefore requires limited resources to set up. However, because the company owns and controls a larger part of the value chain, it can charge more, skim off more value and enjoy greater customer loyalty.[49] However, it can still be challenging to provide long-term value to users and to facilitate recurring trans-actions. One of the key reasons that platforms move from a listings platform to a light marketplace is to facilitate and thus control the payment process. If the payment is conducted over the platform, the platform owner has the additional possibility of taking a percentage of the revenue (e.g. percentage of overall booking price in the case of Airbnb) instead of just transaction fees (e.g. fixed amount per booking in the case of AutoScout24).

Some questions to ask

- In addition to simple listings, can you offer more services such as payment or insurance?
- How can you ensure that payment is conducted over the platform and not settled otherwise?
- Is it reasonable to go beyond asset-light and offer services such as logistics or warehousing?

36 Full-stack marketplace

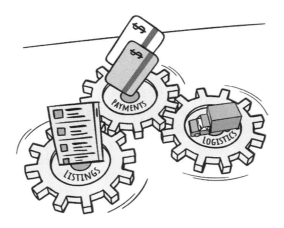

When assuming more of the value creation, platforms start to become asset-heavy. A full-stack marketplace provides a range of additional services that go beyond listings and payment. These might include logistics, marketing or even warehousing. By offering these services, the marketplace becomes asset-heavy but also has more control over the entire user journey. Most often, platforms do not immediately start as a full-stack marketplace. When Amazon became a marketplace in 1998 by opening up to third-party sellers, it was rather a light marketplace. Only after introducing adjacent services, such as logistics, marketing and warehousing to third parties did it become a full-stack marketplace. Amazon now manages the entire process for both the seller (i.e. from customer acquisition, transaction and marketing to logistics) and the buyer. Thereby, it can create and capture much more value, but is also asset-heavy compared with platforms such as Uber or Airbnb which barely own any assets. Ultimately, the user experience of a full-stack marketplace can become so integrated that the underlying platform business model is hardly visible. FlixBus, the company with intercity bus services in Europe and the US, is such an example. While it runs the FlixBus ticket platform and manages the route network and daily bus logistics, buses are mainly owned and operated by regional bus companies. Thus, FlixBus brings bus operators together with travellers via its platform, based on a strong logistics backbone. However, the underlying platform business model is often not recognised as the experience is so seamless and large parts of the value chain are integrated. Contractors are responsible for maintaining and displaying the FlixBus branding on their buses. They are compensated based on transportation mileage. Another example is Jobandtalent, a platform for on-demand work. Compared to listings (StepStone) and light (Indeed) marketplaces, Jobandtalent goes even a step further in the value creation by handling interviews, paperwork and payroll for both sides of the market.

Full-stack marketplaces can also be found in the B2B sector. For example, klarx is a highly integrated marketplace for the rental of construction machinery. On one side of the market, companies can search for machines and request to rent them. On the other side of the market, companies that own equipment can rent it out via the platform. Klarx acts as an intermediary for the entire transaction process and offers logistics services and insurance. Initially, it is not even apparent to the company looking to rent that klarx is not the owner of the machines because the user experience is so integrated.

When and how to apply

By its very nature, a full-stack marketplace requires more capital than asset-light marketplaces, and the platform becomes exposed to a certain degree of operational risk. For example, developing advanced software tools, a logistics network or warehousing requires a significant upfront investment. At the same time, the greater control of the user experience and participation in the value chain offers platforms the opportunity to add and capture much more value.

Some questions to ask

- What asset-heavy services, such as logistics, can you offer to create even more customer value?
- Does the vertical expansion fit with your core competencies? What is your competitive advantage to offer a full-stack marketplace?
- Do you have the resources to offer these services and assume more ownership of the value chain?
- Is it essential that you offer these services or can you integrate third-party services into your offering?

---

37 Market maker

A market maker or iBuyer platform buys and sells assets, such as houses or cars, with the aim of making a profit on the price spread. Thereby, it puts assets on its balance sheet for a limited period and even goes one step further in the platform value creation. Market-maker platforms often act in markets where buying or selling an asset is a complex and long-lasting process. By enabling instant buying and selling experiences and leveraging their large network, they can ask for a lower price and sell for a higher price. So far, this pattern has been particularly prominent in the secondary market for real estate and automotive due to their special characteristics, i.e. lengthy and opaque transactions. The European used car platform Auto1 is a market-maker platform. In contrast to simple listings platforms such as mobile.de or AutoScout24, Auto1 takes on a price-setting role and actively buys cars. With funding of around USD 1.4 billion between 2012 and 2020, this iBuyer platform has been able to temporarily trade on its own books.[50] To do so, it has set up an infrastructure including not only software but also physical logistics. Additionally, the company has developed a strong network of buyers across Europe. As a result of this deep control of the value chain, the process of buying and selling a car has been shortened from an average of around 90 days to 10 days. This means that consumers can sell their cars to Auto1 within 24 hours. Subsequently, the platform resells cars through its wholesale platform for dealers. By doing so, it benefits from the price spreads in its large European network. Throughout the entire transaction process, everything comes from a single source and the contract is signed with Auto1.

Opendoor follows the same principles as Auto1, only in the US secondary market for real estate. Opendoor has streamlined the process of selling a house and shortened it to a few days. As a result, it provides an instant experience in a market where transactions can often take several months. Backed by strong financials and data-driven valuations, it offers to buy your house almost instantly. Sellers do not bother with a long sales process and receive instant cash, while Opendoor can benefit from buying at a discount. Based on its economies of scale and large network, Opendoor then resells these houses on the open market. Market-maker platforms are often focused on a particular geography in which they can build a strong reputation and a large network. For instance, kodit.io has built a market-marker platform for real estate in Finland, Spain and Poland. Kayishha has built a market-marker platform for second-hand cars in Saudi Arabia. Cazoo is a market-maker platform for second-hand cars in the UK.

> Eric Wu, cofounder and CEO at Opendoor on the importance of pricing for a market maker: 'Now, the pricing engine was one of the most critical pieces, which is, how do we build a pricing system that enables us to be able to price a home and purchase it or at least give the customer a quote in minutes. We didn't want the delay. And so, we had to invest very heavily in that pricing system. One of my cofounders is a data scientist, one of the first data scientists from Square. And so, we've always prioritised pricing as a core competency.' (2022)[51]

Examples also exist in other markets, for example, refurbed is a marketplace for second-hand electronics such as smartphones. Instead of linking supply and demand directly, it buys the products, refurbishes them and then resells them through its online shop at a higher price. For the platform business to work, it needs scale and a good understanding of the electronics' condition and respective prices before and after refurbishment. However, becoming a market-maker platform does come with challenges. Like Opendoor, Zillow also offered the opportunity to instantly buy people's homes without any hassle or lengthy process in the US. However, they struggled to generate a commercially viable business. Analysing and predicting real estate prices was difficult, which led to acquiring real estate at higher prices, thereby reducing margins significantly.[52]

When and how to apply

Market-maker platforms require significant financial means and backing to acquire assets in the first place. Secondly, they need in-depth knowledge of asset prices and their development to be able to make financially viable offers (i.e. buy low, sell high). Also, access to a large customer base is needed to make sure a quick resale can be made. By going a step further in value creation and temporarily putting assets on the balance sheet, market-maker platforms are taking on significant risks compared with more asset-light platforms. Imagine a situation where asset prices fall substantially due to a recession. Despite the challenges, market-maker platforms can provide substantial value, especially to the supply side. Once a critical size is reached, network effects are very strong, making it difficult for potential competitors to catch up.

Some questions to ask

- Is your market characterised by long and inefficient sales cycles?
- What measures are key to simplifying and speeding up these processes fundamentally?
- Can a market-maker platform that buys and sells be a decisive differentiator in the market?
- Do you have the financial resources, and can you handle the risks of a market-maker platform?

---

38 E-commerce

E-commerce[53] companies like online fashion stores are focused on trading goods and they do not serve as a platform to connect buyers and sellers.[54] The British online fashion store Asos, for example, can be considered a classic e-commerce store as it selects and buys an assortment of clothes to sell online. This means that the consumer has one place to shop for multiple brands. However, the boundaries between e-commerce and platform business models are blurry and platforms often start as e-commerce companies. Just think about Amazon. It started as an online bookstore and hence an e-commerce business. Then it opened up to third-party sellers and became a light marketplace.

Likewise, Zalando is an established e-commerce company from Germany that buys and sells clothes. The boundaries, however, are fading in the case of Zalando as it has started to open up its e-commerce store to third-party sellers. In essence, Zalando complemented the established e-commerce business model with a platform business model. To do this they have intro-duced 'Connected Retail', a software interface that allows brick-and-mortar shops and other brands to sell their products on the Zalando marketplace. These third-party shops can choose from a continuum of services, from only connecting their inventory and relying on their own fulfilment to outsourcing and even warehousing, or fulfilment as well as logistics handled completely by Zalando.

When and how to apply

E-commerce companies exist in almost every industry. In essence, e-commerce is about purchasing goods from manufacturers and wholesalers and reselling them online to customers for a profit.[55] In contrast to platform business models, e-commerce is about purchasing and selling goods and not matching third-party sellers with buyers. Certainly, the e-commerce business model comes with typical limitations such as lower margins, less scalability and less choice for users. However, platform business models are by no means generally superior to e-commerce business models. E-commerce companies benefit from full control over the user experience and can ensure the quality of products much better than platform companies. More specifically, platforms can scarcely manage the quality of all third-party products, especially if the platform has no control over fulfilment and logistics, as is often the case with listings and light marketplaces.

Some questions to ask

- What are the advantages/disadvantages of e-commerce over platform in your industry?
- How can you complement an e-commerce business with a platform business, or vice versa?
- What are the negative consequences of running both an e-commerce and a platform business?

39 Direct to customer

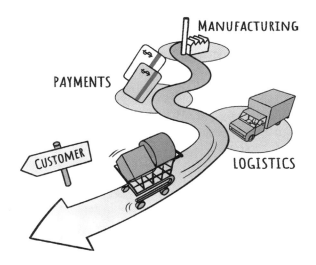

More and more companies want to own the entire value chain from manufacturing the product to selling it to the end customer.[56] For instance, Beyond Meat, the producer of plant-based meat substitutes, has revolutionised the entire food industry. In the US, the company is following a direct-to-customer (D2C) approach selling directly to its consumers.[57] Such an approach often includes running your own online store where the company's products are sold. Many companies such as Whirlpool have moved beyond selling through indirect channels that rely on wholesalers and retailers. While still relying on established channels, they have also built up their own online stores to sell their products directly to end customers (e.g. Whirlpool has a dedicated KitchenAid online store). However, such direct sales through an online store is not a platform business model as it does not facilitate a multi-sided market. Similarly, the internet bank N26 is not a platform business. But with its D2C approach, it has valuable access to and control over consumer touchpoints. While D2C business models are not platform business models, they can complement or evolve into platform business models. Take Amazon as the most prominent example. At its core, Amazon can be considered a full-stack marketplace. However, it still acts as a seller on its own platform and thereby implements a traditional e-commerce business. Ultimately, it also sells its own products on its platform (Amazon Basics), realising a D2C business model.

When and how to apply
A D2C business model is not a platform business model. However, as the example of Amazon illustrates, D2C business models can complement platform businesses. Moreover, just like e-commerce business models, D2C business models can evolve into platform business models. While D2C is certainly not

an asset-light business model, the promise of direct customer interaction and full control over the value chain can facilitate unique customer experiences and profit margins.

Some questions to ask
- Do you have a strong brand to sell products under your own label?
- Can you complement your platform business model with a D2C business model?
- Can you evolve your D2C business model into a platform business model?

Determine innovation platform model

40 Closed core platform

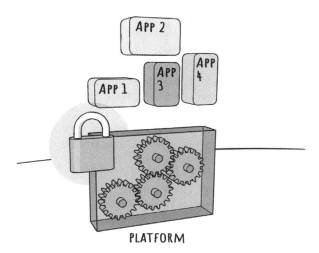

PLATFORM

The operating model of innovation platforms is all about deciding on how much you want to open up to externals.[58] This decision must be made with respect to the platform core (e.g. operating system like iOS, Android, software solutions like Salesforce) and platform complements (e.g. third-party apps, third-party hardware). Closed core platforms do not allow third parties to customise or change the platform core. For instance, the core of the operating systems macOS or Microsoft Windows can only be modified by the platform owner, Apple or Windows, respectively, and not by third parties. Described by the phrase 'walled garden', Apple is very careful about maintaining control over all software installed on its devices.[59] The video game platform PlayStation developed by Sony is also characterised by a closed core. Only Sony, as the owner of the platform, is authorised to modify or change the underlying platform. The start-up Bragi has developed an operating system for headphones and speakers. It allows third parties to develop functionalities or integrate the operating system into its hardware. However, only Bragi can change or modify the underlying source code. There are many other examples of closed core companies, also in the B2B sector. Tesla has its own platform for developing infotainment apps for its electric cars. While most of the apps come from Tesla itself, the platform could potentially open up to third-party developers in the future, much like an operating system for a smartphone, but for a car. However, the core platform with its source code will likely remain closed and tightly controlled by Tesla.[60]

> Elon Musk, CEO, Tesla, back in 2019 on potentially opening up to third-party developers: 'In order for it to be worthwhile for somebody to write an app, there has to be enough of an install base to warrant the effort. Even if you are going to port something, it's still got to be worth the effort. As our number of vehicles grow, it starts to potentially make more sense to develop games and other applications for Tesla. We just need a lot of cars.' (2022)[61]

Another example comes from Bosch Healthcare Solutions (BHCS) which has platformised its existing business and developed an innovation platform for molecular diagnostics. Its diagnostic device Vivalytic can be purchased by pharmacies, doctors and hospitals (market side 1) to perform molecular tests directly at the point of care for respiratory infections, flu or COVID-19, to mention a few. Compared to traditional devices, the portfolio of tests can be expanded without replacing the device. Third parties, so-called biological partners (market side 2) can develop tests (complements) to be offered on the molecular platform in a matter of weeks with the help of so-called test cartridges and a software developer platform. This means that doctors can gain access to a wider portfolio of tests after purchasing the device. While complements can be developed by third parties, the platform core of Vivalytic is closed and fully in the control of BHCS. Hence, it can be characterised as a closed core platform. Other examples, to mention a few, include Tapio (innovation platform for the wood industry), 365FarmNet (innovation platform for the agricultural industry), Zaikio (innovation platform for the printing industry) and Aibo (innovation platform for the robotic dog Aibo).

When and how to apply
At the level of the platform core, you must decide whether you are the only one allowed to change it or whether you allow others to change your platform core. Opting for a closed core platform, sometimes also referred to as a proprietary platform,[62] can bring benefits, such as better control over quality and less friction, as it is easier to provide a seamless user experience. Another major advantage of greater control is the increased ability to capture value. Conversely, a platform core that is too closed can be discouraging for third-party developers as they do not want to be dependent on a large platform owner that controls everything, where third parties have no say, let alone insight

into the platform core. In addition, a closed core platform means that you will most likely be the only one to invest in the platform core. Accordingly, you need the resources and know-how for both the development of the platform core and its long-term maintenance.

Some questions to ask

- Do you have the capabilities and funding to develop your platform core without others?
- Do the platform users trust in a proprietary platform core that is controlled by a single entity?
- Does an open core with a strong developer community outweigh the advantages of a proprietary core?

---

41 Open core platform

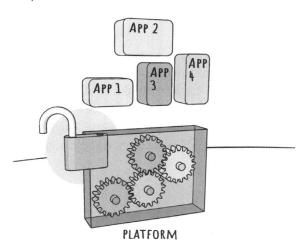

PLATFORM

In contrast to a closed core platform, open core platforms explicitly allow third parties to modify its core. Essentially, third parties can contribute to the development as well as the commercialisation of the platform core. Typically, such platforms are open source and give everyone access to the underlying technology.[63] For example, Linux, the operating system, is open source and fully open. Under the GNU General Public License, everyone can use, extend, modify as well as distribute the operating system as long as no restrictions are placed on further distribution. Linux has become the largest open source project in the world. Android, the operating system for smartphones, is also open to third-party modifications and contributions. Interestingly, Android is based on a version of Linux, as are many other platforms, especially in the B2B sector. Given its open source nature, hardware partners like Huawei or Samsung, as well as software companies, and even competitors, can modify and build upon the Android platform core as part of the AOSP. At the same time, Google does include restrictions for partners in its OHA: Google only certifies Android on a given mobile phone if the Google Mobile Services, i.e. Google Maps and Play Store, are installed by the hardware provider. However, these services are not part of the open core platform.[64]

When and how to apply

At the level of the platform core, you must decide whether you are the only one allowed to change the core or whether others can change and even commercialise it. In the case of an open core platform, you essentially choose to make the source code of your platform publicly available, i.e. open source. This has several advantages. Attracting a strong developer community can lead to better quality and more robust software that benefits both platform owners and users. It can also provide advantages in respect to speed of innovation and extent of individual investment. At the same time, uncontrolled customisation by third parties can lead to incompatible implementations and a bad user experience. Hence, an open core platform can require significant coordination efforts in the end.[65] Due to the increased transparency and freely available source code, both users and third-party developers remain more independent.

> Jared Smith, open source community manager at Capital One (financial service provider), on the reason to invest in an open core platform: 'No matter how many smart people we hire inside the company, there's always smarter people on the outside. We find it is worth it to us to open source and share our code with the outside world in exchange for getting some great advice from people on the outside who have expertise and are willing to share back with us.' (n.d.)[66]

This typically makes it easier to attract developers but comes with a flipside. It is more difficult to capture value from open core platforms. Therefore, open core platforms have tried to introduce some degree of exclusivity. Certain features are not open source and are offered as proprietary services that are add-ons to the open core. That is exactly what Google did with the OHA and its mandatory Google Play Store. This provides Google with the ability to monetise its open core platform.

Some questions to ask
- What monetisation opportunities remain when the core of your platform is available for free?
- How can you attract developers that actively contribute to the core?
- How much friction and coordination effort does an open core bring with it?

42 Single-home platform

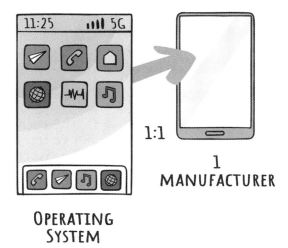

In respect to the platform core, you must also decide whether you want others to distribute the platform core. Single-home platform owners do not allow other players to distribute or use the platform core,[67] meaning that single-home platforms are exclusively distributed by the platform owner itself. This is, for example, the case if an operating system only runs on the platform owner's hardware. Unlike Google with Android, Apple not only owns and controls the operating system iOS but also manufactures complementary hardware. More specifically, it allows third-party app development, but the operating system iOS only runs on Apple hardware, i.e. its iPhone and iPad product line. Hence, iOS is exclusively distributed by Apple. Similarly, Meta is trying to build an in-house operating system for AR and virtual reality (VR) applications, but mainly for its own hardware, the Oculus glasses.

In contrast to the operating system Microsoft Windows, the video gaming platform Xbox only runs on Microsoft hardware, i.e. the Xbox console. The same is true for Aibo developed by Sony. The robotic dog was first introduced by Sony in 1999 but after little commercial success, the product line was stopped in 2006. In 2017, however, the product was revived and transformed into a platform business. Mainly sold in Japan, the Aibo robot dog allows consumers to interact with it in a similar way to a smart speaker (such as Amazon Alexa or Google Echo). Compared with the earlier version, one can now access a developer portal and, for example, use web APIs to make Aibo perform certain actions, connect to other smart devices or recognise something. In contrast to Amazon Alexa which can be integrated into different products, the underlying platform core can only be installed on Sony hardware, i.e. the robotic dog Aibo. B2B examples can be found in the automotive industry, for example, Volkswagen's and Tesla's in-house operating systems for vehicle software and infotainment run exclusively on Volkswagen Group vehicles and Tesla vehicles, respectively. Another example is Microsoft Azure. Companies can subscribe to a range of public cloud services or access the app marketplace with third-party services. However, all services only run on Microsoft servers, and it is not possible to use Azure's entire set of services based on your own computing infrastructure.

When and how to apply

In addition to deciding on an open versus closed platform core, one must also consider the distribution of the platform core. Essentially, you must determine if you are the exclusive provider of the base (e.g. the smartphones) on which the platform core (e.g. the mobile operating system with the app store) runs. If you already have a successful product, or if you want to be in control of the entire innovation platform, becoming a single-home platform can make sense. Selling a bundle of hardware and software can also be financially attractive and you can more easily control the overall customer experience. In the case of Apple, for instance, more than 50 per cent of revenue comes from hardware sales.[68] Often, a closed core platform is accompanied by a single-home platform approach, as in the case of Apple. However, this does not necessarily have to be the case as the examples of Microsoft Windows or Android reveal. By contrast, you need a large installed base, as well as experience with product manufacturing, development and sales to go single home.

Some questions to ask

- Do you have the software/hardware capabilities and resources to realise a single-home platform?
- How can you justify the fixed cost investment which cannot be distributed among other partners, e.g. enough synergies with own products and services?
- Do you have the necessary market access and installed base to go single home?
- How much can you increase adoption by allowing others to use and distribute your platform?

43 Multi-home platform

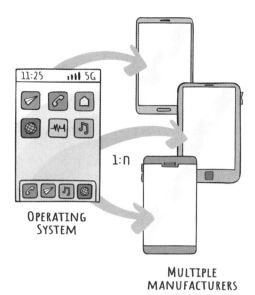

In contrast to single-home platforms, owners of multi-home platforms allow others to distribute the platform. This is, for example, the case of an operating system such as Microsoft Windows that can run on various hardware from different manufacturers. In fact, in Microsoft's case, until the launch of the Surface tablet in 2012, Microsoft did not sell any Windows-compatible hardware at all, and the platform only ran on third-party hardware. Similarly, Android is not tied to one manufacturer. A lot of smartphone producers, such as LG, Motorola or Huawei, can distribute the Android operating system and install it on their devices. In addition, Google manufactures and sells its own phone, Google Pixar. However, like Windows, the very first Android-based phone was not made by Google, but by HTC. While hardware producers can install Android for free, they have to become a member of the OHA to receive access to the Google Play Store. Associated with this membership are certain guidelines and rules set by Google.

Amazon Alexa is also multi home. While Amazon restricts modifications to its smart speaker and voice assistance platform Alexa, it allows hardware partners like Sonos to distribute the Alexa platform by integrating the corresponding software into their devices. Alexa is now supported by more than 60,000 products from more than 7,400 hardware providers.[69] This was only possible because of the easy and seamless implementation of the platform on different hardware devices. The Bosch ctrlX innovation platform is another example of a multi-home platform. In the beginning, the platform for factory automation ran only on Bosch hardware. However, it finally opened up to third-party hardware, becoming a multi-home platform. Bosch developed hardware development kits (HDK) for third parties to facilitate the implementation of ctrlX on their own hardware.

Another example in B2B is 365FarmNet which has followed a multi-home approach in respect to connectivity from the start. In line with its goal to become a neutral innovation platform in the agricultural industry, it did not focus exclusively on the machinery of its parent company CLAAS. 365FarmNet recognised that a farmer's fleet usually consists of a variety of machines from different manufacturers, so it was a natural choice to become open to different machinery brands with the vision of overcoming brand-specific information silos. However, this aim remains challenging as many manufacturers still try to enforce their own solutions. Many other multi-home platforms have emerged, e.g. Azena (an innovation platform for security cameras), Android Automotive OS or Foxconn-initiated MIH Consortium, which announced Project X.

However, the case of Apple reveals that a multi-home strategy does not follow a simple 'the more the better' paradigm. In the early days, Apple faced strong competition from Microsoft's personal computer running on multiple devices. To catch up after losing significant market share, Apple changed its single-home strategy to a multi-home strategy, i.e. an operating system that is open for distribution by third parties. They thought that by licensing they could earn around USD 50 per personal computer sold and double their market share.[70] However, third-party hardware manufacturers, such as Power Computing, Radius and Motorola outperformed Apple's own hardware. This led to a decline in Apple hardware sales and Apple ended up losing more money on unsold hardware than it made from third-party royalties. So it returned to the single-home strategy. Apple pivoted back and today successfully pursues a single-home strategy for its macOS as well as the iOS platform.

> Mike Rosenfelt, former director at Power Computing (one of the hardware manufacturers with built-in macOS), on the reasons why only multi-homing would make Apple successful: 'Is Apple Computer seriously entertaining reversing their policy on being committed to an open macOS platform and continuing the licensing of the OS. This is not an issue about money – it's an issue about preserving customer choice, freedom and doing what's best for the macOS platform. Apple must be successful long term, but it clearly needs partners to fight the battle with – not against.' (1997)[71]

When and how to apply

Allowing multiple third-party manufacturers or operators to run your platform is an effective means of increasing the installed base of the platform and promoting network effects. For example, the more devices that run on your innovation platform, the more attractive it is for third-party developers to add applications to your platform. This, in turn, leads to more users being interested in the hardware as well as the platform itself. However, if you do not offer hardware as a platform owner or leave most of the hardware business to others, you potentially miss out on a significant revenue opportunity. Moreover, leaving the hardware to others, you lose control over key customer touchpoints and need to pay particular attention to maintaining a high-quality user experience.

Some questions to ask

- Which device manufacturers or operators could use and distribute the core of your platform?
- Are these providers willing to pay for the use and distribution of your platform?
- How do you manage conflicts of interest among the different stakeholders of the platform, e.g. technical standards, owning customers, cost allocation?
- Will these providers give you access to their customers so that you can monetise complements?

44 Integration platform

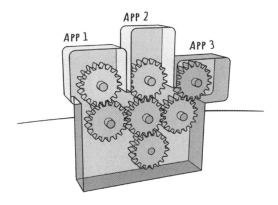

As an innovation platform, you must also decide how you enable others to innovate on top of your platform, i.e. develop complements such as apps. In contrast to platforms that rely on independent co-innovation of complements, integration platforms are characterised by codevelopment and close collaboration between the platform owner and third-party complement providers. In essence, complementors on integration platforms are characterised by a lower degree of autonomy.[72] For instance, on the agricultural platform 365FarmNet, third-party applications are often required to be deeply integrated into the platform to create value, i.e. they are not stand-alone and rely on, as well as coexist with, other components of the system.

Tapio, as another example, is an innovation platform for the wood industry. Partners can develop digital solutions that extend Tapio's platform core, e.g. digital applications to monitor wood machinery or analytics applications to make wood cutting more efficient. Tapio provides a set of community rules and interfaces as well as a few fundamental modules, e.g. a wood materials manager. The value of the platform and its applications relies on the deep integration of different applications. In fact, partner apps can share data with each other or integrate into the already existing applications from Tapio. Hence, codevelopment and integration are key for the Tapio platform.

Another example of a company that is starting to invest into an integration platform approach is Xiaomi, a Chinese competitor to Apple iOS and Google Android, which has seen strong growth in recent years. In 2021, it reached an installed base of roughly 400 million connected devices.[73] While Apple and Google share a set of generic tools (e.g. APIs) to assist app developers in independently creating applications for their mobile operating systems, Xiaomi proactively wants to preserve 'consistent branding and quality standards across its entire product portfolio'.[74] It takes a much more integrated approach, fostering integration across applications. In some cases, the company even invests a minority stake in app developers in return for access to the Xiaomi platform with the complementor's resources.[75]

When and how to apply

In general, innovation platforms want to make it as easy as possible for third parties to build complements such as apps. However, independent complement development is not always possible or effective, for example, if it is necessary that complements are tightly integrated with the platform core or other complements. In these cases, the platform owner and complement providers have to develop more tightly coupled applications, in a codevelopment and partnership style.[76] Integration platforms offer the opportunity to realise a more seamless user experience that is based on rigorous end-to-end engineering and security. Ultimately, however, governance that is too rigid can be harmful to innovation on the platform and can reduce the motivation for third parties to develop complements. While close codevelopment might be necessary to facilitate important use cases, it comes with fundamental challenges: The platform owner can become a bottleneck and hinder the rapid development of new complements such that the ability to scale the platform is limited.

Some questions to ask

- What reasons do you have to be involved in the development of platform complements?
- Do you have the resources to be closely involved in complement development?
- How do you ensure a minimum quality level of your complementor innovations?
- How do you position your platform against fear from lock-in effects from partners on your platform?
- When relying on codevelopment, how can you still enable rapid scaling?

45 Enablement platform

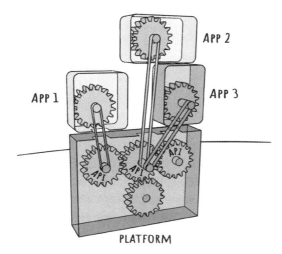

PLATFORM

In contrast to an integration platform, at the heart of enablement platforms is independent co-innovation of complements, such as apps. Essential to this is the provisioning of easy-to-use boundary resources, such as development kits (SDKs), standard interfaces (APIs) or even tacit knowledge in the form of how-to instructions or webinars. Ultimately, the aim is to make complement development for others as easy and as efficient as possible. Aibo, for example, has created an online tool with visual programming (no-code development) so that users can create custom movements for their robot dogs without learning a programming language. Looking at more traditional innovation platforms, Android, for instance, is very open to extensions. Everybody can independently develop applications for Android without the need for close codevelopment with Google. Basically, everyone with the necessary programming skills can develop an application for the Android platform. Only in very exceptional cases is there integration work done by Google. The same is true for Apple. Apple has invested in a new programming language (Swift) to significantly improve developer performance. Since its launch in 2014, Swift has become the new de facto standard as a general-purpose programming language in the iOS ecosystem.

Another example is Roblox, an online gaming platform where users can develop their own games and make them available to the general public. Using a modular component system and the Roblox programming language Lua, users can develop games creatively and independently. Other prominent examples are Bosch ctrlX (innovation platform for factory automation), HERE (the marketplace for navigation data) and Amazon Alexa (the innovation platform for voice assistance applications). The decision to be either an integration or an enablement platform is not always black and white, as the example of Withings shows. The innovation platform relies on connected hardware, e.g. a sleep tracker, weight scale or blood pressure measurement. Third parties like doctors or research institutes can receive access to the medical data (if agreed on by all parties) via an open API. But third parties can also seek closer integration, as in the case of Medable or 8fit, two of its partners. This is especially relevant for Withings' B2B partners. While standard interfaces are a must to become an enablement platform, fewer platforms offer comprehensive education and additional training for third-party developers. For instance, Azena provides video tutorials, webinars and white papers to facilitate the development of video analytics applications for its security camera innovation platform. Similarly, Alexa provides an Alexa Skills Kit with various APIs making it easy for developers to create skills, i.e. voice assistance applications. This is complemented by many how-to videos and readings that are even produced by third parties.

> Philipp Guth, business unit CEO at Bosch Rexroth, on the goals of the innovation platform: 'We want to expand ctrlX AUTOMATION as a leading automation platform over the next years. The fundamentals for this are laid with the open microservice architecture. With this, our customers decide on a future-proof and connectable solution. Of course, we will continuously expand the range of functions and pay high attention to usability. In addition, we are increasingly inviting partners to bring their technology and applications to our platform, thus reducing time to market.' (n.d.)[77]

When and how to apply

In contrast to integration platforms, enablement platforms enable more loosely coupled complement development.[78] Many technical boundary resources to enable developers are at a platform's disposal, from APIs, to SDKs, hardware abstraction layers (HAL) and open source licenses, to publisher terms and conditions, developer guidelines and client libraries, to mention a few.[79] In addition, platforms can draw on educational content to provide more tacit knowledge, e.g. tutorials, webinars, white papers, how-to videos or guidelines. While enablement platforms can attract more developers and increase the ability to scale, they certainly come with trade-offs in respect to cross-complement compatibility as well as integration of complements into the platform core.

Some questions to ask

- Is independent complement development possible or is there a need for tighter integration?
- How can you ensure tight complement integration without codevelopment?
- Which resources do you have to offer third parties for effective complement development?

46 Managed platform

As an innovation platform owner, you have to decide whether and how you validate the quality of platform complements. Managed platform owners review and certify the quality of complements, thereby acting as gatekeepers to enforce rules and policies and, accordingly, generate trust and execute control within the platform ecosystem. Almost every innovation platform provides some underlying guidelines or rules to foster the quality of complements. Managed platforms, however, go beyond this and have, for example, a well-defined certification process in place. Apple iOS can be considered a managed platform. Developers cannot just develop any kind of app as there are strict rules which are enforced by Apple. These guidelines include detailed descriptions of what kind of content or apps Apple does and does not allow on its platform. Apps that leverage user-generated content from YouTube, for instance, must include a mechanism for reporting offensive content or blocking abusive users. Pornography is strictly forbidden as are any potential scams. Before publishing a new or updated app to the App Store, Apple checks and certifies every third-party app. Although the Android core is open source, Google created a set of rules for third-party hardware manufacturers that have to be met to ensure the compatibility of Android applications on their hardware. Similar to Apple, Google also has basic guidelines for third-party app developers but does not enforce them as strictly. In the past, Google has released apps sometimes within minutes, but, as a result, has also received a reputation for being more prone to fraud. B2C innovation platforms can also rely on well-established and rather standardised quality mechanisms such as ratings (Uber) or reviews (Amazon, Airbnb).

Furthermore, many platforms provide quality labels as an additional form of certification.[80] The freelance marketplace Fiverr has launched the 'Fiverr Pro' label which is rewarded to hand-vetted service providers and serves as a strong quality signal for potential service consumers. Similarly, Airbnb introduced the 'Superhost' label to distinguish hosts in a more differentiated way. However, these mechanisms are more challenging to establish in a B2B context. On the Bosch Vivalytic platform, biological partners can independently develop molecular tests using Vivalytic cartridges and a developer portal. Yet, they are strictly bound to the layout of Bosch's cartridges and must adhere to Bosch's specifications. Also, Bosch conducts a diligent certification process before making third-party tests accessible to the platform users. Ultimately, there is a varying degree of how much quality control and management is done. The innovation platform Tapio for the wood industry relies heavily on close codevelopment, and therefore a certain degree of quality control is already carried out in the development phase of the complementary apps.

> Tim Cook, CEO of Apple, on the importance of managing quality: 'The main thing we focus on in the App Store is to maintain our focus on privacy and security. These are the two main principles that create a very trustworthy environment for consumers and developers to come together. If users can trust the developers and the applications are what they say it is, then developers can get a huge user base to sell their software. This is the first item on our list. The others are a distant second. What we are doing is trying to explain the decisions we make, and these decisions are the key to maintaining privacy and security. In the iPhone, there are no sideloading and other methods on the Internet. We do not open iPhone support to uncensored applications. These applications can be listed on the App Store and adopt privacy restrictions.' (2021)[81]

When and how to apply

Through a strictly defined certification process and quality enforcement, platforms can promote trust and execute control over the provided platform complements.[82] As a platform owner, your image and brand are at stake, since the public might hold you accountable even if you have not developed every single application yourself.[83] Certification may sometimes even be required, e.g. in specific industries such as healthcare. At the same time, considerable investments and resources are necessary to implement thorough quality processes. Most often, platforms leverage both incentives and penalties to foster quality and punish bad behaviour as well as potentially harmful complements.

Some questions to ask

- As a platform owner, are you responsible for complement quality from a liability perspective?
- How much is your brand image at risk if you do not manage complement quality carefully?
- How do you assure high-quality complements in an effective and resource-efficient manner?
- What specific quality incentives and penalties can you introduce?

47 Distribution platform

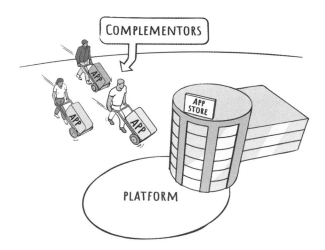

Finally, innovation platform owners must decide how complements are sold and distributed to users. Distribution platforms provide a central distribution channel, such as an app store, for their complement providers. A given distribution channel with a significant number of customers is highly attractive for complement providers. However, these platform distribution channels are generally exclusive, and complement providers have to pay a significant share of their revenue to the platform owner. The alternative is not to provide a central distribution channel and leave it to the complement developers to sell and deliver applications to users on their own. Finally, a hybrid approach is possible. Microsoft Windows, for example, has the Microsoft Store to purchase and download apps but also enables sideloading, i.e. users can buy, download and install applications from any webpage on the Internet, bypassing the Microsoft Store.

Apple is considered a distribution platform as developers must sell their applications through the App Store which is fully controlled by Apple. While developers have access to a multi-billion user market, using the App Store does not come for free. Developers must pay a significant share of their revenue to Apple. In fact, this central distribution serves Apple as a core means for monetisation. The smart speaker software platform Amazon Alexa provides an Alexa Skills Kit that makes it easy for developers to create Alexa Skills (complements). If compliant with Amazon's rules and guidelines, these skills can then be distributed via the Alexa Skills Store, which is available to millions of Alexa users.

Another example is Salesforce which has implemented AppExchange, an app store in the B2B industry. While it is an industrial innovation platform at its core, the Bosch ctrlX platform faced the question of whether it should provide a marketplace for third-party developers to sell and distribute third-party automation applications. They decided to offer an app store but did not make it mandatory.[84] Hence, platform complements can be provided directly by a third-party as well as via an app store. Regardless of origin, however, all third-party automation applications must be certified by Bosch. Similarly, but without additional certification, Google Android applications can be distributed via email or web download, in addition to using the Play Store as the main distribution channel.[85]

When and how to apply

Centralised sales and distribution in the form of a virtual store can certainly be a decisive factor for the monetisation of innovation platforms. It is also an effective way of gatekeeping and controlling quality. However, developers can eventually be deterred if they are obligated to use a central distribution channel, and fees for that channel become too high. Ultimately, the advantages of broad access to users must outweigh the disadvantages for developers, such as negative lock-in effects and usage fees. It is also important to realise that establishing a distribution channel, e.g. in the form of an app store, means establishing a transaction platform on top of an innovation platform. Therefore, it is important to realise that the combination of innovation and transactional platforms adds complexity and increases the challenges of designing and managing your platform.

Some questions to ask

- Is an exclusive distribution channel accepted by the ecosystem? Under which conditions?
- How can you ensure monetisation if you do not operate an exclusive distribution channel?
- How can you effectively manage quality if you do not run an exclusive distribution channel?

Monetise: patterns to capture value as a platform

3

Once the essential decisions about the platform's value creation and delivery have been made, it's time to focus on how to capture value. We therefore present 15 monetisation strategies in three fundamental areas. As a very first step, platforms need to determine their core revenue model. They can build upon direct (A) and/or indirect (B) monetisation strategies (see Figure 2.3.1). Further, platforms can leverage a set of well-established monetisation tactics (C) to foster monetisation. But the presented patterns are not mutually exclusive and are often combined in practice. Since platform businesses build upon two or more market sides, e.g. sellers and buyers in the case of eBay, the appropriate revenue model must be evaluated for each of the sides. Ask yourself who or which sides of the platform you will charge. How will you charge the different sides of the platform? In the case of direct monetisation, revenue is generated by directly charging the customer who benefits from the service or product. For instance, buyers on the Apple App Store are directly charged when purchasing a product. In an indirect monetisation strategy, revenue is generated by charging third parties and not the customer who benefits from the service or product. Facebook revenue, for instance, comes mainly from advertisements, but users do not pay anything to use the platform. After all, one side might be more sensitive to paying money than the other, or one side might be more important for building up strong network effects. Indeed, monetisation can have strategic importance for scaling and includes deciding which type of user not to charge.

Figure 2.3.1 Monetising a platform business (Patterns #48–62)

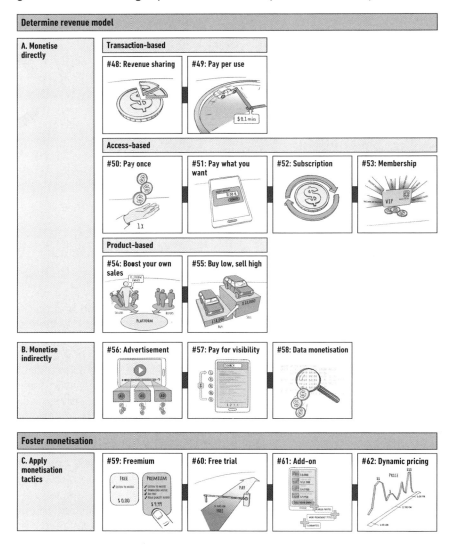

Kevin Systrom, cofounder of Instagram, on its approach to advertising revenue: 'It started only about six months ago. It's beginning, but it's promising. We're happy with the growth so far. We've told everyone we're taking it slow on purpose because we don't want to alienate the community that is so important to Instagram's growth. It's far more important for us to continue the growth worldwide than it is for us to over-monetise it too quickly.' (2014)[1]

Monetise directly

48 Revenue sharing

Platform owners often charge a transaction fee if a product or service is sold over their platform. In the case of revenue sharing, the fee is a fixed percentage of the product or service price, similar to a commission. Hence, revenue is shared between the product or service provider and the platform owner. For instance, developers can offer their apps on the Apple App Store. However, they have to pay a certain percentage of their revenue to Apple. Even though Apple aims for a mutually beneficial relationship with its users, it has faced a lot of criticism for exploiting its market power. Following this debate, Apple adapted its monetisation strategy and reduced the revenue share it charged. Depending on the total sales volume of the developer, this cut now ranges from 15 per cent to 30 per cent of the app revenue. Developers that earn up to USD 1 million can qualify for the reduced commission of 15 per cent instead of 30 per cent.[2] In comparison, the global accommodation platform Airbnb follows a strategy of charging both sides of the platform – the host (producer) as well as the traveller (customers). Homeowners have to pay 3 per cent of the booking value, while travellers are charged a 14 per cent fee on top of the booking value at the checkout.[3]

> Steve Jobs, cofounder of Apple, on the challenge of driving profitability: 'If you get the right strategy, if you have the right people and if you have the right culture at your company – you'll do the right products, you'll do the right marketing, you'll do the right things logistically in manufacturing and distribution and if you do all those things right the bottom line will follow.' (2018)[4]

Revenue sharing can also appear in different forms and may even become a strategic tool, as the example of the gaming platform Roblox shows. While many platforms are not very open about how they make money, Roblox shares and discloses all information to encourage people to join and participate as developers. On their developer portal, they dedicate a whole page to developer economics and revenue sharing. For any transaction on the platform, the creator of a virtual gaming item receives 30 per cent, the seller or distributor gets 40 per cent and the platform Roblox receives the remaining 30 per cent of the transaction value.[5] Revenue sharing is also a common practice in the B2B sector. Tapio (app platform in the wood industry), Azena (operating system for security cameras), ChemDirect (marketplace for chemicals) and klarx (sharing marketplace for machines), for instance, rely on revenue sharing as well.

When and how to apply

With revenue sharing, companies can monetise every single transaction carried out on their platform, and it is probably the most common way for platforms to monetise. But finding the right level of revenue sharing can be difficult. If the share gets too high, platform users might get discouraged and switch to a competitor's platform. In general, the strategy is most easy to apply when platform stakeholders participate in frequent and similar transactions. Most often, the supply and demand sides are also charged with the same share.[6] If implemented correctly, revenue sharing provides distinct advantages as the interests of the platform and its complement providers are aligned. When complement provider sales grow, platform sales grow simultaneously. Additionally, the strategy has a relatively low risk for producers or complementors as money is paid only if transactions are conducted.

> Robert Kalin, founder of Etsy, on the strategic relevance of monetisation: 'There's a 3.5 per cent sales fee on the site. Our goal there is to keep it low, especially below eBay because logically we're competing with them, so we undersell them in price point. But if you search for jewellery on Etsy now, there's about ten times as much jewellery on Etsy as there is on eBay.' (2009)[7]

Some questions to ask
- Are you in full control of the payment process and can therefore apply revenue sharing?
- How price sensitive are your stakeholders, and do you charge the demand and/ or supply side?
- Based on market power and willingness to pay, what revenue share can you claim?

---

49 Pay per use

Pay per use is about usage-based transaction payments. These monetisation schemes can range from a fixed transaction fee on a product marketplace to a predefined price per minute on a car-sharing platform. Uber, for instance, charges its customers on the basis of the time and distance of the route. Platform businesses like to implement this strategy since their customers benefit from flexibility and greater cost transparency.

Unlike other marketplaces, Craigslist wanted to streamline its monetisation from day one. Instead of having a complicated monetisation strategy in place, they simply charged a flat fee for each post. The fees varied, from USD 25 to USD 75 per job listing in certain top cities such as San Francisco to USD 10 per apartment listing, for example in New York City.[8] Similarly, on AutoScout24, a marketplace for cars, sellers are obliged to pay a certain fee for every vehicle they offer on the platform. While this fee varies depending on how the car is presented on the platform, it is independent of the car's value. In general, monetisation strategies are not static. The job marketplace Indeed, for instance, has pivoted its monetisation strategy several times but has always kept platform access free for job seekers. In the beginning, recruiters had to pay a commission for every click on their sponsored job ad and this 'pay-per-click' fee ranged from USD 0.1 to USD 5, depending on the type of offered job. Today, it charges recruiters a commission for every application submitted on their sponsored job ad. This 'pay per application' fee depends on the type and the location of the offered job. Additionally, Indeed offers companies the opportunity to review applications before they are charged, allowing for additional flexibility.[9] Pay per use is particularly common among mobility platforms. The Dutch carsharing platform SnappCar offers a full-service platform for sharing private cars. Compared to well-established rental providers such as Sixt or Europcar, the platform company charges its participants a certain fee per metered usage time. This also enables customers to use a car for a short period of time. Ultimately, customers benefit from a high degree of cost transparency as well as flexibility during the entire carsharing process.

Paul Foster, cofounder of Indeed, on the trend towards performance-based monetisation: 'The benefits of performance-based advertising are now much better understood in the recruitment and HR communities than it was a few years ago. We expect to see a continued migration of recruitment advertising dollars to pay per click (PPC), particularly on search engines.' (2010)[10]

When and how to apply

If you do not have control over payment, it can make sense to introduce pay per use. Also, the nature of some platforms makes it very difficult to collect, count or even define transactions. Think of Facebook for example: Identifying end-to-end conversations (a transaction on Facebook) is rather difficult, and consumers have no willingness to pay for a conversation or, in an even more ambitious model, for a single message. Similar to revenue sharing, pay per use can be well facilitated when platform participants have frequent and similar transactions. In the end, pay per use is more transparent than other forms of monetisation and can therefore drive user experience and platform adoption.

Some questions to ask
- What is your core transaction that you can potentially monetise?
- Can you define the individual transactions and collect as well as count them accurately?
- Do you charge the demand and/or the supply side?
- Why should you favour 'per use' rather than revenue sharing?

---

50 Pay once

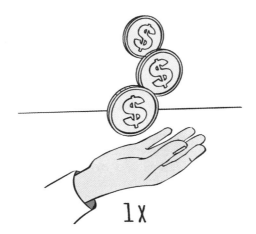

Direct monetisation can also be access-based so that users pay a fee independent of the number of transactions conducted on the platform. Pay once is about charging a one-time fee for platform access. Hence the term 'access fee' is often used. Although such a fee might not be sufficient to cover recurring usage costs, it might help cover initial investments or customer acquisition costs. One-time payments are often used where there is limited willingness to make recurring payments. The Swiss messaging platform Threema guarantees superior encryption and secure communication. Neither a telephone number nor other personal information are required to register with Threema. But to keep its promise, Threema charges a one-time fee of EUR 3.99 to download the app. Similarly, until 2016, WhatsApp charged a small fee of EUR 0.89 for downloading the app and using the platform. Many platforms started to charge a one-time fee in the beginning, but most have dropped such a fee again because it heavily affected their growth. Another pay once example in a sector beyond messaging is the Danish marketplace for rooms in shared apartments, findroommate. dk. It charges room seekers a one-time fee for unlimited access. This ensures high-quality users while keeping advertising to a minimum.

> Roman Flepp, CMO Threema, on why they use direct monetisation: 'Threema has a traditional, honest business model that is not based on collecting and monetising (= 'selling') customer data. [. . .] That's why we rely on revenue. And, hand on heart, we don't understand why people can spend 1,000 francs on a cell phone but are not willing to invest the equivalent of a café crème for the software that makes the phone useful – and prefer to pay with their data instead.' (2021)[11]

When and how to apply

While there is a trend towards free platform access, pay once is often applied in very specific situations, such as when there is a very low willingness to pay on a recurring basis and if transactions are irregular or individualised. Furthermore, pay once is used when a platform wants to attract users who bring a certain willingness to pay. The payment scheme certainly also helps better cover the initial costs of development and production. Notably, pay once often resembles the monetisation strategy of companies that sell connected products in combination with platform services. For example, buying an iPhone for a one-time fee gives you access to the iOS ecosystem and its complements (apps). Similarly, if you buy an Alexa speaker, you get access to the Alexa platform, while usage remains mostly free over its lifecycle. Ultimately, one has to be aware of the disadvantages of pay once, such as discouraging users from joining the platform and realising one-time instead of recurring revenue.

51 Pay what you want

Pay what you want is about customers setting the price, which means that customers can also choose not to pay. Recently, pay what you want has become very popular on peer-to-peer content platforms such as Twitch or YouTube. Content creators receive voluntary donations from their viewers. These donations can easily add up to thousands of dollars per month for popular creators as in the case of the live streaming platform Twitch. Twitch even provides them with a direct donation button on their profiles. Viewers can also go for a monthly creator subscription. While these subscriptions come with additional privileges and features, their value add is often rather limited and they actually have the nature of a recurring donation. Beyond Twitch, the free online encyclopaedia Wikipedia is maintained by a community of volunteer editors. Users can decide how much they want to donate to support the foundation. In the end, Wikipedia generates the majority of its revenue through small fees paid by thousands of private users. Yummy Organics is a marketplace that enables customers to purchase spices from small farmers in Sri Lanka. Through a tracking code on the product, the supply chain can be traced back to the farmer, and customers can virtually meet producers via portraits and videos. Using a slider on the product page, customers can decide for themselves how much the fairly produced products are worth to them. Still, Yummy Organics sets a price corridor, so that customers cannot take unfair advantage of that pricing strategy. Using infographics, customers can see the direct impact of their pricing decision.

The Swiss P2P support platform Mila utilises a slightly adapted version of pay what you want. The platform connects people with professional tech experts (Mila 'Pro') or private tech enthusiasts (Mila 'Friend') to conveniently resolve their tech challenges. When a Mila 'Pro' is booked by a user, the price is defined by Mila and cannot be changed. However, when a Mila 'Friend' is booked, the final pricing is only recommended in the form of a price range provided by Mila. The customer and the Mila 'Friend' can actually define and agree together on the final price.

> Laura Brandt, Founder of Yummy Organics, on 'pay what you want' in practice:
> 'It is very rare that people take advantage of this. Most are happy to pay a fair price if it is well explained to them.' (2022)[12]

When and how to apply

With pay what you want, platforms can tap into the individual willingness of users. However, oftentimes this strategy is only used in a complementary manner, or the nature of business is very unique, e.g. Wikipedia is a non-profit organisation and has a charitable aspect. While being a rather rare strategy, pay what you want can be effective for marketplaces selling products with low marginal costs or with a strong social relationship between its two sides. Often platforms with a social or charitable purpose utilise the pay what you want monetisation strategy, as the social element may positively influence an individual's willingness to pay.

Some questions to ask
- Does your platform have a social or charitable purpose?
- Do your platform participants have a strong social relationship?
- How can you create a high perceived customer value?
- What is the role of social pressure to pay a fair price in your platform model?
- Is it likely that your customers take unfair advantage of the pay what you want strategy?

52 Subscription

Subscription is about charging a recurring fee for access to a platform. The monthly or annual fee must be paid regardless of actual usage or transaction volume. Platforms can benefit from foreseeable and recurring revenue while users can avoid high one-time purchases.[13] For instance, users on LinkedIn can pay a recurring fee to access premium features like unlimited messaging to third-degree connections. However, even if the premium features are not used, the full LinkedIn Premium subscription must be paid. Moreover, LinkedIn offers different types of subscriptions, each tailored to the needs of a particular group of customers: job seekers, sales professionals and recruiters. Hence, the company can take advantage of their individual willingness to pay. The industrial innovation platform Azena has created an operating system for security cameras on which developers can build applications, e.g. object detection and shelf monitoring for retail stores. These applications can be used by customers on an annual subscription basis. The British healthcare platform Babylon offers a subscription plan as an alternative to pay per use for its users (patients) when they join as a member. One can either pay USD 60 for each remote doctor consultation or pay a flat fee of roughly USD 180 per year for unlimited, free remote (video-based) doctor consultations.[14]

> Reid Hoffman, cofounder of LinkedIn, on their pricing intentions: 'Premium services for power searchers, such as recruiters and researchers, have been part of our business plan from the beginning.' (2005)[15]

When and how to apply

To offer a subscription plan, one must have a good understanding of platform usage. For instance, in the case of Babylon, patients might take advantage of more than three consultations a year and therefore profitability of the offering might substantially decrease. Babylon's analysis must have shown that across their user base three consultations on average are a reasonable assumption for their business model. In general, subscriptions must be transparent and provide a distinct advantage so that users do not feel misled by the revenue model or any hidden cancellation policies. At the same time, users typically profit from a lower starting price and more flexibility when opting for a subscription. For the platform, subscriptions can make revenue streams much more predictable and steady.

53 Membership

Membership is a special type of subscription that provides enhanced access to a platform. It is often used by marketplaces that would otherwise only earn money through revenue sharing. Although membership may not be necessary to use a platform, it offers its members exclusive platform features like additional discounts or faster processing on marketplaces. When introducing new platform features, many platforms can use membership to shift their business model from free to fee. Amazon was already running a successful product marketplace when it introduced Amazon Prime, a paid membership with benefits such as faster delivery. With Amazon Prime, Amazon can lock in customers and generate additional revenue. The annual membership fee ranges from USD 69 for students to USD 139 for other customers, and thus considers the individual willingness of its users to pay. The online fashion marketplace

Zalando introduced the membership program Zalando Plus to offer special services to its members. For a yearly fee of EUR 15, members can get style advice, exclusive membership discounts and same-day delivery. Since these members are frequently referred to as 'fans' and are more willing to try out new features or services, Zalando hopes that this bundle binds customers further to Zalando and also helps the company try out new services.

> Lisa Schöner, head of loyalty of Zalando, on their membership strategy: 'Our motivation is to go beyond selling clothes in order to focus on every aspect of what the customer needs. We are already working on ideas for how to integrate additional services in the future.' (2017)[16]

When and how to apply

Only if customers believe that they will receive actual benefits through the membership will they be willing to pay the additional premium.[17] Often, market-places use the membership strategy because they can charge users for special benefits such as additional discounts or better service. In general, platforms can further retain their users, increase share of wallet and better exploit their individual willingness to pay.

Some questions to ask
- Which additional features or services can you offer your customers?
- Which of these features and services can you bundle into a monetisable membership programme?
- Is your membership programme perceived as a real value add or a rip-off?

---

54 Boost your own sales

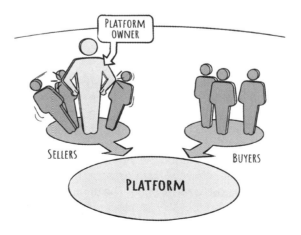

In addition to transaction- and access-based monetisation, the platform revenue model can also be based on product sales. Although this might seem counter-intuitive given that most platforms are only intermediaries, there are examples of platforms that leverage product-based monetisation and take a more active role in the transaction. An owner of a product or service marketplace might consider selling their own products or services on the platform, for instance. While this can be a highly profitable business model, platform owners should be aware that they consequently start competing with their existing platform providers. Eventually, this might lead to negative network effects and providers leaving the platform.

For example, not all products offered on Amazon today come from third-party sellers, as a considerable number of products are sold under the company's own brand. Amazon leveraged its information advantage and analysed its marketplace for products with high margins and high-volume sales. After commissioning other manufacturers, mainly in Asia, to produce these specific products (e.g. power cords), it exploited the Amazon marketplace as a sales channel. Today, Amazon heavily promotes these products under its own brand called Amazon Basics. Similarly, the video streaming platform Netflix began producing its own TV series and movies six years after its foundation in order to generate new sources of income and provide additional value for its users.[18] Like Amazon, it leverages its data insights into what users like or dislike.

Many other examples can be found among traditional product companies that have built up a marketplace, thereby also boosting their own product sales. For example, the German chemical company LANXESS launched CheMondis, which has become a leading B2B marketplace for chemicals. Although it is a cross-dealer and cross-manufacturer platform, LANXESS also offers its own products on the marketplace. Therefore, it is able to leverage CheMondis as an additional sales channel, while other suppliers on the platform also benefit from access to new customers.

When and how to apply

This strategy has been applied in two variations: Either a traditional company develops its own marketplace and utilises it as an additional distribution channel for its existing products or services. Or a platform company with extensive knowledge about its third-party suppliers and their product and service economics starts competing as a complementor or supplier itself.[19] However, the case of Amazon illustrates a very aggressive way of boosting its own sales. Accordingly, critical voices have been raised about market power and unfair information advantages.

Some questions to ask

- Do you have the resources to launch your own product/service brand on your platform?
- Which products and services are particularly suitable for such an offering?
- What is the impact of launching your own product/service brand on your platform ecosystem?

55 Buy low, sell high

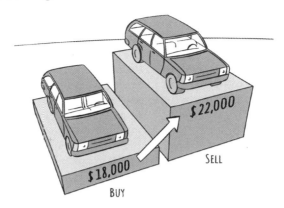

'Buy low, sell high' is about generating revenue from the price spread between supply and demand. The goal is to buy a product at a low price and resell it at a higher price. Although this goes beyond simply brokering a transaction, there are highly capitalised platforms in complex and opaque markets that rely on 'buy low, sell high' strategies.

For instance, Auto1, Europe's largest trading platform for used cars, buys and sells cars in a rather unique approach. In contrast to other used car platforms such as Autoscout24, Auto1 actively buys cars. It creates arbitrage revenue by leveraging regional price differences across Europe and its large network of car dealers. Through the higher level of control in the value chain, Auto1 has shortened the buying and sales process from an average of 90 days to only 10 days. Similarly, the American real estate platform Opendoor buys homes from consumers almost instantly but with a discount of typically 1 per cent to 5 per cent.[20] Leveraging its economies of scale as well as its network, Opendoor then resells these houses on the open market. Thus, Opendoor effectively differentiates itself from its competition while also providing a value-add for its consumers through the faster and much more convenient sales cycle.

When and how to apply

The 'buy low, sell high' strategy includes active buying and selling of products or services. Therefore, only a few platforms, in particular the so-called iBuyer (instant buyer) platforms, use this strategy. Yet, other platforms can also draw inspiration from this strategy. iBuyer platforms usually operate in heterogeneous and opaque markets, so that the active participation of the platform in the deal is accepted and appreciated. However, it requires stable and secure funding and only becomes financially attractive when realised on a very large scale. In fact, the example of Zillow shows that it can be challenging for an iBuyer business model to be financially viable: Zillow also offered a service to instantly buy people's real estate but had to close its iBuyer business Zillow Offers as it became unprofitable due to challenges anticipating asset price development.

Eric Wu, cofounder of Opendoor, on the pricing of its service: 'The structure of the product is that we want to deliver you a valuation that's objective, that's based on data and should inform you on the value that your home is if you sold it today. And we want to charge you a fee for convenience and certainty.' (2022)[21]

Some questions to ask
- Does your market suffer from long, complex and inefficient sales processes?
- Do you have strong financial backing to temporarily put real assets on your balance sheet?
- Are you experienced in the market and confident about reliably realising a significant margin?

Monetise indirectly

56 Advertisement

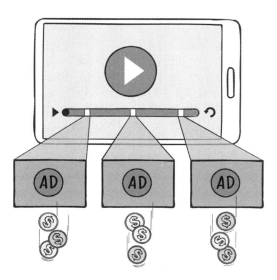

A significant proportion of today's platforms apply indirect monetisation. In an indirect revenue model, revenue is generated by charging third parties rather than end customers or users. The most common form of indirect monetisation is advertisement. It is about charging third parties for placing ads on the platform. These third parties usually cross-finance the free or low-priced offerings that are available to the other platform participants. Therefore, advertisements can finance a platform business even if the willingness of platform participants to pay is low. Users on YouTube do not have to pay if they watch videos. Instead, companies that want to advertise on YouTube pay for the placement of advertisements. The platform sells ad space to third parties and generates revenues on a 'cost per click' or 'cost per view' basis. For example, YouTube charges typically between USD 0.10 and USD 0.30 per view. Ultimately, the advertisers cross-finance the end users. Similarly, Instagram's main source of revenue is advertising. Advertisers pay for advertising campaigns, while the end user can access an ad-based Instagram for free. In fact, with extensive access to user data, such as search behaviour and interests, Instagram can offer third parties highly targeted ad campaigns with accurate performance tracking.

> Stephen Kaufer, former CEO of Tripadvisor, on the challenge of monetisation: 'You look for a hotel in Boston and we had a list of hotels and for each hotel, we had some links to articles or some review. It was really much better than anything else you could find but there was no revenue model behind it. So how did we monetise the traffic? We said we'll put up a banner ad.' (2011)[22]

When and how to apply

Indirect monetisation is considered by some to be the holy grail of platform monetisation since you can offer users free access to your platform while earning money. While advertising is one way of indirect monetisation, it can be rather challenging in practice, as targeted advertising requires a large-scale user base and access to detailed user data. That is why critics also claim that in the end the user still has to pay – not with money, but with his or her user data. Generally, advertisement is very common in the B2C space, where platforms can easily have hundreds of thousands of users (hence many views and clicks), but it can also be applied in B2B. Overall, it is a viable strategy to start with because placing low-key advertisements on your marketplace is quite easy and effortless.

> Susan Wojcicki, CEO of YouTube, on the relevance of advertisers' feedback: 'We're an advertising-supported platform. We want to do the right set of things to build their trust. They're building brands on YouTube, we want to make sure that our brand is a place where they want to build their brand. We've made a number of changes based on the feedback that we have from them. For example, our Google preferred line-up is going to be all curated and reviewed by humans now.' (2018)[23]

Some questions to ask

- Are the users on your platform very price sensitive and therefore direct monetisation is not viable?
- Do you have sufficient and attractive users for advertisers?
- What is the impact of advertisement on user experience and adoption?

57 Pay for visibility

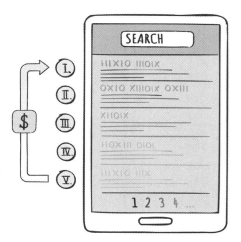

Pay for visibility, another indirect monetisation strategy, is about charging the supply side to be more visible to the demand side. Similar to advertisements, this payment scheme can be applied if platforms have reached a certain size and visibility is a scarce good. At the same time, paying for visibility risks weakening the platform's credibility, as it is not about 'best offers first', but 'paid offers first'.

While it is free for users, the search engine platform Google systematically charges advertisers to be more visible, i.e. to be located higher in the ranking of users' search queries. In fact, the cost per click starts with a few cents but can reach double-digit numbers or even more for popular search topics like loans or other financial services. The social network Facebook also lets companies pay to make their ad or profile page more visible. Thereby, companies, even smaller ones like a local flower or bike repair shop, can pay to increase their reach and visibility among users. Although it is a B2B product marketplace, wind-turbine. com has not yet tapped into the opportunity of revenue sharing. Instead, several years after its foundation, its revenue model still heavily relies on advertisement as well as 'pay for visibility'. When they started, they focused on attracting as many businesses as possible and making the marketplace the most well known in the world, rather than charging customers directly. Advertising was an easy way to make a little money in parallel to cover running costs, but not hinder growth. Today, users who want to sell a used wind turbine can upload it onto the marketplace for free but also have the chance to pay for a dedicated advertisement, i.e. an ad with a link to their sales page on the wind-turbine. com marketplace. The same is true for Amazon or eBay Kleinanzeigen, where (in return for a fee) product offerings can be placed in a more prominent position that is advantageous for the sale of the product.

When and how to apply
Indirect monetisation via 'pay for visibility' can work when a platform is relatively mature and has gained a certain degree of market power. This is because the

supply side has to be convinced that the investment in a more visible placement can actually lead to higher sales. Similar to advertising, platforms need to understand their users' behaviour well in order to target them and offer the best value to those who pay for increased visibility. However, ultimately, 'pay for visibility' rarely stands on its own and is usually a complementary monetisation strategy. Especially when a company is hesitant to advertise, it can be a viable alternative. But it can also risk the platform's credibility if it becomes only about 'paid offer first' and not 'best offer first'.

Some questions to ask
- Is visibility on your platform something providers would pay for?
- How can you increase the visibility of certain offers while maintaining high user experience?
- Is your credibility at risk if you introduce 'pay for visibility' on your platform?

---

58 Data monetisation

Data monetisation is about collecting, analysing and selling user data. Moreover, platforms can use data for their own purposes, e.g. to improve service quality or to design better products. However, with the rise of data privacy concerns and regulations, monetising data is becoming increasingly difficult. In addition to utilising an advertisement strategy, the Finnish job search platform Oikotie systematically collects recruiting data in an anonymised way, such as search queries on its platform. This data is used for benchmark studies and, ultimately, monetised by selling it to third parties as a service or product. After paying a fee, B2B customers like recruiters can see in a dashboard how their job ads perform compared with other players in their industry. While Oikotie has created a new revenue stream, clients can use their promotional budget for job ads more efficiently. Also, Amazon analysed product sales on its marketplace to identify high-margin products that are in demand. Leveraging these insights, Amazon started to offer and sell its own products (Amazon Basics products).

The data-sharing marketplace Farmobile, as another example, links farmers with data purchasers such as seed, chemical, technology or insurance companies. Farmers who use the Farmobile IoT device can capture information about the type and variety of crops grown, the quantity of seeds sowed, the average moisture content and average yields. With this approach, information from more than a million hectares of farmland has been collected and Farmobile monetises this data. Nevertheless, the farmer or producer remains the owner of the user data and can decide not to share their data. Another example is PatientsLikeMe. The company systematically collects data from its patient community on its platform to sell to corporate partners. These corporate partners can use the aggregated and anonymous data about patients and diseases for clinical research or to develop new health interventions, for example.[24]

> Jason Tatge, CEO of Farmobile, on the role of data: 'We started Farmobile based on the belief that data is one of the most valuable things a farmer harvests – it's the infinite commodity. That will never change.' (2018)[25]

When and how to apply

Data is often referred to as the 'new oil' or the 'currency of the future'. At the same time, it is often very challenging to identify use cases where there is actual significant willingness to pay for collected data. Also, privacy concerns or regulations, such as the General Data Protection Regulation (GDPR) in Europe, make it more and more difficult to implement data monetisation. Most importantly, participants' consent is required to share or commercially use the data they generate. Nevertheless, because platforms have access to vast amounts of information, strategies to monetise this data can become very important.

Some questions to ask

- Who are the potential buyers of the data you collect on your platform?
- Do these buyers have a significant willingness to pay for that data?
- Do your users give consent to share and use their data?
- Is data sharing compliant with existing laws, e.g. General Data Protection Regulation (GDPR) in Europe?
- Can you exploit the data for monetisation purposes or for internal purposes?

Apply monetisation tactics

59 Freemium

To foster monetisation, platforms can leverage monetisation tactics such as Freemium. Freemium is about offering a base version of the platform for free, while access to the full version is subject to a fee. This strategy can lower the barriers to entry for potential users. The challenge is to generate enough value with the free version while keeping the value gap between free and premium large enough.[26] Almost every consumer platform builds upon a freemium model and many successful examples can be found. The dating platform Tinder, for instance, offers two options to its users. They can either access the free version of Tinder with limited functionalities, or they can pay for a premium version with unlimited access. Similarly, Spotify has managed to build a large user base through a freemium strategy. In fact, many of its former free users converted to its premium service. Today, Spotify is the world's largest audio streaming platform with more than 430 million monthly active users. Of these, 188 million users are Spotify Premium subscribers, who have access to an ad-free listening experience that can also be used offline.

> Sean Rad, cofounder of Tinder, on the pricing of Tinder: 'The core Tinder experience has been free and will always remain free. And the best way to keep a free and amazing ecosystem is to monetise. We don't expect everyone to use Tinder Plus, in fact, the way we've priced it, it really appeals to some of our more power users.' (2015)[27]

But subscription also works well in the B2B space. For instance, 365FarmNet, a leading innovation platform for the digitised farm, leverages this strategy. It offers a free version with basic functions, such as a field catalogue or cross-compliance documentation, while the premium version provides farmers access to an extended set of features, ranging from crop planning and fertiliser optimisation to a profit manager. As a farmer, you might explore the offering with the free version and then pay to migrate to the premium version.

When and how to apply

By offering a free version with limited functionality, platforms can increase their user base and demonstrate the added value of their premium version. The biggest challenge is to find the right balance between functionality of the free and premium versions. If the additional utility of the premium version it too low, users won't be willing to convert to the premium version. If the premium version is attractive but the free version has very limited functionality, users will not start their usage journey because the free version is perceived as being useless. Platforms in the consumer segment often use freemium to test the willingness of consumers to pay for newly developed software. In general, it can ease the transition from a free to a paid offer and is often combined with other strategies such as subscription.

Some questions to ask
- Which features should be free and which should be premium?
- Are the benefits of the premium offer clear, convincing and easy to communicate?
- How can you increase the conversion rate from free to premium?
- How many features should the free version have in order to be attractive enough for users but still allow the premium version to be distinct and attractive as an upgrade?
- Are your premium users able to cross-finance your free users?

---

60 Free trial

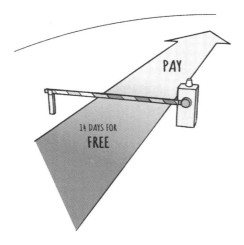

Free trial is about offering free access to the platform, but only for a limited period of time. After this period ends, users must pay for access. Companies use a free trial to attract users and hope to convert them into paying customers after the trial period expires. Similar to freemium, it lowers entry barriers as users get the opportunity to experience the functionalities and test the platform.

For instance, the B2B marketplace for mobility data Caruso offers a free trial period of three months for the purpose of prototyping. During this period, third parties have full access to the offering. Once expired, companies must choose from three paid service packages which are offered as subscriptions. Similarly, students can sign up for a one-month trial with free access to course content at Udacity. However, to continue and complete an online course, students must become paying customers once the trial period has ended. Also, users on LinkedIn are offered a free trial of the LinkedIn Premium subscription that provides access to additional features, such as unlimited people browsing or teaching videos. But this trial period runs for one month only. In the end, a free trial is offered as a supplement by many platforms, such as Fitbit (3 months), Chegg (1 month) or DoorDash (3–12 months) to mention a few, and comes in other variations, as well. For example, by distributing codes with very high discounts, FlixBus gained high awareness and led many customers to test long-distance bus travel for almost free before becoming paying customers in the long run.

When and how to apply
A free trial can help foster monetisation and is an established tool for many platforms. However, one must achieve a solid conversion rate from the free trial period to paying customers for this strategy to be successful. Therefore, platforms aim to provide a particularly high value during the trial period. To achieve a high conversion, a smooth and frictionless user onboarding is required. Good customer support or even an active customer onboarding can increase conversion.

Some questions to ask
- What are the full costs associated with a free trial and is it financially viable for your business?
- How long is the trial period for users to fully experience the platform?
- How can we create a lock-in effect which dissuades users from exiting the platform, e.g. convenience, loyalty, emotion, lack of attention?
- Do you apply an opt-in (no payment information necessary upfront) or an opt-out free trial?

61 Add-on

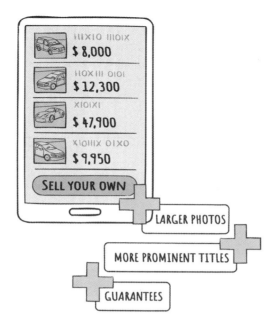

Add-on is about complementing a base product with optional, high-margin extensions (add-ons). Often, the base product just satisfies a core need at a competitive price. Complementary add-ons that cost extra are offered with the aim of increasing revenue and margin.[28] Sellers on eBay can upload products for free, but to increase the chances of a successful auction, add-ons can be purchased, such as larger product photos, more prominent titles or listing of the product in two distinct categories. Similarly, the online car marketplace mobile.de offers both sellers and buyers complementary add-ons to enhance the car buying process, such as financing for the vehicle, while the core functions are mostly free. The core value of Upwork is to bring businesses and freelancers together. Upwork charges its corporate users a monthly or annual subscription fee in addition to the usage-based service fee, which is calculated as a percentage of the individual transaction volume. However, Upwork offers and sells add-ons such as Upwork Plus, Upwork Payroll and Managed Services to companies to increase its margin.

When and how to apply
Typically, for this strategy to work, the base product or service is offered at a relatively low price to attract and lock in customers. To cross-finance the base product, users need to be convinced of the relevance of add-on products or features. Hence, the add-ons must provide a real value-add for the users. Value-adding services or products are often identified along the customer journey and are those that have a particularly high margin, e.g. additional insurance. To apply this strategy, a good understanding of your customers' buying behaviour and willingness to pay is necessary.

62 Dynamic pricing

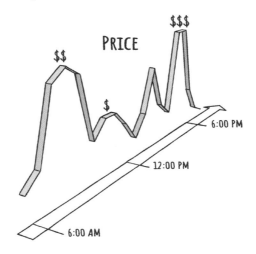

Dynamic pricing is about adjusting prices based on actual demand and supply. Higher demand leads to higher prices, lower demand leads to lower prices. Platforms can leverage their knowledge of current demand and supply to adjust prices so that market equilibrium is assured while fostering monetisation. One night, the ridesharing platform Uber had trouble recruiting enough drivers to match the demand in Boston. That's when Mike Pao, Uber's general manager in Boston at the time, manually asked the drivers via email to drive for double the payment. After a huge success, Uber rolled this out to all cities and started to make use of dynamic pricing on a large scale.[29] In periods of high demand, prices were increased to attract additional drivers and vice versa. Today, to adjust prices in real time, Uber heavily relies on its data on drivers and passengers, and it has become a highly automated process. Also, Google determines the price of ads based on the current search interest of users as well as seasons and events. For example, the keyword combination 'gift ideas' is priced higher during the Christmas season.

Travis Kalanick, cofounder of Uber, on dynamic pricing: 'We feel like we're doing a lot of interesting work on pricing in an industry that has operated with fixed supply and fixed pricing for 100 years. We think dynamic supply and flexible pricing is a better way to do things, and we're learning a lot about how that works in practice.' (2014)[30]

When and how to apply

Knowing your customers becomes crucial if you want to make use of dynamic pricing. In fact, to develop an effective pricing algorithm, it is essential to track customers' behaviour and understand how they react to price changes (price elasticity). In particular, mobility or logistics platforms, like Uber, FlixBus, DoorDash or InstaFreight, have mastered this strategy to balance their fluctuating demand and supply. At the same time, platforms must be careful that their prices are not perceived as being exploitative, and that the change in price does not create too much uncertainty for the users on either side. Therefore, upper or lower price caps can be introduced.

Some questions to ask

- Can dynamic pricing help you to balance demand and supply on your platform?
- Do customers accept dynamic pricing, or will it upset customers who have to pay more?
- Do we know roughly the price elasticity of demand and supply?
- What is the base for price variations?
- What is the magnitude of price fluctuations your customers will accept?

4

Scale: patterns to scale a platform

Network effects are fundamental to the success of platforms. As described above, they refer to the dynamic that more users on the platform leads to greater platform value. Network effects follow a self-reinforcing dynamic: More users leads to more value so that even more users are attracted. Without scaling there are no network effects and platforms become dead on arrival. Platforms either grow or die. Most incorrect assumptions about platforms have to do with the scaling phase. It is much easier to attract nerds, fans and early pioneers who are interested in the new platform than reach the majority of the target market, both on the demand and supply sides. That is why network effects can be difficult to kickstart at first. In the case of a product marketplace like Amazon, for example, you cannot attract sellers without having buyers on your platform, and you cannot attract buyers without sellers. The same is true for innovation platforms. If there are no third-party developers on Android, there are no complementary apps, and the innovation platform stays unattractive to users, and vice versa. Every platform is confronted with this so-called chicken-and-egg problem, which is considered to be one of the biggest barriers to the successful implementation of a platform business model.[1] In the following section, we present 14 scaling strategies in five domains that can help you systematically overcome the chicken-and-egg challenge and deadlocked situations (see Figure 2.4.1). This includes traditional strategies that focus on one side first (A), attract key users (B), leverage existing assets (C) and focus on both market sides simultaneously (D), as well as the opportunistic strategies (E). Even though it can be challenging, there are platforms that have kicked off network effects very successfully. The payment platform PayPal, for instance, subsidised users by offering them USD 20 when they signed up (Pattern #66). This strategy boosted the initial acceptance rate and spurred the adoption of PayPal. Moreover, PayPal integrated its payment platform into eBay to leverage eBay's existing user base (Pattern #71).

Figure 2.4.1 Scaling a platform business (Patterns #63–76)

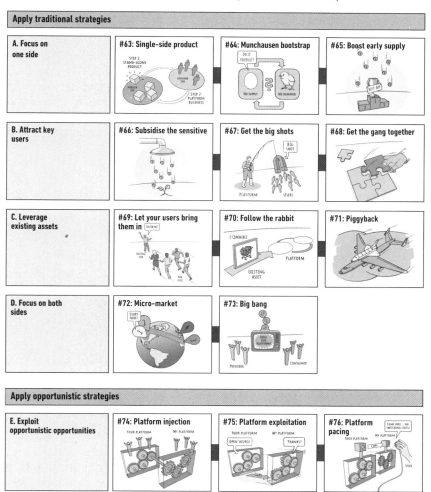

Peter Thiel, co-founder of PayPal, on the beginnings of PayPal: 'We needed to achieve escape velocity, we needed to grow so quickly that it would discourage anybody from even trying to compete with us. On the one hand, you have to race really hard to scale fast, but then the benefit if you do it is that you're sort of achieving escape velocity from the black hole that is hyper-competition. There are two types of businesses. There are companies that are purely competitive; they do not make any money, think a restaurant. And then there are businesses that do not compete. They are monopolies, and they do very well. And even though this is not the way people want to talk about it on the inside, you always want to have a monopoly on the inside. You never want to be in the restaurant business.' (n.d.)[2]

Certainly not all strategies are applicable to each and every case, and they must be adapted to the individual characteristics of the innovation or transaction platform. Also, the presented scaling patterns are loosely coupled. This means that the depicted strategies may be applied simultaneously, subsequently, jointly or separately. A good starting point is, therefore, to analyse what strengths and assets you currently have available. Ultimately, you should address core questions like, 'Which market sides (platform players) are difficult to attract?', 'Which are easy to attract?', 'Can we get access to one or more market sides by providing a product or service that provides stand-alone value?', 'Which one to three growth strategies can be applied to address the chicken-and-egg problem?'.

Focus on one side

63 Single-side product

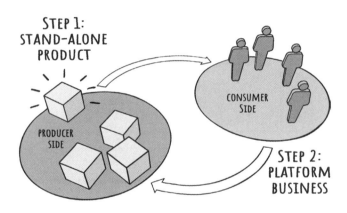

One way of systematically scaling your platform is to focus on one of the market sides first. This can be done by creating a single-side or a stand-alone product for one market side first, while already striving for a two-sided market.[3] As soon as a critical mass of users for this stand-alone offering is reached, the product business model is extended to a platform business model. The second group of users can be onboarded more easily as they are attracted by the existing customer base. Salesforce, for instance, began by selling software for customer relationship management (CRM) before establishing the app-store-like marketplace, AppExchange, where third-party developers could offer complementary B2B apps. The first set of users was attracted by the stand-alone value of the CRM solution, and network effects were not present at this point in time. By creating an app store, Salesforce moved from a stand-alone product to a two-sided platform. External developers were attracted because they saw the potential of selling their B2B applications to an already existing and large customer base. With this transition, network effects started to emerge: Additional users were attracted by the large number of developers (and the resulting complementary apps), and vice versa.

Another well-known example is OpenTable. Already at its foundation in 1998, its management had the idea of simplifying the process of booking a table at a restaurant by connecting restaurants and customers. However, OpenTable realised that the industry was not yet digital enough and many bookings were still made using pen and paper. They pivoted as a result and instead created stand-alone restaurant management software. By 2006, more than 4,500 restaurants had been persuaded by the software's stand-alone value, i.e. improving a restaurant's operations, sales and marketing. Only once the customer base of restaurants was large enough was a marketplace set up where diners could book a table at the already connected restaurants. Users were soon drawn to the OpenTable platform to search for and book a restaurant, attracted by the critical mass of restaurants available via their restaurant software business. In fact, the company registered strong growth over the following years and by 2019 surpassed 134 million seated diners per month on average.[4]

Similarly, the platform HoneyBook initially started with an online album service for wedding photographs. It was opened to consumers only after a critical mass of professionals had joined and used the online album service. Over time, it has evolved into the go-to marketplace for wedding services following the credo 'come for the tool, stay for the network'.[5] The start-up Parkdepot provides camera technology to analyse the utilisation of commercial parking spaces, e.g. at grocery stores or hotels. As of now, the technology is sold as a stand-alone product, but it would be an easy step to move towards a marketplace by offering vacant parking spaces to customers that need a parking space. Thereby, Parkdepot brings owners of vacant parking lots and car riders seeking a parking space together on a marketplace. Other examples that have taken advantage of this strategy include InstaFreight in the logistics sector, Bosch ctrlX in the industrial sector and Amazon Alexa in the smart home segment.

> Mike Xenakis, former managing director of Europe of OpenTable, on the relevance of starting with the right platform side: 'We ultimately discovered if we had enough restaurants in a market, we'd have enough value for the diner to use OpenTable. Dining is local, so concentration was key. A rule of thumb was that if we could get to 50–100 concentrated restaurants in a city, we had enough for a consumer to land on the site, cast a wide net, and get a consideration set that was meaningful enough to not be disappointed.' (2019)[6]

When and how to apply

In a variety of contexts, including B2C and B2B, the single-side product strategy has proven to be effective. Some companies envision their journey from a stand-alone product to a platform business model early on. Others identify this opportunity once they are established and mature. Hence, they transition to a platform at a later stage after they have already generated substantial revenue.

The strategy is frequently used in the context of B2B and connected products, where companies offer a physical product – often subsidised – to a certain set of users. Once the installed base is large enough, they attempt to expand to a multi-sided platform business, e.g. by establishing an app store. Critical for the success of this strategy is a superior stand-alone value and achieving a critical mass of users from one market side before moving to the platform.

> **Some questions to ask**
> - Can you offer a strong stand-alone product to build up a viable customer base?
> - Can you leverage the customer base to establish a two-sided market?
> - How can you attract providers that are willing to leverage the existing customer base?

64 Munchausen bootstrap

In the well-known fairy tale, Baron Munchausen pulls himself out of a swamp by his own hair. Platforms can follow this logic by kickstarting the supply side themselves. Similar to start-ups that bootstrap their business, this strategy is all about kickstarting network effects without external help. As early supply is often limited, platforms often generate content themselves, make the supply look bigger, or even 'fake it till they make it' and simulate supply in the beginning.[7] The objective is to create initial demand that is attracted by this simulated supply. This in turn draws external producers and supply to the platform. With this strategy, platforms can also illustrate the nature and quality of products they want third parties to generate on their platform.[8]

> David Rosenthal, board member of Rover, on internally kicking of supply: 'All early supply was from employees.' (2019)[9]

The Q&A platform Quora initially had difficulties attracting people to answer questions. To overcome this deadlock, Quora hired people to answer the initial inquiries, thereby leveraging the Munchausen bootstrap. As a result, Quora's own employees facilitated the initial activity on the platform. With a growing customer base, more and more platform users answered inquiries themselves, and Quora personnel could be relieved of this task. The social media platform Reddit, founded in 2005, provides user-generated content such as images, videos, links and text postings. Similar to Quora, Reddit's success depends heavily on interaction and content from the community. It also utilised the Munchausen bootstrap as employees created 'normal' accounts and posted links, images and voted posts up and down, in order to stimulate activity.[10] Thereby, Reddit also demonstrated the type of content they would prefer to see on their platform. This consequently drew users who were interested in comparable content, resulting in a high-quality network community. After years of rapid growth, Reddit in fact has become one of the most visited websites in the world. Another example is Apple. When Apple launched its App Store in 2008, it already offered 500 native apps at the start, most of them for free.[11] By offering applications from the beginning, Apple increased the popularity of the App Store and laid the foundation for third-party developers to join, as well as create new and better applications. AutoScout24 founder Joachim Schoss went to a used car store and took pictures of all the cars to put on the platform. Moreover, he included many used car ads from local newspapers to get a first critical supply.

> Sander Daniels, founder of Thumbtack, on the relevance of the platform's supply side: 'When we were starting out, we looked at the biggest marketplace companies – eBay, Craigslist, Amazon. There were two things in common: (1) they had all the supply and (2) they had ugly products and brands. The lesson we took away from this was that all that matters is supply. So we decided to focus on that above all else. We postponed building brand and delightful product until we had liquidity. Dozens of other start-ups took another direction. Case after case, it proved a mistake. Creating scaled supply early on matters more than anything.' (2019)[12]

When and how to apply

Munchausen bootstrap is applied at an early stage of the platform journey but can come in different forms. It can even be a very analogue and manual process as the example of wind-turbine.com demonstrates. Instead of waiting for sellers to join his marketplace, wind-turbine.com founder Bernd Weidmann transferred all wind turbine listings found in physical ads onto his marketplace manually. If the self-created activity or supply is not driven by actual users, one needs to be very careful to meet the needs of early adopters.

65 Boost early supply

By boosting early supply, the platform owner incentivises producers to generate high-quality offerings in the early stages of the platform lifecycle. This strategy has been frequently employed by innovation platforms to encourage third-party app development (but is not limited to these kinds of platforms). Contests with cash prizes, for instance, are one popular way to promote early supply. Since starting with the supply side is vital for platform success, this strategy is well known and commonly applied to kickstart network effects at a very early stage.[13]

In order to catch up with the Apple App Store, Google started the Android app development competition in 2008. The contest was designed to support the developer community and award cash prizes to the winning top ten apps. This resulted in high-quality mobile applications and, ultimately, in the necessary momentum to catch up with the Apple App Store. Similarly, in 2018, the multinational engineering and technology corporation Bosch launched Azena, a marketplace for smart security cameras and safety solutions. It provides an operating system for security cameras that any camera manufacturer can use. Thereby, it provides the opportunity for third parties to develop video analytics applications on top. Similar to Android, a challenge was launched to incentivise developers to create applications for the platform. The three developers with the best application each received prize money of EUR 10,000. Hence, Azena executed the 'boost early supply' strategy in order to activate the supply side and obtain an initial set of high-quality applications. The artwork platform Redbubble has also held a number of competitions, including the Redbubble Art Party, which engaged both the supply side and the demand side. Users shared images of their favourite things on Instagram with the hashtag #RedbubbleArtParty. The supply side (artists) could pick up those ideas and then draw inspiration from them to produce real artwork which then was uploaded and sold via the Redbubble marketplace. The top three customer–artist collaborations each received a prize. Another example that has taken advantage of this strategy is Bosch ctrlX in the industrial segment (B2B), which started a developer challenge in 2022.

> Andy Rubin, founder of Android, on the reason why they started the developer challenge: 'We believe that the Android platform offers developers a unique opportunity to create truly innovative mobile software. We're challenging developers to stretch their imaginations and skills to leverage the full capabilities of this new platform and to create something amazing.' (2007)[14]

When and how to apply

Establishing a vital supply side early on is key to platform success. Boosting early supply can therefore be essential at the beginning, particularly if the nature of the platform requires upfront investments or commitment from third parties, as in the case of innovation platforms. Most often, this strategy relies on significant financial incentives that must be provided. Furthermore, in the case of competitions, there must also be a set of rules.[15] Android, for example, allocated prize money to specific categories in order to steer the variation of apps and topics. However, there are also other ways to boost early supply, as the example of DoorDash shows. So-called 'launchers' did research on the street and went door-to-door to recruit potential partner restaurants and persuade them to join the DoorDash platform as early suppliers. Blockchain platforms have also developed an alternative incentive scheme by giving away tokens to their first developers so that they can benefit from the platform's success in the long term. In fact, giving away actual shares or large amounts of (crypto) money to early developers can be a very strong supplier incentive scheme.

Some questions to ask

- Can you attract third-party producers to your platform by having competitions?
- What monetary incentives do you have to offer to assure significant provider contributions?
- How can you ensure that the contributions have the desired variety?

Attract key users

66 Subsidise the sensitive

'Subsidise the sensitive' is about subsidising those users who are highly price sensitive, yet of utmost relevance for the growth of the platform. While the demand side is more frequently subsidised than the supply side, subsidisation can be applied to any side of a platform. Due to the nature of its business model, PayPal heavily relies on network effects: If your relevant businesses and friends are not signed up, there is no need for you to use PayPal as a payment platform. PayPal's management knew early on that a key challenge would be to convince consumers to share their personal information, i.e. email and credit card details, for user-friendly and instant payments. Thus, management tried to partner up with traditional banks. However, that was either too expensive or too bureaucratic. After securing Series C funding of USD 100 million in the year 2000, they started offering USD 20 to every person who signed up and another USD 20 when they referred a friend. They gradually phased out these bonuses and lowered the rate to USD 5 but registered daily growth rates of around 7 per cent to 10 per cent during this period. Even though PayPal successfully attracted millions of users, this strategy cost them around USD 60 million.[16]

Similarly, Uber used external funds to keep pricing competitively low and driver compensation above existing industry standards, thereby indirectly subsidising both the supply and demand sides. One of the most expensive parts was the acquisition of drivers. In the very beginning, Uber even paid drivers a bonus ranging from USD 2,000 to USD 5,000 in key cities to sign up on the platform.[17] This also helped achieve a balance between supply (drivers) and demand (riders) on the platform. While Uber gained a lot of traction, it also accumulated significant losses through the expensive acquisition process and is still not profitable as of today. The Chinese platform Pinduoduo is well known for its subsidy programmes. Despite making deficits, it continuously subsidises its users on a large scale. In 2019, it spent RMB 10 billion to give away discounts with the goal of broadening its target group and attract higher income customers.[18] In 2020, it spent millions of yuan for users to cope with the coronavirus. Also, FlixBus attracted customers with strong discount codes and low-priced tickets in its first business years. Through coupons distributed at German universities or placed on widely used consumer products, such as Nutella jars, FlixBus gained general awareness and led many customers to use long-distance bus travel as an alternative to trains or planes.

When and how to apply

Subsidising one side of users has proven to be very effective for building up network effects. However, it often requires a significant amount of capital. Platforms like Napster or Skype, for instance, have made their offering completely free after charging for it for years. However, in return they had to rely on advertisement. Subsidies can also be implemented indirectly, for example, in the form of a reduced revenue share or discounts. Subsidising is all about understanding the price sensitivity of the different market sides as well as their importance in respect to network effects. Moreover, platform providers must realise when the time has come to reduce subsidy to a minimum. Ultimately, they have to demonstrate that their business model relies on more than subsidised demand and supply.

Some questions to ask

- Do you understand the importance and price sensitivity of your key customer segments?
- What is the relationship between the level of subsidies and customer uptake?
- How many price-sensitive customers do you need until the momentum for growth is reached?
- Do you have sufficient funding to keep subsidies in place long enough to make a substantial effect?

---

67 Get the big shots

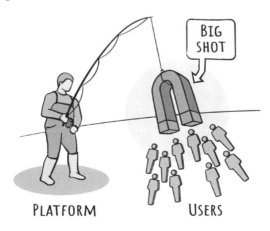

PLATFORM   USERS

A second way of systematically scaling your platform is to attract key users to your platform. With 'get the big shots', the platform owner tries to attract key providers or users who bring their own networks to the platform.[19] For the greatest effect, the engagement of such key players should be exclusive to the platform. By leveraging the 'get the big shots' strategy, Microsoft managed to increase the adoption of their gaming console Xbox and attract many users to its platform. It acquired the video game company Bungie Studios and made its signature game Halo exclusive to the Microsoft platform. Today, Microsoft also pays high premiums to other developer studios if they provide their games solely on the Xbox platform. Dedicated players who want to play those games must purchase an Xbox console. TaskRabbit, a platform for local freelancing tasks, has brought IKEA onto its platform and extensively promoted this partnership. Naturally, IKEA contributed its own large customer base to the platform's success. The implementation ultimately led to the acquisition of TaskRabbit by IKEA.

Similarly, food delivery platform DoorDash tried to connect large partners with its own existing network on both market sides. It tried to partner with renowned food chains like McDonald's or Wendy's by negotiating exclusive agreements. The objective was to attract customers to those food chains and indirectly benefit from their brand's identity and reputation. It also partnered with the insurance company Chase, distributing millions of DashPass subscriptions free of charge to Chase customers. Another popular example is Adobe whose management convinced the US federal government to utilise their PDF solution to issue US tax forms, making it quickly the de facto standard for reading and sharing documents.

When and how to apply

This strategy is all about the identification of partners that bring a valuable set of users or reputation and credibility with them. Once these potential partners are identified, the core challenge is to attract such key users to the platform. Typically, this only works through a larger financial commitment. The exclusivity of products may even lead to an acquisition as in the case of Microsoft. However, if there is exclusivity, this strategy can have a very strong, positive impact on network effects. The strategy can also be observed in health platforms that try to convince key opinion leaders (e.g. respected professors or well-known doctors) or 'cool kids' to promote their platform and attract users.

Some questions to ask

- Who/What are the big shots that are relevant for your platform?
- How can you get these key players to utilise and adopt your platform?
- Is there a key producer you could even acquire?

---

68 Get the gang together

Platforms frequently start as an ecosystem with a few relatively equal partners. The objective of 'get the gang together' is to develop a collaborative, innovative value proposition with complementary partners. However, with the growing success of the platform and the rising number of partners, it is common that one platform owner emerges who will eventually dominate the ecosystem.

In 2007, Google founded the open platform Open Handset Alliance, which consisted of 34 initial partners, with the objective of creating a novel mobile operating ecosystem.[20] In the beginning, the strategic focus was on aligning each partner's interests for the benefit of the alliance. Once the network grew and numerous partners joined, Google started to dominate the alliance and set the rules. For example, to protect itself, Google requested that its hardware partners only produce devices that were compatible with Android. Similarly, only after Nokia sold HERE to a consortium consisting of several automotive companies like Daimler, BMW and Audi did the mapping and location data platform gain the necessary momentum. The ecosystem of automobile manufacturers and suppliers ensures that the platform has strong access to traffic data and that their services are used by a variety of manufacturers. Essentially, it makes sure that everybody has an incentive to make the platform succeed.

> Michael Bolle, former CTO of Bosch, on the platforms' dilemma: 'No one wants to be trapped on someone else's platform. Everyone wants to create their own platform. That's why platforms don't scale and fail in most cases.' (2021)[21]

When and how to apply

'Get the gang together' is vital when the platform idea is too big for one single company to pursue. As a result, platform managers seek out complementary partners in the ecosystem. However, coordinating interests and convincing complementary parties to join forces is rather challenging and requires outstanding alignment and negotiation. One must showcase and provide value add for each partner. Also, a sustainable long-term proposition has to be set forth for the individual partners. Finally, the tendency of platforms to become single owner–driven monopolies has to be addressed appropriately early on.

> **Some questions to ask**
> - Does the core value proposition of your platform business depend on multiple partners?
> - Are the necessary partners willing to join forces and are they allowed to (antitrust law)?
> - How do you address the challenge of one partner becoming the dominant platform owner?
> - What value can you provide to each participating industry player?

Leverage existing assets

69 Let your users bring them in

A third way of systematically scaling your platform is to leverage existing assets. First, you can leverage your own platform assets. With 'let your users bring them in', platform owners incentivise existing platform participants to bring in new participants. Platform owners can, for example, pay referral fees or grant exclusive sales conditions. Moreover, the motivation to get other users on board might be inherently integrated into the platform's business model. This is the case, for example, with crowdfunding platforms.

Owners of a Kickstarter crowdfunding campaign naturally heavily promote their campaign as they want to bring their supporter base to the platform. This serves as an additional marketing activity for Kickstarter as a side effect. The promotion of campaigns stimulates traction across the entire platform and drives new users to the crowdfunding platform. Similarly, on Pinduoduo, a

Chinese platform that connects farmers with consumers directly, users naturally have an incentive to attract more users. Instead of purchasing a product on your own, you can be part of a 'team purchase' which means you wait until a certain number of users desire the same product and in return you get a discount once the product is purchased by the 'team'. The supplier profits from selling a bulk order instead of individual ones. The strategy is not limited to the consumer segment, as the example of Unite (formerly Mercateo) showcases. Unite is a B2B marketplace with the goal of simplifying procurement. However, in the beginning, Unite was struggling to convince companies to participate on their platform. Suppliers were particularly afraid of losing control of their individual client relationships. As a response, Unite started to grant special sales conditions to those suppliers that brought their own customers onto the platform. They offered that they would always have 'the last word' in a bidding competition.[22] This led to a strong increase in the number of customers. The game innovation platform Roblox also heavily rewards users to attract new players. By sharing promotional links, users get rewards. In fact, for every in-game purchase made by the referred new member, the original referrer receives a certain share of the proceeds, for all upcoming purchases over the entire lifecycle of the new user.[23]

When and how to apply
Incentivising your users to bring in new ones has become an integral part of almost every platform, from B2C to B2B. For instance, on Uber and Airbnb 10 per cent to 15 per cent of new users come from referrals.[24] Ultimately, however, incentive programmes only pay off if there is a platform that users love and are satisfied with.

> **Some questions to ask**
> - What types of incentives can you offer your users to bring in new ones?
> - How can you assure that users can bring in new ones effortlessly?
> - Are there ways to create incentives that do not require financial rewards?

70 Follow the rabbit

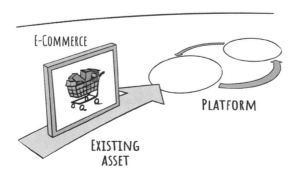

With 'follow the rabbit' you can leverage existing, non-platform assets from your own company. In the novel *Alice in Wonderland*, Alice follows a white rabbit down a hole, thereby discovering a new world and finding her true destiny.[25] Similarly, companies can explore and go beyond what they originally intended. This strategy is about leveraging existing, non-platform assets, such as a strong customer base, a world-class e-commerce infrastructure, or technology to develop a platform business. The objective is to build upon unique assets in your company that competitors do not have access to and that give you an early competitive advantage when moving towards a platform business model.

Amazon started as an e-commerce business selling books. It chose to sell books since they were relatively easy to source, package and distribute compared to other goods. Soon it started selling products in other categories like music CDs, DVDs and electronics. But in order to succeed as an online retailer, Amazon knew it would need to scale and grow fast. While other bookstores such as Barnes & Noble focused on their own online bookstores, Amazon launched its third-party seller marketplace in 1999. The online store was essentially turned into an open marketplace with third-party merchants. Since this transition was not part of the goal at the beginning, Amazon went beyond the 'imaginary'. Looking back, this transition was a crucial element in the successful scaling of Amazon. Klöckner & Co is another example of how a company can leverage its assets and knowledge to develop a platform business. Because the materials industry was characterised by low and decreasing margins, Klöckner & Co was looking for alternative revenue streams and new competitive advantages. After its management got inspired in Silicon Valley, they fostered the creation of XOM Materials, a procurement platform for all the products and services associated with the materials industry. Having a long history in steel, metals and plastic distribution, they already had the essential infrastructure in place and were familiar with the different needs of the involved parties. With this existing expertise and infrastructure, they transformed XOM Materials into one of the leading one-stop-shop platforms in the industry. Two other well-known examples come from the wearables and fitness market. Both Fitbit and Withings started by designing and selling connected devices to end consumers. Only in a second step did they open up to healthcare professionals and external developers. More specifically, they leveraged their unique access to customers and their data and developed an innovation platform based on their connected devices. They thereby created new opportunities for B2B customers, a completely new market for both companies.

> Gisbert Rühl, former CEO of Klöckner & Co, on the internal challenges of an incumbent: 'We launched XOM separately because it turns out it is rather difficult to really disrupt yourself. [. . .] As an incumbent, you always spend the money where you earn the money, and when you earn the money with certain products, it's really difficult to invest in something that could disrupt your core business.' (2021)[26]

When and how to apply

'Follow the rabbit' requires thinking outside the box. In the end it is all about an existing infrastructure, asset or expertise in your company that can be leveraged to develop a platform business. Therefore, it is particularly suited for established or mature businesses that want to transition into or build a complementary platform business. In general, 'follow the rabbit' can come in many forms since the asset or infrastructure can be diverse or specific to the company at hand. The timing is also an important success factor. Schneider Electric, for example, only moved its EcoStruxure product ecosystem to an open and interoperable IoT platform when the company already had strong traction and scale, i.e. more than four million connected devices, 50 per cent annual growth and a stable technology.[27]

> ## Some questions to ask
> ● What are your unique assets that make you stand out?
> ● How can you leverage your unique assets to build up a platform business model?
> ● Are you willing and able to potentially disrupt your core business while building up a platform?

71 Piggyback

Piggybacking is about connecting with an existing user base from a different platform. Instead of leveraging your own assets, it is about leveraging another platform's assets. Many platforms have succeeded in this by creating a symbiotic win–win offering with other platforms, e.g. by creating an integrated, more convenient user experience. PayPal, for instance, became successful only after it was deeply integrated into eBay. In the early 2000s, purchases on eBay were paid using money orders/checks with the U.S. Postal Service, which often led to product shipment delays.[28] Once PayPal with its user-friendly payment service was integrated into eBay, users began benefiting from the most convenient payment solution at the time. Most eBay users rapidly adopted

PayPal and even demanded commercial partners beyond the eBay ecosystem to integrate the payment service. In turn, this integration provided PayPal access to the vast customer base of eBay that signed up and started using PayPal.

Another example is Amazon's innovation platform that revolves around its smart speaker Echo and the voice assistant Alexa. While Alexa can perform web searches, create calendar invites, order products and do other tasks, most users simply wanted to play music and make use of Spotify in the beginning. Therefore, Amazon decided to integrate Spotify into Alexa, providing users with a convenient way to access their favourite music. In fact, it was one of the first preinstalled applications. Essentially, Alexa piggybacked on Spotify's existing user base, but Spotify also profited from a larger reach. However, piggybacking can also take different forms as the example of Babylon illustrates. The British healthcare platform wanted to connect patients remotely with doctors but struggled to onboard patients in the beginning. They overcame the challenge when they entered into a partnership with the National Health Service (NHS) in the United Kingdom in 2017. In this win–win situation, Babylon got linked to the national healthcare database of users and was able to provide more convenient and efficient access to health care. Babylon continued with the piggyback strategy by integrating into Tencent's WeChat platform, as well. However, a mutual win–win in the long run is not always easy to achieve. Although value was created for both sides of the market, the two partnerships were discontinued. The economics of the partnerships simply did not pay off for Babylon as sufficient scale was not achieved fast enough.

> Tim Rideout, UK general manager at Babylon, on the economic importance of scale: 'We do a lot of economic modelling and we can sustain the position – [. . .] but what we can't do is expand it. And ideally we would . . . So if we were incentivised we would expand and everyone would win – the service would save money and patients would have great access to primary care but the economics just don't allow us to do that.' (2022)[29]

When and how to apply

The key success factor for the piggyback strategy is to create a mutual win–win situation. On the one hand, it must be ensured that one has access to and can profit from the user base of the established 'carrier' platform. On the other hand, the carrier platform needs to recognise the value add for its users and accept a synergic platform in its immediate environment. Ideally, one has such distinct usability and value add that users from the carrier platform demand to integrate your service.

Some questions to ask

- Would another platform and its users benefit from your platform?
- Can you create a win–win situation for you and the established 'carrier' platform?

- How big is the support from the platform 'carrier'?
- How do you cope with the dependency on the 'carrier' platform in the short and long term?
- What are the exit scenarios from the platform 'carrier'? Do exit clauses exist?

Focus on both sides

72 Micro-market

A fourth way of systematically scaling your platform is focusing on both sides of the platform simultaneously. Micro-market is about starting a platform in a small, often local market. The objective is to attract a critical user mass and establish strong network effects in a distinct market first. Once this goal is reached, the objective is to expand into a second and third micro-market to ultimately integrate them.[30] Micro-markets can be based on local regions but also dedicated product categories.

Facebook's initial market, for instance, was Harvard University. In this closed community, it could focus on improving the interaction and network quality. Only after it gained traction at Harvard did it expand to other Ivy League universities. While users were only able to connect within their specific campus, Facebook soon allowed inter-campus connections. Finally, Facebook was rolled out to other universities and high schools. Only then did Facebook develop into a global platform. Similarly, the healthcare job platform MedWing applied the micro-market strategy. It started out in Berlin and gained strong traction in this market covering 80 per cent of the hospitals.[31] As the platform started to allow international applicants to access the platform, the market also grew within Europe. The next locations were London and Paris, for which the platform had received requests from healthcare facilities. Other well-known examples are Airbnb (marketplace for vacation homes), Rover (marketplace for vetted pet sitting) and DoorDash (food delivery platform), which all started in one city first, gained traction there and then grew from city to city. In fact, DoorDash actively tracked and focused on suburbs and smaller cities where there was less competition at the time. However, micro-markets do not necessarily have to be geographically limited. In 2012, the Chinese company Didi started as a platform to connect passengers and local drivers. After reaching a critical mass of users in this specific segment, Didi expanded into other on-demand services such as (food) delivery, car rentals and bike sharing.

> Doron Reuveni, founder of uTest (software testing platform), on the importance of starting small: 'I formed the company in April 2007 and launched a beta a year after in April 2008. The adaptation from ecosystem was easy because the message was polished, and right. We started with a pilot to only 10 companies that were different in size and nature. We listened to them closely and spent 3–4 months on implementing quickly.' (2009)[32]

> David Rosenthal, board member at Rover, on the importance of organic growth: 'We started in Seattle, kept it focused, learned about the dynamics of the market [. . .] then we flipped the switch and went national. [. . .] When we saw organic growth bubbling up in a new market, that informed where we would go next. For non-activated markets, we knew that performance was going to be bad because liquidity was low. We were willing to let it ride.' (2019)[33]

When and how to apply

The micro-market strategy is not unique to platforms, but it is particularly relevant to companies that rely on network effects. It also facilitates learning opportunities and feedback in each micro-market and gives you the opportunity to showcase success in a niche market (e.g. for investors). In some cases, it may even be necessary not to scale up too quickly, e.g. in a legally complex or highly regulated environment.[34] Starting in a confined geographical market is particularly important for platforms that rely on local interactions (e.g. delivery platforms). Ultimately, the long-term objective is to overcome micro-markets (be it a geographical or category micro-market) and merge the different market segments, a process called 'bridging'.[35]

> An executive at Xiaomi on its expansion strategy: 'We have been very disciplined in managing our ecosystem scope and charting our expansion path. To grow, we need to enter and invest in new product categories; yet, investment in too many categories will stretch our resources thin. Oftentimes, this means saying no to a lot of seemingly attractive opportunities that do not fit into our business model.' (2021)[36]

73 Big bang

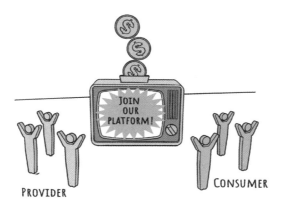

With the big bang approach, platform owners apply one or more push marketing strategies, such as TV or web advertisements, to kickstart two or more market sides simultaneously. The objective is to sign up very high volumes of participants in a very short amount of time. Traditional channels such as TV are often forgotten, but they are still of great importance and should at least be considered complementary for overcoming the chicken-and-egg challenge.

The microblogging platform Twitter accomplished its breakthrough after advertising itself during the 2007 South by Southwest festival. By live streaming its tweets on a large-scale TV, Twitter was able to reach thousands of influential visitors. The marketplace for travel bookings Expedia invests heavily in push marketing in order to grow its business. For example, in its record year 2019, it spent about USD 6 billion on marketing, including online advertisement and TV spots. Thereby, Expedia significantly promotes its brand. The same is true for booking.com, which invested almost USD 5 billion in the same year on marketing activities that ranged from TV commercials to online marketing.[37] A large part of the expenditure is on performance marketing, the use of online search engines, metasearch and travel research services, as well as affiliate marketing. Etsy, the marketplace for handmade or vintage items, has kicked off network effects similarly but with the advantage that an Etsy user can be both a supplier and consumer. One of its first actions to get media attention was initiating an 'Etsyday' when participants engaged on multiple social media channels which attracted a significant number of users. Also, features about Etsy sellers on TV shows, like that by Martha Stewart (a prominent US television host and chef) have boosted the marketing and image of the Etsy platform among both sellers and buyers.

> Nate Moch, VP at Zillow, on the relevance of traditional marketing: 'At scale we continue to invest in the areas above (PR, SEO (search engine optimisation), mobile), but we also added paid marketing. We added paid late in our company timeline, but it made a big difference when we turned it on.' (2019)[38]

When and how to apply

Targeting both sides of the platform at the same time is a particular challenge but can be especially effective for platforms where the demand and supply sides consist of the same type of user, e.g. Airbnb, where users can both offer and book apartments. Ultimately, this strategy can go very well hand in hand with other scaling strategies and extend to very different activities, such as performance marketing, SEO, conversion optimisation, TV or even public relations.

Some questions to ask
- Does your demand and supply come from the same type of users?
- What are the most relevant advertisement channels to reach your users?
- Can you address all segments of your target market effectively with the big bang?
- How can we use marketing guerrilla strategies to maximise the big bang effect?
- Do you have the resources to go big bang, i.e. run a large-scale advertisement campaign?
- How do you manage the risk of a failed big bang strategy? Are there risk mitigations?

Exploit opportunistic opportunities

74 Platform injection

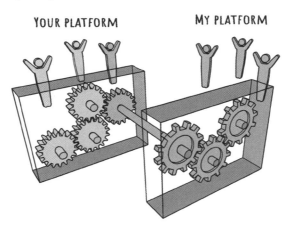

YOUR PLATFORM   MY PLATFORM

In addition to traditional scaling strategies, there are also opportunistic strategies that try to leverage existing platforms and take advantage of their openness. With platform injection, a platform integrates itself into another platform. This strategy exploits the other platform's openness, similar to a Trojan horse. In contrast to the piggyback strategy, the integration is not necessarily a mutually symbiotic win–win and can be seen as an unfriendly attack. The entrant might compete with the value capturing of the inhabited platform.[39]

Everyone can download the e-reader application Kindle from the Apple App Store. However, if you purchase a book on Amazon and read it on an iPhone, Apple receives no commission or revenue share. In essence, Amazon injected Amazon Kindle into the iPhone ecosystem. The same was true for Audible in the beginning. Instead of allowing in-app purchases of audiobooks, users are transferred to Audible's own external marketplace via a link. Hence, Amazon aimed to save the revenue share that goes to Apple, which would normally be applied for any iOS in-app purchase. Also, the marketplace Airbnb injected itself into another platform: Once a host was ready to publish a room or apartment on the marketplace, Airbnb allowed them to also publish the offer on Craigslist. Craigslist used to be one of the most popular go-to marketplaces for all sorts of things, from jobs and housing to services and more. It was as simple as pressing the button 'Publish on Craigslist', but anyone responding to the offer on Craigslist was still able to reach the host through Airbnb.[40] In addition, Airbnb sent mass emails to hosts on Craigslist to recruit them and invite them to Airbnb. Thus, Airbnb, without paying anything for it, exploited Craigslist's huge, existing user base in a rather aggressive way, with the result that many users became interested in Airbnb and switched to the platform in the long term.

When and how to apply

Essentially, platform injection is about finding a host platform with a compelling user base and exploiting that user base for your own platform's purposes. However, because this exploitation can potentially be harmful for the host platform, potential fighting back has to be expected. In the case of Airbnb, for example, Craigslist, after recognising this behaviour, started to fine similar activities.[41] However, unlike other opportunistic strategies, platform injection often requires fewer resources and could be attractive to start-ups that have nothing to lose.

Some questions to ask

- Are there platforms with a similar user base or similar offering that you can integrate into?
- What specific opportunities do you have to integrate into these platforms?
- How will the affected platform react to your injection?
- Do you create superior value by drawing users away from your competitor's platform?

---

75 Platform exploitation

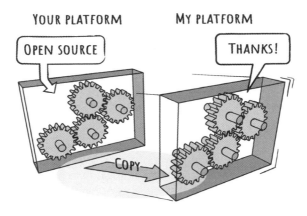

Platform exploitation is about copying the core of an open source platform for the benefit of your own platform. Even if the platform doing the copying does not violate any laws, this strategy is often seen as exploiting an existing platform in a highly opportunistic and unfriendly way.[42] This is especially the case when the new entrant does not offer any value add, but only aims to compete with the existing platform. Ultimately, by copying one or more resources of an existing platform, platform exploitation can dramatically reduce development costs and help a company catch up with the existing platform quickly. In order to release its tablet computer Amazon Fire, Amazon had to develop an operating system. However, instead of developing the platform from scratch, Amazon just copied the open source operating system Android from Google. This was only possible since Google deliberately chose to make its source code publicly available and open source. In the end, Amazon was able to save large amounts of time and money and developed a competing platform while staying outside of Google's highly regulated OHA. Sailfish is another example of this strategy and also an operating system for smartphones and tablets. Jolla, the company behind the operating system Sailfish, is built upon the open source software Mer. Furthermore, it utilised Android components such as the Android runtime environment. Thus, users may run Android applications on the Sailfish operating system.

> Andy Rubin, founder of Android on Alibaba, on exploiting the openness of Android: 'We agree that the Aliyun OS is not part of the Android ecosystem and you're under no requirement to be compatible. However, the fact is, Aliyun uses the Android runtime, framework and tools. And your app store contains Android apps (including pirated Google apps). So there's really no disputing that Aliyun is based on the Android platform and takes advantage of all the hard work that's gone into that platform by the OHA.' (2012)[43]

When and how to apply
When there is an established standard in place and the underlying basis is open source, an emerging platform can copy and exploit the open source for its own

purposes. Copying and adopting an incumbent's platform is less expensive and requires shorter development time. Conversely, dedicated developer skills are still needed as the copied source code must continuously be updated and the act of copying can also fall into a legal grey zone.[44]

Some questions to ask

● Are there open source platforms that you can potentially leverage by copying their source code?

● What is the impact of copying an open source platform, e.g. in respect to reputation or legal actions?

● How much is the dependence of your platform from the open source code?

● Does the open source platform limit your future value-capturing strategy, e.g. patenting?

● Do you have the skills and the resources to maintain the code and keep up with the original platform?

76 Platform pacing

Platform pacing is about copying boundary resources and interfaces of well-established innovation platforms. Compared with platform exploitation, it is about the interfaces (APIs or SDKs) and not the entire source code.[45] The goal is to make it as easy as possible for customers and complementors to switch to one's own platform – imagine that you keep the same power socket but replace the energy supply system behind it. The strategy is most often applied in the domain of open source software platforms.

When Android was created in 2003, it was the first operating system for digital cameras.[46] Due to the declining size of the digital camera market, they pivoted their strategy to developing a mobile operating system. Subsequently, Google acquired it creating an initial momentum. However, since its competitor Apple was already ahead in building an operating system, Google knew they needed to boost innovation on their operating system. They wanted to design an open platform that could be offered to third-party smartphone manufacturers free of charge. But they needed third-party developers who would invest time and money into the development of apps and complements. To jumpstart innovation on its innovation platform, Android copied about 11,500 lines of code and APIs from Java, the most popular developer platform at the time.[47] As a result, Java developers could easily migrate and develop apps for Android. In the meantime, Oracle, one of the largest enterprise resource planning (ERP) software providers in the world, acquired Sun Microsystems, which originally developed and later open sourced Java. Since Oracle considered Google's activities to be illegal and hostile, they filed a USD 9 billion lawsuit against Google claiming violation of Oracle's copyright. However, in April 2021, the US Supreme Court ruled in favour of Google.[48]

Similarly, since its foundation, Microsoft Azure was in close competition with Amazon's cloud services, Amazon Web Services. In order to scale fast and gain momentum, Microsoft applied platform pacing for its own database services. For instance, Microsoft used the same interfaces as MongoDB, the most popular NoSQL database at that time, for its own offerings. In turn, developers ended up switching from MongoDB to Azure with just a few clicks.

When and how to apply

Platform owners who want to employ the platform pacing strategy should be aware that their user base is identical to the competitor's original platform. Moreover, in order to facilitate long-term attractiveness, they are required to continuously update any modifications on the copied boundary resources. For example, if the original platform integrates a new feature into its API, one needs to rapidly copy and incorporate the new function to avoid falling behind the original or losing compatibility.

Some questions to ask

- Are there platforms with an attractive user base that provide services which you could also provide?
- Is there already a standard for APIs and SDKs in your field that you can benefit from?
- Can you copy their boundary resources (e.g. APIs) without significant negative side effects?
- Why would users prefer your platform over the existing one?

Manage: patterns to manage a platform

5

As platforms become more successful and mature, unique challenges and new competitors arise. Managers need to adapt to developing customer needs and novel offerings that have the potential to disrupt the market. Positive network effects can also quickly turn into negative ones. Overall, competitive dynamics are very high in the platform economy. Hence, platforms, for instance, are aggressively looking to extend their user base and capture share from their rivals. We present 12 guidelines and best practices in four domains for how to stay competitive and become a sustainable platform business (see Figure 2.5.1). On the one hand, platforms must further grow their platform business through continuous innovation (A) while defending the platform (B). On the other hand, platforms must maintain network effects (C) and monitor platform performance (D), which requires different approaches and tools compared with traditional pipeline businesses. In addition to concrete strategies, this step includes many universal guidelines that are important to consider and refine. We, therefore, recommend picking three to five patterns that you think are most relevant for your case.

Kevin Systrom, cofounder and former CEO of Instagram, on their innovation efforts: '[. . .] true innovation is like looking around at the world and putting the ingredients together and figuring out how to execute on it, market it, scale it. The amount of work that goes into making these things work at scale, at 700 million users around the world, that's where the magic is every single day. Making it work in different countries, on different networks. The reason why we're seeing the growth we have [. . .].' (2017)[1]

Figure 2.5.1 Managing a platform business (Patterns #77–88)

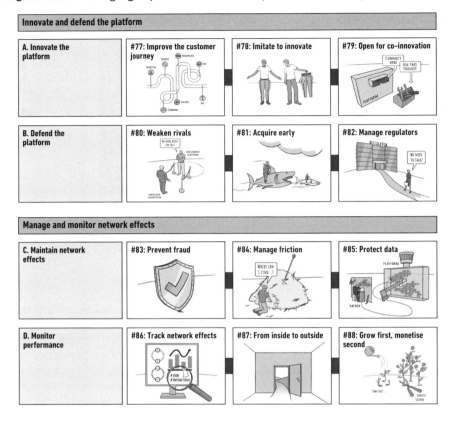

Innovate the platform

77 Improve the customer journey

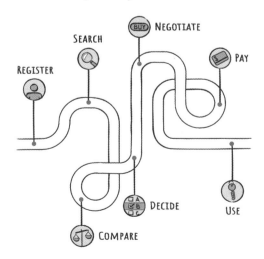

Even though a core offering has been successfully established, platforms need to keep innovating. One opportunity lies in extending a platform's scope and innovating along the customer journey. Platforms can do this organically or through acquisitions. The core aim of improving the customer journey is to provide a seamless end-to-end experience for both sides of the market (e.g. consumers and providers) and to create stronger interdependencies between your individual services.[2] Through this, platforms can increase both customer as well as provider loyalty and also facilitate monetisation with greater control over the customer journey.

Over time, the accommodation marketplace Airbnb has continuously expanded its offerings across the provider and consumer journey. It implemented a variety of features to benefit its users, from photo services (before the stay) and vacation experiences, e.g. city tours offered to the traveller (during the stay) to insurance offerings (during/after the stay). In response to the market downturn during the Corona crisis, Airbnb also expanded its offering to include monthly stays. This, for instance, allowed people living in densely populated cities to rent flats or houses in the countryside and enjoy more freedom. The marketplace eBay is another example of a platform successfully improving its customer journey. While eBay's core is about listing products and matching supply and demand efficiently, payment is a fundamental pillar to capturing value for eBay. When it first started, many users tried to exploit the marketplace by finding a buyer or seller on the marketplace but then conducting the payment transaction outside the platform. This disintermediation can be very harmful to platforms as they are cut out from the financial transaction. To counteract this user behaviour, eBay tried to improve the payment experience and invested heavily in convenient and secure payments. It developed its own payment peer-to-peer payment platform called Billpoint and later replaced it with PayPal (as it provided even more frictionless payment).

> Brian Chesky, cofounder of Airbnb, on the importance of going beyond transactions: 'However we first entered this community, we all know that getting in isn't a transaction. It's a connection that can last a lifetime. That's because the rewards you get from Airbnb aren't just financial – they're personal – for hosts and guests alike.' (2021)[3]

> Dan Schulman, CEO of PayPal, on the importance of expanding your value proposition: 'The key to stopping people from leaving the platform is engagement right and engagement has to do with expanding our value proposition into new applications like, for instance, buy now pay later.' (2020)[4]

Similarly, on the freelancing platform Upwork, freelancers and clients frequently try to circumvent Upwork as they find and contact each other outside of the platform. This is particularly the case when they engage in a second contract and already know each other from before. Upwork tries to reduce the risk of disintermediation by providing incentives as well as additional services for freelancers. If they stay on the platform to conduct all conversations on the marketplace, they can build up a brand and awareness, thereby improving access to future work opportunities. Complementary services include service help desks, customer satisfaction insurance, loyalty programmes and access to customer data. Steam initially aimed to provide users with automated updates for a selected number of games. Later, Steam transformed into a marketplace for selling and buying digital games. Management constantly reviewed the customer journey and expanded, e.g. launched community features such as in-game voice, chat functionalities and broadcast streaming. These improvements allowed Steam to become a strong gatekeeper and one of the most popular platforms among gamers in the world. The platform MedWing, which helps bring together health workers and health facilities for short- and long-term placements, offers a range of services across the user journey to both market sides. Employers can receive technical support and access to resource planning and optimisation software, while employees receive feedback on their CVs and career coaching.

Jörg Hellwig, former CDO of LANXESS (mother company of the B2B market-place CheMondis), on the need for continuous innovation: 'We are proud that CheMondis is number one already in the Western world. But if we don't contin-uously improve, someone else will take over as number one. So there needs to be a constant push to change and to optimise.' (2020)[5]

Jeff Bezos, founder of Amazon, on customer focus being most important: 'The first and by far the most important one is customer obsession as opposed to competitor obsession, [. . .] I have seen over and over again companies talk about being customer focused, but really when I pay close attention to them I believe they are competitor focused, and it's a completely different mentality, by the way.' (2019)[6]

When and how to apply

While horizontal marketplaces often grow by expanding their product portfolio first, vertical marketplaces (niche marketplaces) instead seek to maximise value creation by offering additional services along the customer journey. Platforms like Airbnb have been very successful in this endeavour as they added services like insurance or cleaning services to their portfolio to satisfy adjacent customer needs along the customer journey. In essence, improving the customer journey is all about knowing your customer and identifying unmet or adjacent customer needs, and then expanding the platform's offerings accordingly. However, the focus should not only be on the journey of one user side, but on both user sides of the market (e.g. consumer and provider, seller and buyer). This strategy can be important for platforms struggling with capturing a share of value with their current offering. When extending the user journey and taking more control, in particular of the payment processes, monetisation opportunities are opened up through the provision of additional benefits for users.

Some questions to ask
- What does the customer journey of your consumers and providers look like?
- What are the gains and pains of the users on both sides? How can the platform improve the user experience along his/her journey?
- What are the sweet spots in the customer journey, important for the customer and addressable with limited effort?
- When and why do users try to circumvent your platform services?
- What additional services across the customer journey could complement your existing offering?
- Is it reasonable to increase the value proposition of your platform by offering these services?

---

78 Imitate to innovate

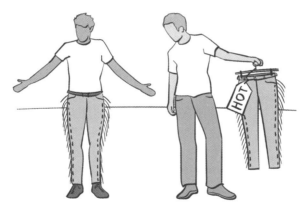

In traditional industries, copying competitors' features are often considered a weakness or even unethical. Platform companies, in contrast, often do not refrain from imitating different functions of competing platforms. And it is not limited to imitating simple features but can also include more complex imitations such as copying an entire business model.[7] Since competition in the platform economy is very dynamic, platforms actively monitor their rivals as well as platforms with an overlapping or similar user base. When promising features or new business models emerge, they consider quickly imitating these changes while often slightly amending them.

Although Instagram had high growth rates after its acquisition by Facebook, it faced a serious competitor. The social network Snapchat, launched shortly after Instagram, also attracted a significant number of users during its first few years. A large part of the strong user growth could be attributed to 'Snapchat stories'. This feature allowed users to share photos and videos with friends that would disappear after 24 hours. This led to much longer user retention compared to simple photo sharing on Instagram. Because its competitor Snapchat posed a significant threat to its social network, Instagram (Facebook) wanted to acquire Snapchat but could not agree on a deal. Therefore, Instagram changed its approach and simply adopted and improved some of Snapchat's most popular features, including the sharing of stories that would disappear after 24 hours. As a result, Instagram attracted many Snapchat users. Another example is Stack Overflow, a Q&A platform for professional programmers to share knowledge, exchange ideas or solve coding problems. One of the reasons Stack Overflow became such a popular platform was its convenient and intuitive search that was based on a peer-review and hashtag system. However, both concepts had already proven themselves on other platforms. The idea of ranking up questions and answers had already been implemented by Reddit. The hashtag function was already used by Flickr (who imitated it from del.icio.us).[8] Ultimately, the combination of those adopted features was a driver for the success of Stack Overflow.

> Chad Hurley, cofounder of YouTube, on the power of learning from other platforms: 'Touching on our experience at PayPal, we saw the power of simplifying processes and giving everybody a solution. Being the early employees at PayPal, we did that for payments. We saw the same opportunity in the video space.' (2006)[9]

BeReal is an example of a company that faced imitation. It focuses on authenticity online, as users can share content with their friends, but only once a day. The platform BeReal decides when that is. Users have two minutes to create a video or photo using the front and back cameras of the phone simultaneously. The emerging platform now has over 10 million daily users, and TikTok considered it a major threat. So, it simply mimicked the feature and launched TikTok Now, which is basically the same as BeReal.

When and how to apply
As seen in Instagram's imitation of 'Snapchat stories', copying only one feature can already help drive users to your platform. In general, imitation has become an integral part of competitive battles in the platform economy and often goes beyond imitating simple features. Platforms should, therefore, closely track their competitors' technology, strategy and business models, and be aware of the need to react and copy quickly. Although such continuous screening of the market requires time and resources, it is effective and, in the end, often mandatory to stay relevant in rapidly developing markets.

79 Open for co-innovation

After an initial phase of growth, platforms often open up for further co-innovation. In essence, they invest in the enablement of third-party complements by providing boundary resources, such as interfaces or tool kits, to external companies or individuals. Moreover, opening up can also mean establishing dedicated organisational units to build and maintain partnerships as well as developer communities. For example, Facebook focused primarily on attracting users to its social media platform in the early years. After building up a network of 50 million users, in 2007, it introduced an application developer platform with interfaces for external developers to complement Facebook's core.[10] Companies and external developers could now integrate games or other applications on the social media platform. Just months later, hundreds of new apps were added to Facebook every day. Since then, Facebook has continuously expanded its platform with additional tools and interfaces. This co-innovation approach significantly boosted Facebook's growth and helped it to outpace its competitors like Myspace, although they likewise opened up shortly after Facebook did. Also, Alibaba's revenue started really taking off once they opened up their marketplace and gave complementors more freedom.[11] The company HERE started as a rather closed platform for location-based services in navigation systems. However, the company opened up to external developers and today offers a comprehensive development portal that makes it easy for external developers to create location-based applications based on the HERE platform.

Many other platforms are using this strategy to innovate and increase access to their platforms. Twitter, YouTube, LinkedIn, Airbnb and Expedia, to name a few, have all started offering APIs for their platforms after establishing themselves as potent marketplaces. Currently, as part of the 'Made for iPhone' (MFi) Programme, Apple also continues to open up its products to accessory companies. Previously only hardware produced by Apple was able to be tracked on its 'Find My' app. A year after the AirTag was successfully adopted by many iPhone users, Apple announced that it would let other hardware companies, e.g. bike manufacturers, build the technology into their products, as well. As a result, other products (e.g. bikes) can now also be located via the 'Find My' app without the use of an AirTag.

> Bob Borchers, VP product marketing of Apple, on opening up: 'For more than a decade, our customers have relied on 'Find My' to locate their missing or stolen Apple devices, all while protecting their privacy. Now we're bringing the powerful finding capabilities of 'Find My', one of our most popular services, to more people with the 'Find My' network accessory programme. We're thrilled to see how Belkin, Chipolo, and VanMoof are utilising this technology, and can't wait to see what other partners create.' (2021)[12]

When and how to apply
Open up for co-innovation is often applied by mature transaction platforms to evolve from a two-sided to a multi-sided platform. In essence, marketplaces open up to external developers or content producers so they can enrich the offering of the platform core. However, with this, marketplaces also become innovation platforms. Thereby, they have to master the complexity of both transaction and innovation platforms.

Some questions to ask
- What kind of complements would your existing users appreciate?
- Do you have a marketplace with a strong user base so that you can attract complementors?
- What boundary resources are necessary to enable third parties to provide those complements?
- How can we create a win–win situation for all?

Defend the platform

80 Weaken rivals

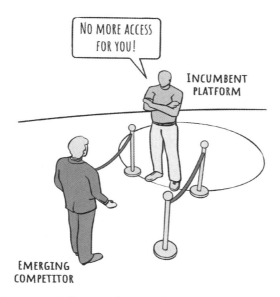

To defend their core, platforms often actively weaken existing or emerging competitors. This strategy goes back to Michael Porter's concept of comparative competitive advantage: In an oligopolistic market – that means only a few players are active – companies can gain competitive advantage when they get better, or the competitors are weakened.[13] Therefore, strategies often aim to make the life of competitors as difficult as possible, rather than to protect a company's own product features.[14]

Several strategies are at the disposal of platform companies in this regard. They can, for one, move into an adjacent platform's market by extending their core offering. Thereby, they apply 'platform envelopment' and can offer a multi-platform bundle.[15] Apple, for example, has enveloped multiple platforms in the past. It leveraged its iPhone/iPad platform to attack numerous competitors including gaming platforms (e.g. Nintendo Gameboy), eBook platforms (e.g. Amazon Kindle) or streaming platforms (e.g. Netflix). Apple bundled in one ecosystem all the functions that had previously been provided individually by the existing rival platforms. With its payment service Apple Pay, it tried to envelop the payment platforms MasterCard and Visa, and with the launch of Apple Music, Apple directly aimed to compete with Spotify. Even though Spotify is currently the largest music streaming platform in the world, Apple was able to sign up 60 million active users within few years.[16] In essence, a better or broader and integrated set of functionalities (that goes beyond just music) is offered to incentivise users to switch between platforms. Therefore, this strategy primarily helps capture users of a rival platform and strengthen your own network effects.[17]

Mike Jones, former CEO of Myspace, on its competitive fight with Facebook: 'The real problem was that the world had been trained by MySpace that social networking was interesting, but the actual product had been perfected by Facebook.' (2015)[18]

Similarly, by integrating features and value propositions from emerging competitors into its platform, Amazon Web Services made niche players obsolete while simultaneously defending its position. However, this only works because AWS already offers a wide range of services and serves a large user network. Another example is Facebook. In its early days, Facebook's offering was very similar to that of other social platforms such as Myspace. However, its broader scope enabled Facebook to slowly 'envelop' the competing platforms and win their users.

Additionally, to defend their core, platforms can fight or even try to prohibit multi-homing, which refers to the situation when users take advantage of two or more competing platforms simultaneously. Uber and Lyft, for example, are vulnerable to multi-homing since the costs from switching between Uber and Lyft are quite low for drivers and riders. Hence, drivers and riders multi-home, i.e. use both apps at the same time. To combat this behaviour and prevent drivers multi-homing, Uber and Lyft have integrated features that offer drivers potential new customers as close as possible to the drop-off point of the current ride – even before the current ride ends. In addition, both platforms have introduced subscriptions for drivers to further lock them in and reduce multi-homing. Uber has been combating multi-homing even more aggressively by hiring third-party providers to book Lyft rides only to cancel them shortly before the actual ride, creating a negative vicious cycle of interaction errors and driver churn for Lyft.[19] Moreover, apps always compete for screen time. Uber, therefore, tries to fight multi-homing with respect to navigation apps, such as Google Maps. Uber has developed in-app navigation and is constantly trying to make it so convenient that drivers consistently use the Uber app rather than Google Maps.[20]

Alibaba followed an even more aggressive strategy when they punished providers on their marketplaces that wanted to sell their goods on competing platforms as well. Alibaba called this practice *er xuan yi* which translates to 'choose one out of two'.[21] However, as it actively abused its dominant position, the company was severely disciplined by the regulator and fined 455 million yuan.[22] While rather uncommon, in order to defend their core business, platforms may furthermore selectively close interfaces (APIs) to exclude competitors from their platform.[23] For example, Apple restricted its interfaces on Adobe's Flash Player, Twitter prohibited competitor platforms, especially other social media platforms, from integrating tweets on their platforms via its APIs,[24] and Facebook excluded its competitor Vine, a platform for sharing short video clips, from accessing its APIs.[25]

When and how to apply

First of all, platforms need to constantly review their own markets in addition to adjacent markets to identify emerging competitors with an overlapping user base. While enveloping an incumbent platform can be effective in defending your platform and attacking competitors, it can also be resource intensive, especially compared to simply copying individual functions. Ultimately, the challenge is to create a multi-platform bundle that blends seamlessly and delivers superior value. Weakening rivals is also about actively and carefully tracking user behaviour, especially the degree of multi-homing. A direct ban or penalties for multi-homing is not always enforceable, as the case of Alibaba shows, and platforms often have to rely on incentives for retention instead.

Some questions to ask
- How can you strategically weaken your competitor's platform?
- Can you attack rival platforms by providing the same type of platform services?
- Are your platform users multi-homing and how can you prevent this?
- Are rival platforms accessing your platform for their benefit? If so, can you prevent this?

---

81 Acquire early

Platform companies are known to acquire early. Mergers and acquisitions have been central to the success of many platforms.[26] Acquiring another platform is particularly reasonable if the target platform has a similar user base. In that case, network effects can be strengthened through buying users and extending the company's own platform through compelling features while decreasing a competitor's network. Another objective may be to gain access to a new user group or an adjacent market. In addition, platforms have acquired complementors to further increase their value capture.[27] Over time, all the leading platform companies, including Amazon, Apple, Facebook, Alibaba and Google, have systematically acquired hundreds of companies to grow their platform businesses.[28]

The social media platform Facebook acquired Instagram since there was a strong overlap in product and user base. Facebook noticed that its users were heavily shifting towards mobile devices. Although Facebook developed a mobile app, it did not have the same lock-in effect as Instagram. Facebook acquired Instagram very early which prevented – in retrospect – the rise of a mighty rival. The same applies to the takeover of WhatsApp by Facebook. Since its founding, Amazon has acquired more than 100 companies averaging approximately five deals per year.[29] All of these acquisitions strategically complemented its portfolio of platforms. To mention a few, Amazon acquired Audible, an audiobook platform, Twitch, the world's largest video game and live streaming platform, and Ring, a leading home security and smart home platform.

> Jennifer Newstead, general counsel of Facebook, on the reason for its acquisitions: 'When we acquired Instagram and WhatsApp, we believed these companies would be a great benefit to our Facebook users and that we could help transform them into something even better. And we did.' (2020)[30]

Alphabet (Google) is also among the most active acquirers, with more than 260 acquisitions in its history.[31] Some of its most prominent acquisitions were the video platform YouTube, the navigation platform Waze, the hardware company Motorola and the fitness platform Fitbit. Salesforce, by contrast, has acquired several of its platform complementors. For instance, Salesforce acquired Heroku in 2005 (an application platform), Slack (a messaging platform) in 2020 and Vlocity in 2021 (one of its largest complementors).[32]

However, it is not only big platform companies that use the strategy of acquiring early. For example, in January 2015, FlixBus and MeinFernbus merged and became the market leader in German long-distance bus transport in the same year. This was the starting point for a successful scaling through acquisitions. To further grow internationally, the platform repeatedly acquired existing bus companies in other countries, from Sweden to the US. One of the largest acquisitions was the US-based Greyhound Lines, the market leader in long-distance bus transport in the US. However, FlixBus also acquired companies to improve their business operations. One example is the acquisition of the German start-up Liinita, a technology company for shared mobility and route optimisation. In addition to FlixBus, there are many other examples of smaller platform companies that have taken advantage of acquisitions, e.g. CoachHub, Paytm and Indeed, to name a few.

When and how to apply

Early mergers and acquisitions play an important role in platform development, especially if the acquired platform has a similar user base. Although acquisitions are an essential part of platform development, they require strategic foresight and strong financial backing. By their very nature, platforms have the potential to become monopolies or oligopolies. The acquisition of a competing platform may therefore trigger intervention by the authorities. Indeed, regulators in the EU and the US have been keeping an eye on competition between platforms and potential M&A deals. Therefore, in the end, acquisitions are always about the right timing. Many argue, for example, that the acquisition of Instagram might not have been successful if Facebook had waited longer. However, if you are too early, it is difficult to properly estimate the business potential of a platform, but, conversely, if you wait too long, your competitor's platform might become too big, making a potential acquisition expensive or leading market regulators to prohibit it altogether.

Marc Zuckerberg, founder of Facebook, on the relevance of acquisitions: 'It is better to buy than compete.' (2020)[33]

Some questions to ask
- Is there an emerging rival or an existing competitor that you could buy?
- Can an acquisition give you access to a new user group or an adjacent market?
- What are the synergies between the two companies?
- What benefit does the M&A activity have regarding the previous strategies in design, scale and monetising patterns?
- Will market regulators approve the acquisition?

82 Manage regulators

By their nature, many platforms have the potential to become monopolies or oligopolies. This might call for regulators to intervene as the examples of Amazon, Apple or Google reveal. Moreover, platforms might challenge existing businesses, such as the taxi or hotel industry, in a way that can, ultimately, conflict with existing law or induce the need for new regulations. Therefore, emerging platforms need to work closely with regulators at an early stage. This is particularly important in light of existing legislation, such as the General Data Protection Regulation (GDPR) and Digital Markets Act (DMA) in the European Union. By engaging early in discussions with regulators and local authorities, platforms can mitigate potential future conflicts.[34]

Airbnb engages, for example, with city authorities around the world to ensure that its rentals do not conflict with local housing laws and regulations. There are also tax issues, as providing accommodation often involves hotel or tourist taxes that are not sufficiently addressed on the Airbnb platform. The ride-hailing platform Lyft has invested in campaigns to prevent legislators from classifying its drivers as full-time employees. This way, workers remain independent contractors and are not entitled to full labour protections.

> Logan Green, cofounder of Lyft, a ride-hailing platform, on dealing with regulators: 'When it comes to the regulatory environment, being a jerk doesn't get you very far, because the folks that you have to work with are the ones making the decisions.' (2015)[35]

When and how to apply

Platforms, especially big tech platforms, are increasingly in the focus of regulators because of their monopolistic positions. This led governments, e.g. in the European Union, to introduce reforms to limit their power. Other areas where platforms often come into conflict are labour law, data protection or tax law. This also means having to continuously screen the regulatory environment and build up good relations with regulators as early as possible.[36] In fact, what is often forgotten is that digital platforms can also reinvent collaboration between public and private entities to solve societal challenges, as the example of Velocia shows. Velocia is a platform to reward sustainable mobility behaviour by connecting end users, public transit agencies, micro-mobility service providers and municipalities.

> Hamid Akbari, chairman of Velocia, on the relevance of public–private partnerships: 'Some of the most interesting problems our societies face – like transport and mobility – cut across different policy areas, and link the private and public sectors in new and exciting ways. Velocia's purpose is to create an open ecosystem that rewards the positive behaviour of urban commuters, who respond to the inducements that both public- and private-sector organisations can offer. Our job is to provide a platform that connects the players, incentivises collaboration and improves urban mobility.' (2019)[37]

Some questions to ask

- What legislation affects your platform and respective industry?
- What potential conflicts between your business model and (future) legislation might arise?
- How does the platform company become a 'good citizen'?
- How can we do good and communicate about it?
- How can you engage with regulators or authorities to mitigate potential conflicts early on?
- How can we create long-term relationships with relevant administrations and governments?

Maintain network effects

83 Prevent fraud

Fake reviews, fake profiles, password phishing, identity theft, credit card misuse and much more: With the growing success of a platform, fraud becomes a fundamental challenge that must be dealt with. Whether it's PayPal, eBay or Amazon, there is hardly any successful platform that has not had to deal with fraud – among users as well as from the outside. Fraud destroys trust, the most important resource for a platform. Trust is very difficult to build and often needs many years. But a single big fraudulent event can destroy all trust within a few days.

Hence, platforms heavily invest in preventing fraud with the overall goal of maintaining network effects. For example, they deploy special teams to protect their IT infrastructure and their users from systematic and organised cyber attacks. If not handled carefully, fraud can lead to mistrust in the platform's network which eventually results in negative network effects. For instance, at Amazon, human moderators and machine-learning tools analyse more than 10 million reviews weekly to fight fake reviews and inflated ratings. Thus, the authenticity of product reviews and ratings is maintained.

> Dan Schulman, CEO of PayPal, on the risk of cyber attacks: 'Financial firms get attacked millions of times practically every day. What you really need to do is not only have very high walls and towers to prevent people from coming in. But if ever people come in, you have to have very sophisticated data analytics to prevent information and data and money from moving out so it's a two-tiered defense system.' (2020)[38]

With more than 430 million active users,[39] PayPal is a popular target for fraudulent attacks. Fake emails asking for user credentials are a core challenge for PayPal. To address this, PayPal has invested heavily in fraud prevention and improved transaction security, e.g. through two-factor authentication. In the end, increased transaction security has helped PayPal build trust in its brand. The platform Shopify also provides its merchants on the marketplace with different fraud prevention mechanisms. By developing a risk analysis algorithm, Shopify can detect whether a transaction has a high, medium or low risk of being fraudulent. This feature, among others, has reduced uncertainty and fraud on the Shopify platform. In the first weeks after the introduction of AirTags, Apple was confronted with unlawful behaviour: Strangers were using the AirTag to stalk others. By planting the AirTag in somebody's bag, for example, they were able to track their location. This greatly threatened the acceptance of AirTags, so Apple had to develop new technical features to address this. Now, if there are unidentified AirTags in the vicinity of your iPhone, the user is notified and warned based on a unique identifier for each AirTag.

Preventing fraud is also about establishing strong standards for what is allowed and what is not. Such rules can come in the form of a code of conduct or terms and conditions, for example. However, it is not enough just to establish rules, platforms must also enforce them. A well-known example is the app I am Rich from the early days of the Apple iPhone. The app cost USD 999.99 in the App Store but was nothing more than a glowing picture of a red diamond. After iPhone users accidentally clicked 'buy app', they were charged the full amount and were furious. After some time, Apple deleted the app from its store. Today, both Google and Apple have a similar set of rules on their marketplace, yet Apple enforces the rules much more strictly. A similar app like the I am Rich app was uploaded to the Play Store but was not deleted by Google. In fact, today, Apple does diligent monitoring of every new or updated app before publishing. To ensure a minimum quality standard on Airbnb, each offer was manually checked at the beginning against a 12-point checklist before it could be uploaded. Airbnb creates additional incentives for high-quality supply today with its 'Superhost' label. Similarly, the B2B marketplace for chemicals CheMondis checks each company that registers on its marketplace for legality, its address and tax numbers, etc.

When and how to apply

Preventing fraud can be expensive, but it is an important aspect of platform management and critical to maintaining trust. Innovation platforms like Google Android in particular face the trade-off between being more open and being more restrictive. Openness can promote co-innovation, but it can also foster fraud. To prevent or mitigate fraud, there are various options, from easy-to-implement codes of conduct, terms and conditions and additional layers of security (e.g. two-way authentication) to AI-based or even human-moderated observers. Enforcement of the rules is equally important, e.g. through screening or certification systems. However, even though fraud prevention is important, it oftentimes adds friction to the user journey. Hence, an appropriate balance needs to be achieved between fraud prevention and frictionless user experience.

84 Manage friction

While platforms depend on network effects, there is a flipside to growth. The more a platform grows, the more friction it usually creates. Friction may range from overly complex sign-up processes to security procedures and overloaded navigation menus. Also, more consumers and providers can lead to friction. For example, too much supply can make it difficult to find the product you want. Take Amazon as an example. With a growing number of suppliers and offerings, it became increasingly difficult to find the desired product. Different suppliers were offering the same product under different labels and consumers had problems understanding the differences between the various offers.

In the end, too much choice and growing non-transparency can create consumer confusion, which results in users even switching to other platforms and losing trust. For this reason, many niche marketplaces are currently emerging that focus on a specific product niche (e.g. smart home products) and offer a high degree of curation and individual customer consultation. Certainly, Amazon has benefited from the ever-growing number of products and sellers. But given the increased friction, Amazon had to invest heavily to ensure consistent labelling of offerings and easy product comparisons to be able to compete with emerging niche marketplaces. Additionally, Amazon integrated filter options to mitigate the risk of too much friction and thus optimised the user journey. Amazon has also recognised that being aware of recurring buying habits can help reduce friction. For example, someone who has bought a product from the marketplace in the past is much more likely to buy that product again in the future. For this reason, a 'buy again' button was introduced. Similarly, after an initial phase of growth, the Q&A platform Quora suffered from a lack of transparency. Hence, it decided to introduce an upvote system to improve its matchmaking algorithm and the usability of its platform. Ultimately, this curation mechanism allowed the community to maintain and improve the structure of Quora and therefore enhance the usability of the platform.

When and how to apply

Platforms need to manage friction throughout the user journey, from onboarding and matchmaking to closing a transaction. Particularly, it is the quality of match-making that is crucial for platforms' success.[40] Hence, platforms constantly need to look out for curation features that lead to better matchmaking and user experience. However, avoiding friction at any cost, e.g. by not performing essential quality checks, can lead to low-quality offerings and fraud. Ultimately, however, a balance needs to be achieved in both directions, as too little friction can also be damaging, e.g. little friction in onboarding can lead to an inferior offer or fraudulent behaviour.

Some questions to ask
- Where do users experience friction and frustration throughout the customer journey?
- Where are the sweet spots to eliminate perceived friction?
- What type of friction do users experience (e.g. high search costs, cumbersome onboarding)?
- What measures can you take to mitigate friction?

---

85 Protect data

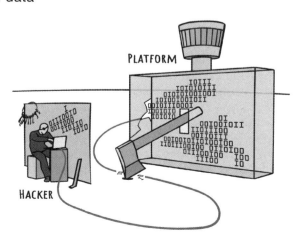

People get more and more sensitive about data protection, and for good reason. On 16 May 2016, for example, 117 million LinkedIn accounts were found to be up for sale on a hacker site.[41] Given access to a wide range of data, including sensitive user data, platforms must take all measures to ensure privacy and data protection. This may seem trivial at first glance, but destroyed trust in a platform is difficult to restore and can significantly harm network effects. For instance, Facebook's image and trust were severely damaged after the Cambridge Analytica scandal where user data was abused on a large scale. The mistrust and bad publicity have had a strong, negative impact on the entire ecosystem including WhatsApp and Instagram, even years later. Another example is Clubhouse. Launched in 2020, the social platform focuses on audio-only conversations and initially had severely limited access, with individuals only able to join the platform via an invitation from an existing member. This created a big initial hype around the platform with immense demand, but Clubhouse lost many users when it became known that it accesses users' smartphones, especially the contacts in your address book.

> Tim Cook, CEO of Apple, on the strategic importance of trust: 'We believe privacy is a fundamental human right, and the best technology is one that people can trust. At Apple, we're constantly innovating to give our users more control over how their data is used and the choice with whom to share it.' (2022)[42]

Establishing 'digital trust' has become a strategic imperative for companies as consumers consider trust and data protection to be almost as relevant in their purchasing decisions as classic factors such as price.[43] In 2020, Apple introduced a set of privacy principles, including 'data minimisation' with the aim of protecting users from unnecessary data collection and sharing, and increased transparency about what data is collected and what it is used for. Its enhanced privacy rules do not only fulfil legal requirements, e.g. the GDPR in Europe, but also provide a value add to those users who are privacy conscious. Apple advertises its privacy and security strategy very prominently to promote trust among its customers. Thus, the privacy principles may further help maintain Apple's network effects. However, there has also been criticism that Apple's heavy marketing is clouding its true intentions and that its new rules are supposed to hinder third parties, including its core competitors, from making money from personalised advertising on the iOS platform.[44] Nevertheless, Google has followed Apple's lead and highlighted its privacy efforts and principles to promote trust in its ecosystem of platforms.[45] Altogether, trust receives more and more attention in competitive battles between platforms.

Compared to WhatsApp, the messaging platform Signal follows a strict data policy with a focus on data protection and encrypted communication. While WhatsApp is still one of the market leaders, Signal won over many former WhatsApp users (installs jumped to 4,868 per cent),[46] when WhatsApp updated its privacy policy and required its users to share metadata in order to continue using the app. Lastly, trust can also be an important lever to manage vested interests among partners as an intermediary, in particular in B2B where competitors are especially hesitant to join each other's platforms.[47] For example, Tapio, the industrial innovation platform in the wood processing industry, puts heavy emphasis on data sovereignty. Although data sharing is necessary for the development and provision of services by third-party providers, Tapio leaves all power and decision making to users over what happens to their data. They can choose not to share their data from their machinery. This gives Tapio the possibility of being respected as a neutral party in the industry bringing different manufacturers and partners together on one platform. At the same time, there are also counter-examples, such as WeChat (the most popular social media platform in China), which is highly successful without giving substantial data protection promises. Instead, WeChat claims that collecting data is required to offer their services.[48] In this case, the respective network effects are so strong and articulated customer concerns are rather low, so WeChat does not have to fear losing users.

> Aruna Hard, COO of Signal, on its data privacy strategy: 'Unlike other popular messaging apps, Signal does not have access to users' contacts, social graph, group data, group membership, profile name, profile avatar, location data, gif searches, etc. [. . .] We want you to own your own data.' (2021)[49]

When and how to apply

In addition to legal requirements, users' expectations in terms of data protection and data security are becoming more demanding. Therefore, regardless of their nature, more and more platforms go beyond legal requirements and provide enhanced data protection as a superior value offering to their users. Nevertheless, it is often a trade-off: either you collect data to be able to offer additional services to users, or you limit yourself and cannot offer such services. Caution is required as soon as data is sold to third parties, or interactions involve or contain sensitive or personal data, as in the example of PatientsLikeMe, a platform where patients share health issues with each other on a very personal level.

> Ben Heywood, former CEO of PatientsLikeMe, a social media platform for patients, on the trade-off between user value and privacy: 'The biggest downside potentially for participating in our site is around privacy. We do have a very open model, where patients are sharing incredible amounts of information about themselves. I think what's great is that patients understand that and we are very explicit and transparent about that, but they understand the value outweighs that risk.' (2008)[50]

Monitor performance

86 Track network effects

When developing a platform business, many companies struggle with establishing the right KPIs to track and manage performance. Platform businesses are different from pipeline businesses and need specific metrics. Network effects are at the heart of platform value creation and, hence, platform KPIs often focus on network effects and activities that foster them. Also, negative network effects need to be identified quickly to prevent a negative vicious circle. Typical platform KPIs are aimed at users and their growth (e.g. active users, percentage of active users), as well as interactions and their quality (e.g. number of successful interactions, value of interactions). Moreover, liquidity on the platform, i.e. the balance between supply and demand, is often tracked constantly (e.g. producer-to-consumer ratio).

> Dara Khosrowshahi, CEO of Uber, on choosing the right metrics to track network effects: 'The driver is probably the most important element of the actual consumer experience: If you've got happy drivers, then consumers in cars are

treated well etc. We have been on a programme to consistently improve the drivers' experience. We introduced tipping [. . .], changed how much drivers get paid for wait times [. . .] we adjusted the cancellation fee.' (2017)[51]

Salesforce started as a CRM software company but became an innovation platform. External parties, from software companies, and consultancies to systems integrators, can offer B2B applications that complement Salesforce's CRM software. In 2005, they introduced AppExchange, an app store where third parties can directly sell their applications to B2B customers. Thereby, third parties became essential to the value creation of Salesforce. Once Salesforce realised that its AppExchange is heavily driving growth, it started to track network effects by looking systematically at the number and growth of developers, API calls (i.e. the number of requests sent to access a platform's interfaces) as well as third-party revenue and downloads. Since its beginnings, the ride-hailing platform Uber has tracked how long drivers and users must wait to provide or take a ride, i.e. the liquidity on the platform. Uber bases its operations and business decisions on network effects and focuses on a single metric, the number of rides per week. When it realised that the driver is the most important lever to increase this metric, it introduced financial incentives to provide rides in cases of high demand and vice versa. Furthermore, based on the peer-to-peer rating system, it can quickly assess the quality of each ride (interaction). Another example is Facebook, which tracks the number of daily active users on its platform. It also analyses how strong the connections between its users are and how often they interact with each other, e.g. the number of messages sent. This provides the social network with valuable information on how to manage its platform and, for example, fight fake accounts. Very similarly, YouTube tracks interaction on its video and streaming platform. One of its key metrics is the average screen time per user and month. With 23.1 hours on average, YouTube is the social network with one of the longest average screen time per user and month in the world.[52]

When and how to apply

While traditional companies tend to select many KPIs when managing performance, platforms often rely on just a few or one single KPI with a specific focus on network effects. In fact, many successful platforms focus on a so-called North Star metric, from Airbnb (booked nights), Amazon (repeated purchases), Slack (daily active users) and PayPal (total payment volume) to 365FarmNet (monthly active users × frequency of usage).[53] The chosen metric reflects how users naturally behave when they love the platform. Ultimately, it is important to reflect that there are leading and lagging KPIs. While leading KPIs capture important antecedents of success (e.g. user activity), lagging indicators depict current performance (e.g. revenue). Both leading and lagging platform KPIs should be tracked. However, young emerging platforms focus on leading rather than lagging KPIs, specifically when network effects have not fully developed and platform growth is still a key concern.

87 From inside to outside

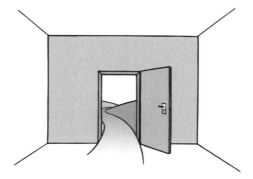

A platform's value creation heavily depends on external resources. Compared to traditional businesses, the primary aim of platforms is not the efficient value flow within a given platform organisation but to enable efficient transactions between providers and consumers. Hence, when tracking and managing performance, platforms must pay specific attention to external resources instead of their own. Essentially, all areas in a company, from product development to finance, have to be aligned so that external value creation is enabled and supported.[54] Often, it is easier to quantify internal procedures, such as in the case of corrective-action tracking where the elapsed time between registering a complaint in the database and its removal from the database is commonly measured, rather than the duration between when the user encounters the issue and when it is resolved for the user.

Take Apple as an example. While internal developer efficiency is certainly important for Apple, even more vital for its iPhone business is a compelling app portfolio and hence (external) app developer productivity. The core questions are: How long does it take for an external developer (complementor) to develop or update an iOS app? How much time do developers need to learn the necessary programming language? Since the programming language Objective-C did not perform well enough in respect to these questions, Apple invested millions in the development and introduction of a new programming language, Swift, in 2014. This made developing apps easier and faster for developers and assured competitiveness against Google Android.

To manage its platform ecosystem and foster growth, YouTube also pays close attention to the productivity of its content providers. In the end, the platform derives most of its value from content that is created and uploaded by individuals. Whereas traditional TV producers create and distribute their own content, YouTube creates its value by enabling interactions between content providers and content consumers. In fact, YouTube considers both providers and consumers as users of its platform. As a result, everything they do is focused on making it easy to create, share and market videos (provider side), and as convenient and entertaining as possible to watch videos (consumer side). This is also the reason why YouTube deliberately does not charge its content providers directly to upload videos.

> Craig Federighi, SVP software engineering of Apple, on the advantages of Swift: 'Now Objective-C has served us so well for 20 years. We absolutely love it. But we had to ask ourselves the question what would it be like if we had Objective-C without the baggage of C? Well, we did more than think about it. We have a new programming language. The language is called Swift and it totally rules. Swift is fast. It is modern. It is designed for safety. And it enables the level of interactivity in development that you've never seen on the platform. When it comes to speed, Swift is great. Compare Python, a popular scripting language, with Objective-C, when it comes to something like, let's say complex object sort. Objective-C is a lot faster. But Swift is faster still.' (2014)[55]

The same is true with Airbnb where value creation relies on the hosts' offering. Therefore, Airbnb is using the 'side switching rate' as one important KPI. It tracks how many travellers become hosts, i.e. offer apartments themselves. Ultimately, Airbnb's core values from the platform are the resources from their participants and complementing interactions. Only a few months after the launch of Apple's App Store in July 2008, Google introduced the Android Market, which later became the Google Play Store. Google quickly realised they can only catch up with Apple if they are able to engage developers on their platform. To make it as easy as possible for developers to join the Android platform, Google decided to build upon the very popular Java programming language. To foster engagement even further, Google started a developer challenge with prize money to encourage third-party developers to join.

> Nate Moch, VP at Zillow, an iBuyer marketplace for houses, on the relevance of changing the entire culture: 'Picking your core goal is more than just selecting the most accurate metric. You want to have a goal that is easy to understand, memorable and inspiring because you are trying to change the culture.' (2016)[56]

When and how to apply

The core of any platform is its ecosystem of producers and consumers and their respective resources. Therefore, instead of focusing on internal platform provider productivity, platforms need to manage the productivity of their users. And both sides of a platform must be considered. Take Instagram as an example. Although users can both create and consume, Instagram needs to separately think about the two sides. Today, it offers the supply side an opportunity to make money and the demand side easy consumption as well as a personalised experience. Traditional pipeline companies tend to focus their platform ambitions on the end customer (app users in the case of an app store), forgetting that platform providers (app developers in the case of an app store) are the second group of customers which, in contrast to a traditional supply chain, cannot be tightly managed and controlled.[57]

> **Some questions to ask**
> - What is essential to put external resources to effective use on your platform?
> - What metrics best capture effective value creation by your providers and consumers?
> - How can you ensure effective value creation for your providers and consumers?

88 Grow first, monetise second

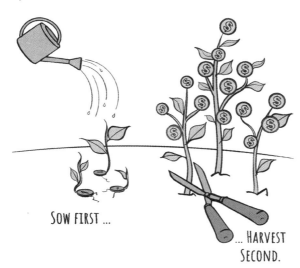

SOW FIRST ...

... HARVEST SECOND.

Platforms can only be successful if they build upon strong network effects. In fact, the value of a platform depends on the number of its users. Therefore, platforms prioritise growth over profit in their early stages, as long as the platform is creating user engagement and user stickiness.[58] Still, most platforms have a rigid long-term strategy for monetisation from the beginning. Although monetising too early can harm network effects and hinder long-term success, platforms still track and manage financial metrics such as revenue, platform transaction volume, customer acquisition and retention costs from day one.

One prominent example is Uber. Despite still not being profitable after many years, Uber has created one of the strongest networks and thousands of jobs. Accordingly, the overall satisfaction and customer retention are very high. Also, many of Amazon's operations were initially unprofitable, and management sacrificed monetisation for building up a compelling multi-platform offering. For example, it invested billions in one-day shipping even though profits fell. And even when one business unit started making profits, these profits were reinvested in growth projects and customer retention. While in the early days it did not focus on profitability, Amazon still looked at gross merchandise volume (GMV) and free cash flow as core management metrics. The same is true of WhatsApp. While the core services (e.g. messaging, and sending photos) remain free, the social media platform has introduced WhatsApp Business and WhatsApp Pay (in some countries) to monetise its platform almost 10 years after its foundation. With more than 2 billion active users, WhatsApp is now one of the most popular applications in the world.[59]

> David Wu, VP strategy of Pinduoduo, a Chinese product marketplace, on the question of what to prioritise: '[It] is not so much growth versus monetisation, but rather on engagement. We are convinced that by having strong user engagement and good user experience, monetisation will follow [. . .]' (2019)[60]

> Christian Bertermann, founder of Auto1, an iBuyer marketplace for cars, on the relevance of focusing on long-term profitability: 'We can't afford to be more expensive than others. The beauty for the customer is the absolute price transparency in this market. Our cars have to be competitive, otherwise customers won't buy them. [. . .] It pays off in the long run. The idea that you start directly with a profit is wrong. We will invest significantly in the brand, also in the infrastructure and the delivery process. These are large amounts. We are very grateful that our investors are willing to support this vision. And you can see in the USA with comparable players like Carvana or Carmax that there are definitely interesting margins in this business in the long term.' (2020)[61]

Facebook also started by focusing on the growth of its network. It did not think about monetising early members beyond making money through advertising. This is even more apparent when comparing it with Myspace, its early competitor. Many people thought that Myspace would win the battle, especially because of its size. By 2006 it became the most visited website in the US and attracted more users than Facebook. However, it lost the battle to Facebook after it was sold to News Corporation, at that time one of the largest media groups in the world. Management began to run Myspace as if it was a traditional pipeline company. In 2008, a revenue target of USD 1 billion was confidently announced, representing a 56 per cent increase over the previous year.[62] While there are certainly different reasons, in retrospect, the decline of Myspace can certainly be attributed to wrong prioritisation of monetisation over growth by News Corporation.

When and how to apply
Platform managers need to look at performance management from a different perspective than pipeline companies. In the platform economy, scale matters, and establishing network effects is of utmost importance. Hence, platforms defer profits in favour of growth. As a consequence, it might be mandatory to prioritise growth KPIs over profit KPIs. You want to attract and bind users to your platform, but you expect long-term profits from the installed base of platform users.

> Jeff Bezos, founder of Amazon, on investing free cash flow: 'Amazon is a collection of several businesses and initiatives, and we have some very profitable more established businesses that are free cash flow generating very significantly. Fortunately, we have lots of opportunities to invest in new initiatives and we take advantage of those opportunities.' (2019)[63]

Some questions to ask
- How do you track platform growth, engagement and monetisation?
- Given your current situation, how should you prioritise growth, engagement and monetisation?
- What is your long-term monetisation strategy and how do you track progress until then?

[PART THREE]

Finished reading?
Let's get to work!

A canvas to bring everything together

1

Every strategy is only as good as its implementation. To drive platforms and their implementation, we have developed a few tools in addition to this book. We offer a physical card set of the 88 patterns. It has proven to be very effective in corporate innovation workshops, consulting workshops and in teaching (bachelors, masters, MBA). Additionally, several teaching videos and a canvas are available online.*

As a supplement to the patterns, the platform canvas can be used to capture the platform idea in a clear and structured manner (see Figure 3.1.1). It has proven to be very helpful in starting a platform project. The canvas builds upon traditional business model building blocks, such as value proposition (what do we offer?), value creation (how do we create value?) and value capturing (how do we monetise and capture value?). It also integrates platform-specific components, such as value flow between the different market sides, the chicken-and-egg problem and platform management. In the end, we believe it is important to highlight the key findings from your workshop and document them in a clear and digestible way, e.g. based on our concise canvas. This will not only support communication with your stakeholders but also helps discussing, testing and refining the platform idea further, for example, with your customers and partners.

* You can download the canvas and order physical pattern cards at www.iot-lab.ch/the-platform-navigator/ and www.bmilab.com/resource.

Figure 3.1.1 The platform canvas brings everything together

How to bring everything together? The canvas

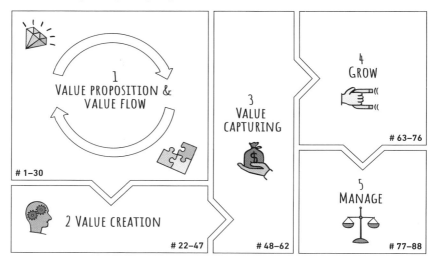

Step 1: value proposition & value flow

Browse through the ideate patterns (# 1–21) to identify opportunities for your own business. Looking at the specific examples mentioned on the patterns, you could ask yourself:

- How would platform X conduct our business?
- Can we transfer the business model of platform X into our industry?
- Should we build our own platform X or is it more feasible to become a complementor or user in an existing one?

At the heart of any platform business model are the transactions between the different market sides (customer groups). Therefore, write down the platform participants and make the core transactions and the value flow between the market sides explicit. Sketch them onto the canvas and discuss the following questions:

- What is the core value proposition and mission of the platform?
- Which different market sides (platform players) does the platform bring together?
- What are the core interactions and value flows between the different platform players?

In addition, put yourself in your users' and partners' shoes and answer the following questions (for all market sides):

- What do we offer as a platform to the particular market side?

- What is their motivation to join the platform ecosystem?
- What is their contribution to the platform ecosystem?

Step 2: value creation

Depending on the platform type (transaction versus innovation), discuss the platform's extent of value creation and its operating model. Use the design patterns (# 22–47) to discuss the following questions:

- How is the platform value proposition being implemented?
- What is the ownership model of the platform? Can we establish our platform ambitions as a single company, or do we have to establish a consortium?
- What is the operating model of our transaction platform? Are we going asset-light or asset-heavy?
- What is the operating model of our innovation platform? Do we allow others to develop, enhance and distribute our innovation platform? How do we ensure quality and distribution of complements?

Step 3: value capturing

Discuss the pros, cons and feasibility of different monetisation options by putting yourself in the shoes of the different market sides. Do not forget that you can also combine several patterns. Use the monetise pattern cards (# 48–62) to define your revenue model and answer the following questions:

- Who or which sides of the platform will we charge?
- How will we charge the different sides of the platform?
- What direct and/or indirect revenue streams can be monetised?
- What monetisation tactics can be utilised?

Step 4: grow

Browse through the scale patterns (# 63–76) to explore how you can overcome your chicken-and-egg problem. Discuss the following questions:

- Which market sides (platform players) are difficult to attract, which are easy to attract?
- Which one to three growth strategies can be applied to address the chicken-and-egg problem?
- Should the growth strategies be applied simultaneously or in a specific order?

Step 5: manage

The long-term perspective of managing a platform is often forgotten. Not only do you need to constantly innovate, but you also need to defend your position and maintain quality and trust. Use the manage patterns (# 77–88) to brainstorm specific actions and ideas for the following questions:

- Which KPIs are core to managing our platform journey effectively?
- How can we defend our platform business against existing or emerging rivals?
- What measures do we have in place to mitigate fraud and maintain trust?

In summary, the canvas is a tool to bring all your ideas together across the different steps of the Platform Business Navigator, and the 88 patterns will facilitate the discussion and help to fill in the blank canvas. The example of Airbnb as a very successful transaction platform can illustrate this in a simplified way (see Figure 3.1.2).

Figure 3.1.2 The platform canvas in action

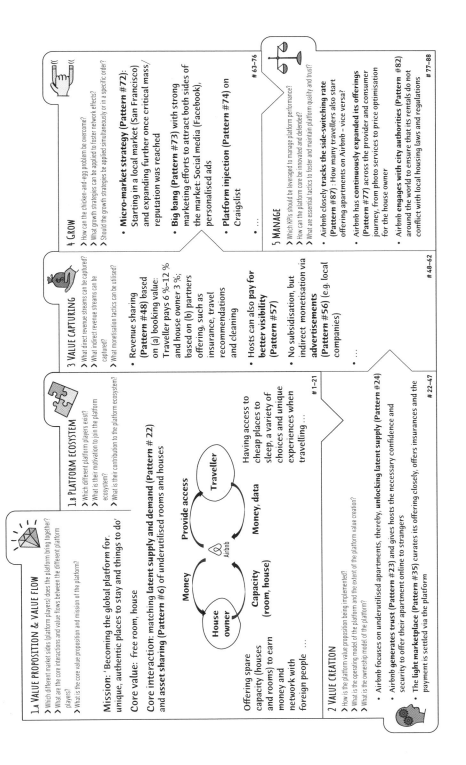

1.A VALUE PROPOSITION & VALUE FLOW
➤ Which different market sides (platform players) does the platform bring together?
➤ What are the core interactions and value flows between the different platform players?
➤ What is the core value proposition and mission of the platform?

Mission: 'Becoming the global platform for. unique, authentic places to stay and things to do'

Core value: free room, house

Core interaction: matching **latent supply and demand (Pattern # 22)** and **asset sharing (Pattern # 6)** of underutilised rooms and houses

Offering spare capacity (houses and rooms) to earn money and network with foreign people …

Money   **Provide access**

House owner   Airbnb   **Traveller**

Capacity (room, house)   **Money, data**

Having access to cheap places to sleep, a variety of choices and unique experiences when travelling …

1–21

1.B PLATFORM ECOSYSTEM
➤ Which different platform players exist?
➤ What is their motivation to join the platform ecosystem?
➤ What is their contribution to the platform ecosystem?

2 VALUE CREATION
➤ How is the platform value proposition being implemented?
➤ What is the operating model of the platform and the extent of the platform value creation?
➤ What is the ownership model of the platform?

- Airbnb focuses on underutilised apartments, thereby, **unlocking latent supply (Pattern #24)**
- Airbnb **generates trust (Pattern #23)** and gives hosts the necessary confidence and security to offer their apartment online to strangers
- The **light marketplace (Pattern #35)** curates its offering closely, offers insurances and the payment is settled via the platform

22–47

3 VALUE CAPTURING
➤ What direct revenue streams can be captured?
➤ What indirect revenue streams can be captured?
➤ What monetisation tactics can be utilised?

- **Revenue sharing (Pattern #48)** based on (a) booking value: Traveller pays 6 %–12 % and house owner 3 %; based on (b) partners offering, such as insurance, travel recommendations and cleaning
- Hosts can also **pay for better visibility (Pattern #57)**
- No subsidiation, but indirect monetisation via **advertisements (Pattern #56)** (e.g. local companies)
- …

48–62

4 GROW
➤ How can the chicken-and-egg problem be overcome?
➤ What growth strategies can be applied to foster network effects?
➤ Should the growth strategies be applied simultaneously or in a specific order?

- **Micro-market strategy (Pattern #72):** Starting in a local market (San Francisco) and expanding further once critical mass/reputation was reached
- **Big bang (Pattern #73)** with strong marketing efforts to attract both sides of the market: Social media (Facebook), personalised ads
- **Platform injection (Pattern #74)** on Craigslist
- …

63–76

5 MANAGE
➤ Which KPIs should be leveraged to manage platform performance?
➤ How can the platform core be innovated and defended?
➤ What are essential tactics to foster and maintain platform quality and trust?

- Airbnb closely tracks the **side-switching rate (Pattern #87)** : How many travellers also start offering apartments on Airbnb – vice versa?
- Airbnb has **continuously expanded its offerings (Pattern #77)** across the provider and consumer journey, from photo services to price optimisation for the house owner
- Airbnb **engages with city authorities (Pattern #82)** around the world to ensure that its rentals do not conflict with local housing laws and regulations

77–88

2

Working with the pattern cards

Organise a creative workshop

For optimal use of the Platform Business Navigator, we recommend utilising the physical 88 pattern cards in a workshop setting that complements using the book (see Figure 3.2.1 for an overview of all patterns). The physical pattern cards aid brainstorming, encourage collaboration and make business model innovation more tangible. It is beneficial to divide larger groups into smaller groups. A diverse group of three to five participants is ideal. Select participants from a wide range of backgrounds to boost creativity and out-of-the-box thinking. Take care that people are open minded and creative. These smaller groups can then independently work through the steps outlined in the Platform Business Navigator with the goal of comparing the results at the end (Option 1). Alternatively, if an initial platform business model idea is already sketched out, smaller groups can focus on selective steps of the Platform Business Navigator to integrate the outcomes into a cohesive overall picture (Option 2).

Create the right atmosphere

Start by setting clear objectives for the workshop and communicating them to the participants. This will help them understand the purpose of the session and what is expected of them. Choose a venue that is comfortable, spacious and conducive to creativity and collaboration. Establish ground rules at the beginning of the session to ensure that everyone is on the same page. Encourage participants to actively participate, respect each other's opinions and avoid distractions during the session. For instance, let participants write

Figure 3.2.1 The 88 patterns at a glance

No.	Pattern	Step
#1	Crowdfunding platforms	Ideate
#2	Open innovation platforms	Ideate
#3	Co-innovation platforms	Ideate
#4	Industrial innovation platforms	Ideate
#5	Data harvesting platforms	Ideate
#6	Asset sharing platforms	Ideate
#7	Product marketplaces	Ideate
#8	Application and data marketplaces	Ideate
#9	Service marketplaces	Ideate
#10	P2P support platforms	Ideate
#11	Social media platforms	Ideate
#12	Content and review platforms	Ideate
#13	Collaboration platforms	Ideate
#14	Education platforms	Ideate
#15	Freelance platforms	Ideate
#16	Payment platforms	Ideate
#17	Lending platforms	Ideate
#18	Investment platforms	Ideate
#19	Technology platforms	Ideate
#20	Application platforms	Ideate
#21	Open source platforms	Ideate
#22	Aggregate demand and supply	Design
#23	Generate trust	Design
#24	Unlock latent supply	Design
#25	Unlock scarce supply	Design
#26	Create a complementor ecosystem	Design
#27	Open up the platform core	Design
#28	Establish a platform vertical	Design
#29	Facilitate local interactions	Design
#30	Enable an instant experience	Design

Figure 3.2.1 *Continued*

No.	Pattern	Step
#31	Single owner	Design
#32	Consortium	Design
#33	Peer-to-peer community	Design
#34	Listings platform	Design
#35	Light marketplace	Design
#36	Full-stack marketplace	Design
#37	Market maker	Design
#38	E-commerce	Design
#39	Direct to customer	Design
#40	Closed core platform	Design
#41	Open core platform	Design
#42	Single-home platform	Design
#43	Multi-home platform	Design
#44	Integration platform	Design
#45	Enablement platform	Design
#46	Managed platform	Design
#47	Distribution platform	Design
#48	Revenue sharing	Monetise
#49	Pay per use	Monetise
#50	Pay once	Monetise
#51	Pay what you want	Monetise
#52	Subscription	Monetise
#53	Membership	Monetise
#54	Boost your own sales	Monetise
#55	Buy low, sell high	Monetise
#56	Advertisement	Monetise
#57	Pay for visibility	Monetise
#58	Data monetisation	Monetise
#59	Freemium	Monetise

Figure 3.2.1 *Continued*

No.	Pattern	Step
#60	Free trial	Monetise
#61	Add-on	Monetise
#62	Dynamic pricing	Monetise
#63	Single-side product	Scale
#64	Munchausen bootstrap	Scale
#65	Boost early supply	Scale
#66	Subsidise the sensitive	Scale
#67	Get the big shots	Scale
#68	Get the gang together	Scale
#69	Let your users bring them in	Scale
#70	Follow the rabbit	Scale
#71	Piggyback	Scale
#72	Micro-market	Scale
#73	Big bang	Scale
#74	Platform injection	Scale
#75	Platform exploitation	Scale
#76	Platform pacing	Scale
#77	Improve the customer journey	Manage
#78	Imitate to innovate	Manage
#79	Open for co-innovation	Manage
#80	Weaken rivals	Manage
#81	Acquire early	Manage
#82	Manage regulators	Manage
#83	Prevent fraud	Manage
#84	Manage friction	Manage
#85	Protect data	Manage
#86	Track network effects	Manage
#87	From inside to outside	Manage
#88	Grow first, monetise second	Manage

down platform ideas immediately without judgement. Only in the end, evaluate and shortlist one to three ideas. A devil's advocate is only helpful after initial results have been derived. Finally, a facilitator who is familiar with the Platform Business Navigator and its structure is important to keep the session focused and on target. Ideally, participants should also familiarise themselves in advance with some platform basics (e.g. Part One of our book).

Pick your playing field

We recommend thinking through all five steps at once. However, feel free to adjust the overall process to your specific setting and requirements. The Platform Business Navigator is designed so that you can take out only those sections that are most important for you. If you have had few touchpoints with platform business models so far, you could focus only on the ideate step. If your platform activities are more mature, you could jump directly into the design or scale steps to refine and challenge an existing idea. If you already know that a transaction platform will be most suitable for you, you can discard the innovation platform patterns. Specifically, there are three starting points for you: If you do not have a specific platform idea yet but want to brainstorm multiple ideas, use the ideate pattern cards (Starting Point 1). If you have a viable platform idea but need to design the underlying platform business model, use the design and monetise pattern cards (Starting Point 2). If you have a specific platform business model in mind which you would like to implement now with concrete measures, use the scale and manage pattern cards (Starting Point 3).

Think beyond the pattern cards

Feel free to adjust the overall process to your specific setting and requirements. You can also combine different pattern cards if you find it useful. You should also be aware that not all patterns are equal. While some provide a very concrete strategy (e.g. piggyback), some are more general and only provide guidance in the form of a principle (e.g. grow first, monetise second). This means that some pattern cards will be more relevant than another – or not relevant at all – for your business or setting. However, for a holistic view on platforms, we believe they are all important to know for a (future) platform manager. Moreover, platform business models are not static and implementing one is a continuous journey. It can take time and require multiple iterations through our five steps. The examples of Amazon and Android illustrate well how platform companies keep moving through this cycle again and again. Nevertheless, we believe the best way to start is by thinking an idea through from the beginning to the end.

Sources and further reading

3

Should you be interested in reading more about platform business models, the underlying theories and frameworks, we recommend the following literature, in particular *Platform Revolution*, *The Business of Platforms* and *Winning the Right Game*, which inspired us when developing the Platform Business Navigator.

Part One

Chapter 1

Adner, R. (2021) *Winning the Right Game: How to Disrupt, Defend, and Deliver in a Changing World*. Cambridge, MA: The MIT Press.

De Reuver, M., Sørensen, C. and Basole, R. (2018) 'The digital platform: A research agenda'. *Journal of Information Technology*, 33(2), 124–135.

Eisenmann, T., Parker, G. and Van Alstyne, M. (2006) 'Strategies for two-sided markets'. *Harvard Business Review*, 84(10), 92–101.

Gawer, A. and Cusumano, M. (2014) 'Industry platforms and ecosystem innovation'. *Journal of Product Innovation Management*, 31(3), 417–433.

Gregory, R., Henfridsson, O., Kaganer, E. and Kyriakou, H. (2021) 'The role of artificial intelligence and data network effects for creating user value'. *Academy of Management Review*, 46(3), 534–551.

Jacobides, M., Cennamo, C. and Gawer, A. (2018) 'Towards a theory of ecosystems'. *Strategic Management Journal*, 39(8), 2255–2276.

McIntyre, D. and Srinivasan, A. (2017) 'Networks, platforms, and strategy: Emerging views and next steps'. *Strategic Management Journal*, 38(1), 141–160.

Parker, G., Van Alstyne, M. and Choudary, S. (2016) *Platform Revolution: How Networked Markets Are Transforming the Economy and How to Make Them Work for You*. New York: W. W. Norton & Company.

Van Alstyne, M., Parker, G. and Choudary, S. (2016) 'Pipelines, platforms, and the new rules of strategy'. *Harvard Business Review*, 94(4), 54–62.

Chapter 2

Boudreau, K. and Lakhani, K. R. (2008) How to manage outside innovation'. *MIT Sloan Management Review*, 50(4), 69–76.

Cusumano, M. (2020) 'Guidepost: The evolution of research on industry platforms'. *Academy of Management Discoveries (June)*, 1–15.

Cusumano, M., Gawer, A. and Yoffie, D. (2019) *The Business of Platforms: Strategy in the Age of Digital Competition, Innovation, and Power*. New York: Harper Business.

Dealroom.co (2020) 'Online marketplaces entering the next phase'. Available at: https://dealroom.co/uploaded/2020/06/Marketplaces-2020-vFINAL.pdf

Markfort, L., Arzt, A., Kögler, P., Jung, S., Gebauer, H., Haugk, S., Leyh, C. and Wortmann, F. (2022) 'Patterns of business model innovation for advancing IoT platforms'. *Journal of Service Management*, 33(1), 70–96.

Porter, M. E. and Heppelmann, J. E. (2014) 'Smart, connected products are transforming competition'. *Harvard Business Review*, 11, 64–68.

Täuscher, K. and Laudien, S. M. (2018) 'Understanding platform business models: A mixed methods study of marketplaces'. *European Management Journal*, 36(3), 319–329.

Zhao, Y., von Delft, S., Morgan-Thomas, A. and Buck, T. (2020) 'The evolution of platform business models: Exploring competitive battles in the world of platforms'. *Long Range Planning*, 53(4).

Chapter 3

Gassmann, O., Frankenberger, K. and Choudury, M. (2020) *The Business Model Navigator: The Strategies Behind the Most Successful Companies* (2nd ed.). FT Publishing.

Hagiu, A. (2014) 'Strategic decisions for multisided platforms'. *MIT Sloan Management Review*, 55(2), 4–13.

Hodapp, D., Hawlitschek, F., Wortmann, F., Lang, M. and Gassmann, O. (2022) 'Key lessons from Bosch for incumbent firms entering the platform economy'. *MIS Quarterly Executive*, 21(2), 115–129.

Parker, G., Van Alstyne, M. and Choudary, S. (2016) *Platform Revolution: How Networked Markets Are Transforming the Economy and How to Make Them Work for You*. New York: W. W. Norton & Company.

Snihur, Y., Thomas, L. D. W. and Burgelman, R. A. (2023) 'Strategically managing the business model portfolio trajectory'. *California Management Review*, 65(2), 156–176.

Teece, D. (2017) 'Dynamic capabilities and (digital) platform lifecycles'. *Advances in Strategic Management*, 37, 211–225.

Weking, J., Hein, A., Böhm, M. and Krcmar, H. (2020) 'A hierarchical taxonomy of business model patterns'. *Electronic Markets*, 30(3), 447–468.

Part Two

Chapter 1

Boudreau, K. and Lakhani, K. R. (2008) 'How to manage outside innovation'. *MIT Sloan Management Review*, 50(4), 69–76.

Chan, H., Zeng, K. J. and Yang, M. X. (2022) 'Review platforms as prosumer communities: Theory, practices and implications'. *European Journal of Marketing*, 56(10), 2698–2720.

Chnar, M. and Subhi, Z. (2021) 'Sufficient comparison among cloud computing services: IaaS, PaaS, and SaaS: A review'. *International Journal of Science and Business*, 5(2), 17–30.

Cusumano, M., Yoffie, D. and Gawer, A. (2020) 'The future of platforms'. *Sloan Management Review*, 61(3), 46–54.

Drewel, M., Özcan, L., Koldewey, C. and Gausemeier, J. (2021) 'Pattern-based development of digital platforms'. *Creativity and Innovation Management*, 30(2), 412–430.

Einav, L., Farronato, C. and Levin, J. (2016) 'Peer-to-peer markets'. *Annual Review of Economics*, 8, 615–635.

Gassmann, O., Frankenberger, K. and Choudury, M. (2020) *The Business Model Navigator: The Strategies Behind the Most Successful Companies* (2nd ed.). FT Publishing.

Grieger, M. (2003) 'Electronic marketplaces: A literature review and a call for supply chain management research'. *European Journal of Operational Research*, 144(2), 280–294.

Hagiu, A. and Altman, E. J. (2017) 'Finding the platform in your product: Four strategies that can reveal hidden value'. *Harvard Business Review*, 95(4), 95–100.

Hagiu, A. and Wright, J. (2020) 'When data creates competitive advantage'. *Harvard Business Review*, 98(1), 94–101.

Jin, L. and Chen, A. (2018) 'What's next for marketplace startups?' Future from A16z. Available at: https://a16z.com/2018/11/27/services-marketplaces-service-economy-evolution-whats-next/

Kenney, M. and Zysman, J. (2016) 'The rise of the platform economy'. *Issues in Science and Technology*, 32(3), 62–69.

Porter, M. (1985) *Competitive Advantage*. New York: The Free Press.

Täuscher, K. and Laudien, S. M. (2018) 'Understanding platform business models: A mixed methods study of marketplaces'. *European Management Journal*, 36(3), 319–329.

Taylor, T. A. (2018) 'On-demand service platforms'. *Manufacturing & Service Operations Management*, 20(4), 704–720.

Wichmann, J. R. K., Wiegand, N. and Reinartz, W. J. (2022) 'The platformization of brands'. *Journal of Marketing*, 86(1), 109–131.

Wirtz, B., Schilke, O. and Ullrich, S. (2010) 'Strategic development of business models'. *Long Range Planning*, 43(2–3), 272–290.

Wirtz, J., So, K. K. F., Mody, M. A., Liu, S. Q. and Chun, H. H. (2019) 'Platforms in the peer-to-peer sharing economy'. *Journal of Service Management*, 30(4), 452–483.

Chapter 2

Alaei, A. M., Taleizadeh, A. A. and Rabbani, M. (2022) 'Marketplace, reseller, or web-store channel: The impact of return policy and cross-channel spillover from marketplace to web-store'. *Journal of Retailing and Consumer Services*, 65, 1–17.

Amit, R. and Zott, C. (2001) 'Value creation in e-business'. *Strategic Management Journal*, 22(6–7), 493–520.

Bakos, Y. (1998) 'The emerging role of electronic marketplaces on the Internet'. *Communications of the ACM*, 41(8), 35–42.

Baldwin, C. Y. and Woodard, C. J. (2009) 'The architecture of platforms: A unified view'. In A. Gawer (Ed.), *Platforms, Markets and Innovation* (pp. 19–44). Glos, UK: Edward Elgar Publishing.

Bergman, R., Abbas, A. E., Jung, S., Werker, C. and de Reuver, M. (2022) 'Business model archetypes for data marketplaces in the automotive industry'. *Electronic Markets*, 32(2), 747–765.

Brunn, P., Jensen, M. and Skovgaard, J. (2002) 'E-marketplaces: Crafting a winning strategy'. *European Management Journal*, 20(3), 286–298.

Buchak, G., Matvos, G., Piskorski, T. and Seru, A. (2020) 'iBuyers: Liquidity in real estate markets?' *SSRN Electronic Journal*, March, 1–81.

Cusumano, M., Gawer, A. and Yoffie, D. B. (2019) *The Business of Platforms: Strategy in the Age of Digital Competition, Innovation, and Power*. New York: Harper Business.

Dealroom.co (2020) 'Online marketplaces entering the next phase'. Available at: https://dealroom.co/uploaded/2020/06/Marketplaces-2020-vFINAL.pdf

Eisenmann, T., Parker, G. and Van Alstyne, M. (2006) 'Strategies for two-sided markets'. *Harvard Business Review*, 84(10), 92–101.

Eisenmann, T., Parker, G. and Van Alstyne, M. (2008) 'Opening platforms: How, when and why? *HBS Working Paper 09-030*.

Gassmann, O., Frankenberger, K. and Choudury, M. (2020) *The Business Model Navigator: The Strategies Behind the Most Successful Companies* (2nd ed.). FT Publishing.

Gawer, A. (2020) 'Digital platforms' boundaries: The interplay of firm scope, platform sides, and digital interfaces'. *Long Range Planning*, 54(5), 102045.

Hagiu, A. (2014) 'Strategic decisions for multisided platforms'. *MIT Sloan Management Review*, 55(2), 4–13.

Hein, A., Schreieck, M., Riasanow, T., Setzke, D. S., Wiesche, M., Böhm, M. and Krcmar, H. (2020) 'Digital platform ecosystems'. *Electronic Markets*, 30(1), 87–98.

Hein, A., Weking, J., Schreieck, M., Wiesche, M., Böhm, M. and Krcmar, H. (2019) 'Value co-creation practices in business-to-business platform ecosystems'. *Electronic Markets*, 29(3), 503–518.

Karhu, K., Gustafsson, R., Eaton, B., Henfridsson, O. and Sørensen, C. (2020) 'Four tactics for implementing a balanced digital platform strategy'. *MIS Quarterly Executive*, 19(2), 105–120.

Katz, B. M. L. and Shapiro, C. (1985) 'Network externalities, competition, and compatibility. *The American Economic Review*, 75(3), 424–440.

O'Mahony, S. and Karp, R. (2022) 'From proprietary to collective governance: How do platform participation strategies evolve?' *Strategic Management Journal*, 43(3), 530–562.

Täuscher, K. and Laudien, S. M. (2018) 'Understanding platform business models: A mixed methods study of marketplaces'. *European Management Journal*, 36(3), 319–329.

Tiwana, A. (2014) *Platform Ecosystems: Aligning Architecture, Governance, and Strategy*. Amsterdam: Morgan Kaufmann.

Chapter 3

Bakos, Y. and Katsamakas, E. (2008) 'Design and ownership of two-sided networks: Implications for internet platforms'. *Journal of Management Information Systems*, 25(2), 171–202.

Brunn, P., Jensen, M. and Skovgaard, J. (2002) 'E-marketplaces: Crafting a winning strategy'. *European Management Journal*, 20(3), 286–298.

Dushnitsky, G., Piva, E. and Rossi-Lamastra, C. (2020) 'Investigating the mix of strategic choices and performance of transaction platforms: Evidence from the crowdfunding setting'. *Strategic Management Journal*, 1–36.

Eisenmann, T., Parker, G. and Van Alstyne, M. (2006) 'Strategies for two-sided markets'. *Harvard Business Review*, 84(10), 92–101.

Gassmann, O., Frankenberger, K. and Choudury, M. (2020) *The Business Model Navigator: The Strategies Behind the Most Successful Companies* (2nd ed.). FT Publishing.

Hagiu, A. and Wright, J. (2020) 'When data creates competitive advantage'. *Harvard Business Review*, 98(1), 94–101.

Meier, P. (2019) 'How do digital platforms make their money?' Alexander von Humboldt Institute for Internet and Society. Available at: https://www.hiig.de/en/how-do-digital-platforms-make-their-money/

Parker, G., Van Alstyne, M. and Choudary, S. (2016) *Platform Revolution: How Networked Markets Are Transforming the Economy and How to Make Them Work for You*. New York: W. W. Norton & Company.

Pauwels, K. and Weiss, A. (2008) 'Moving from free to fee: How online firms market to change their business model successfully'. *Journal of Marketing*, 72(3), 14–31.

Trabucchi, D., Buganza, T. and Pellizzoni, E. (2017) 'Give away your digital services'. *Research-Technology Management*, 60(2), 43–52.

Weking, J., Hein, A., Böhm, M. and Krcmar, H. (2020) 'A hierarchical taxonomy of business model patterns'. *Electronic Markets*, 30(3), 447–468.

Wirtz, B. and Kleinecken, A. (2000) 'Geschäftsmodelltypologien im Internet'. *Wirtschaftswissenschaftliches Studium*, 29(11), 626–634.

Chapter 4

Boudreau, K. and Lakhani, K. R. (2008) 'How to manage outside innovation'. *MIT Sloan Management Review*, 50(4), 69–76.

Büge, M. and Ozcan, P. (2021) 'Platform scaling, fast and slow'. *MIT Sloan Management Review*, 62(3), 40–46.

Currier, J. (2019) '19 tactics to solve the chicken-or-egg problem and grow your marketplace'. Available at: https://www.nfx.com/post/19-marketplace-tactics-for-overcoming-the-chicken-or-egg-problem

Dou, Y. and Wu, D. J. (2018) 'Platform competition under network effects: Piggybacking and optimal subsidization', *Information Systems Research*, 32(3), 820–835.

Eisenmann, T., Parker, G. and Van Alstyne, M. (2006) 'Strategies for two-sided markets'. *Harvard Business Review*, 84(10), 92–101.

Evans, D. (2009) 'How catalysts ignite: The economics of platform-based start-ups'. In A. Gawer (Ed.), *Platforms, Markets and Innovation*. Glos, UK: Edward Elgar Publishing.

Gawer, A. and Cusumano, M. (2008) 'How companies become platform leaders'. *MIT Sloan Management Review*, 49(2), 68–75.

Ghazawneh, A. and Henfridsson, O. (2013) 'Balancing platform control and external contribution in third-party development: The boundary resources model'. *Information Systems Journal*, 23(2), 173–192.

Karhu, K. and Ritala, P. (2021) 'Slicing the cake without baking it: Opportunistic platform entry strategies in digital markets'. *Long Range Planning*, 54(5), 1–18.

Luca, M. and Zervas, G. (2016) 'Fake it till you make it: Reputation, competition, and yelp review fraud'. *Management Science*, 62(12), 3412–3427.

Parker, G., Van Alstyne, M. and Choudary, S. (2016) *Platform Revolution: How Networked Markets Are Transforming the Economy and How to Make Them Work for You*. New York: W. W. Norton & Company.

Rachitsky, L. (2019) 'How to kickstart and scale a marketplace business'. Lenny's Newsletter. Available at: https://www.lennysnewsletter.com/p/how-to-kickstart-and-scale-a-marketplace

Rochet, J.-C. and Tirole, J. (2003) 'Platform competition in two-sided markets'. *Journal of the European Economic Association*, 1(4), 990–1029.

Stummer, C., Kundisch, D. and Decker, R. (2018) 'Platform launch strategies'. *Business & Information Systems Engineering*, 60(2), 167–173.

Veisdal, J. (2020) 'The dynamics of entry for digital platforms in two-sided markets: A multi-case study'. *Electronic Markets*, 30(3), 539–556.

Zhu, F. and Iansiti, M. (2019) 'Why some platforms thrive, and others don't'. *Harvard Business Review*, 97(1), 118–125.

Chapter 5

Aversa, P., Haefliger, S., Hueller, F. and Reza, D. G. (2021) 'Customer complementarity in the digital space: Exploring Amazon's business model diversification'. *Long Range Planning*, 54(5).

Boudreau, K. and Lakhani, K. R. (2008) 'How to manage outside innovation'. *MIT Sloan Management Review*, 50(4), 69–76.

Byers, J., Proserpio, D. and Zervas, G. (2013) 'The rise of the sharing economy: Estimating the impact of Airbnb on the hotel industry'. *SSRN Electronic Journal*, 1–45.

Casadesus-Masanell, R. and Hałaburda, H. (2014) 'When does a platform create value by limiting choice?' *Journal of Economics and Management Strategy*, 23(2), 259–293.

Casadesus-Masanell, R. and Hervas-Drane, A. (2015) 'Competing with privacy'. *Management Science*, 61(1), 229–246.

Eisenmann, T., Parker, G. and Van Alstyne, M. (2011) 'Platform envelopment'. *Strategic Management Journal*, 32(12), 1270–1285.

Gawer, A. (2020) 'Digital platforms' boundaries: The interplay of firm scope, platform sides, and digital interfaces'. *Long Range Planning*, 54(5).

Gu, G. and Zhu, F. (2021) 'Trust and disintermediation: Evidence from an online freelance marketplace'. *Management Science*, 67(2), 794–807.

Hagiu, A. and Wright, J. (2020) 'When data creates competitive advantage'. *Harvard Business Review*, 98(1), 94–101.

Karhu, K., Gustafsson, R. and Lyytinen, K. (2018) 'Exploiting and defending open digital platforms with boundary resources: Android's five platform forks'. *Information Systems Research*, 29(2), 479–497.

Lang, N., Lechner, C., Wurzer, C. and Dexheimer, M. J. (2020) 'Four strategies to orchestrate a digital ecosystem'. Available at: https://www.bcg.com/publications/2020/four-strategies-to-orchestrate-digital-ecosystem

Luca, M. and Zervas, G. (2016) 'Fake it till you make it: Reputation, competition, and Yelp review fraud'. *Management Science*, 62(12), 3412–3427.

Pidun, U., Reeves, M. and Wessel, E. (2021) 'How healthy is your business ecosystem?'. *MIT Sloan Management Review*, Special Issue, 9–16.

Reinhold, S. and Dolnicar, S. (2021) 'The evolution of Airbnb's business model'. In S. Dolnicar (Ed.), *Airbnb Before, During and After COVID-19* (pp. 17–78). University of Queensland.

Rietveld, J. and Schilling, M. A. (2020) 'Platform competition: A systematic and interdisciplinary review of the literature'. *Journal of Management*, 47(6), 1528–1563.

Staub, N., Haki, K., Aier, S., Winter, R. and Magan, A. (2021) 'Acquisition of complementors as a strategy for evolving digital platform ecosystems'. *MIS Quarterly Executive*, 20(4), 237–258.

Trischler, M., Meier, P. and Trabucchi, D. (2021) 'Digital platform tactics: How to implement platform strategy over time'. *Journal of Business Models*, 9(1), 67–76.

Zhao, Y., von Delft, S., Morgan-Thomas, A. and Buck, T. (2020) 'The evolution of platform business models: Exploring competitive battles in the world of platforms'. *Long Range Planning*, 53(4).

Zhu, F. and Iansiti, M. (2019) 'Why some platforms thrive, and others don't'. *Harvard Business Review*, 97(1), 118–125.

Zhu, F. and Liu, Q. (2018) 'Competing with complementors: An empirical look at Amazon.com'. *Strategic Management Journal*, 39(10), 2618–2642.

Notes

Part One

Chapter 1

1   PwC. (2022) Global Top 100 companies by market capitalisation. Available at https://www.pwc.com/gx/en/services/audit-assurance/publications/global-top-100-companies.html (accessed August 2023).

2   CNN Money. 'Fortune 500: Our annual ranking of America's largest corporations'. Available at: https://money.cnn.com/magazines/fortune/fortune500/2011/performers/companies/biggest/ (accessed August 2023).

3   Rochet, J.-C. and Tirole, J. (2003) 'Platform competition in two-sided markets'. *Journal of the European Economic Association*, 1(4), 990–1029.

4   Parker, G., Van Alstyne, M. and Choudary, S. (2016) *Platform Revolution: How Networked Markets are Transforming the Economy and How to Make Them Work for You*. New York: W. W. Norton & Company.

5   Cusumano, M. A., Gawer, A. and Yoffie, D. B. (2019) *The Business of Platforms: Strategy in the Age of Digital Competition, Innovation, and Power*. New York: Harper Business; Van Alstyne, M. W., Parker, G. G. and Choudary, S. P. (2019) 'A study of more than 250 platforms reveals why most fail'. *Harvard Business Review*, 2–6; Van Alstyne, M. W., Parker, G. and Choudary, S. P. (2016) '6 reasons platforms fail'. *Harvard Business Review*, 31(6), 2–6; Zhu, F. and Iansiti, M. (2019) 'Why some platforms thrive and others don't'. *Harvard Business Review*, 97(1), 118–125.

6   Gawer, A. and Cusumano, M. (2002) *Platform Leadership: How Intel, Microsoft, and Cisco Drive Industry Innovation*. Boston, MA: Harvard Business School Press.

7   Eisenmann, T., Parker, G. and Van Alstyne, M. (2006) 'Strategies for two-sided markets'. *Harvard Business Review*, 84(10), 92–101; Rochet, J.-C. and Tirole, J. (2003) 'Platform competition in two-sided markets'. *Journal of the European Economic Association*, 1(4), 990–1029; Caillaud, B. and Jullien, B. (2003) 'Chicken & egg: Competition among intermediation service providers'. *The RAND Journal of Economics*, 34(2), 309–328.

8   Gassmann, O. and Ferrandina, F. (2021) 'Die Win-Win-Win Formel'. *Harvard Business Manager*, 6(6), 30–41.

9   Gawer, A. and Cusumano, M. (2014) 'Industry platforms and ecosystem innovation'. *Journal of Product Innovation Management*, 31(3), 417–433.

10 Van Alstyne, M. W., Parker, G. and Choudary, S. P. (2016) 'Pipelines, platforms, and the new rules of strategy'. *Harvard Business Review*, 94(4), 54–62.

11 Zhu, F. and Iansiti, M. (2019) 'Why some platforms thrive and others don't'. *Harvard Business Review*, 97(1), 118–125.

12 Eisenmann, T., Parker, G. and Van Alstyne, M. (2006) 'Strategies for two-sided markets'. *Harvard Business Review*, 84(10), 92–101; Van Alstyne, M. W., Parker, G. and Choudary, S. P. (2016) 'Pipelines, platforms, and the new rules of strategy'. *Harvard Business Review*, 94(4), 54–62.

13 Zhao, Y., von Delft, S., Morgan-Thomas, A. and Buck, T. (2020) 'The evolution of platform business models: Exploring competitive battles in the world of platforms'. *Long Range Planning*, 53(4), 101892.

14 Van Alstyne, M. W., Parker, G. and Choudary, S. P. (2016) 'Pipelines, platforms, and the new rules of strategy'. *Harvard Business Review*, 94(4), 54–62; Eisenmann, T., Parker, G. and Van Alstyne, M. (2006) 'Strategies for two-sided markets'. *Harvard Business Review*, 84(10), 92–101.

15 Parker, G., Van Alstyne, M. W. and Choudary, S. P. (2016) *Platform Revolution: How Networked Markets Are Transforming the Economy and How to Make Them Work for You*. New York: W. W. Norton & Company; Van Alstyne, M. W., Parker, G. and Choudary, S. P. (2016) 'Pipelines, platforms, and the new rules of strategy'. *Harvard Business Review*, 94(4), 54–62.

16 Eisenmann, T., Parker, G. and Van Alstyne, M. (2006) 'Strategies for two-sided markets'. *Harvard Business Review*, 84(10), 92–101.

17 Gawer, A. and Cusumano, M. (2014) 'Industry platforms and ecosystem innovation'. *Journal of Product Innovation Management*, 31(3), 417–433.

18 Van Alstyne, M. W., Parker, G. and Choudary, S. P. (2016) 'Pipelines, platforms, and the new rules of strategy'. *Harvard Business Review*, 94(4), 54–62.

19 Eisenmann, T., Parker, G. and Van Alstyne, M. (2006) 'Strategies for two-sided markets'. *Harvard Business Review*, 84(10), 92–101.

20 Rochet, J.-C. and Tirole, J. (2003) 'Platform competition in two-sided markets'. *Journal of the European Economic Association*, 1(4), 990–1029.

21 McIntyre, D., Srinivasan, A., Afuah, A., Gawer, A. and Kretschmer, T. (2021) 'Multisided platforms as new organizational forms'. *Academy of Management Perspectives*, 35(4), 566–583; Afuah, A. and Tucci, C. (2000) *Internet Business Models and Strategies: Text and Cases* (2nd ed.). McGrawHill; Zhang, X.-Z., Liu, J.-J. and Xu, Z.-W. (2015) 'Tencent and Facebook data validate Metcalfe's law'. *Journal of Computer Science and Technology*, (30), 246–251.

22 Reed, D. P. (2001) 'The law of the pack'. *Harvard Business Review*, 79(2), 23–24; Chen, A. (2021) *The Cold Start Problem: How to Start and Scale Network Effects*. Penguin. See also https://a16z.com/2021/11/22/beyond-metcalfes-law-for-network-effects/ (accessed August 2023).

23 Parker, G., Van Alstyne, M. W. and Choudary, S. P. (2016) *Platform Revolution: How Networked Markets Are Transforming the Economy and How to Make Them Work for You*. New York: W. W. Norton & Company; Wirtz, J., So, K. K. F., Mody, M. A., Liu, S. Q. and Chun, H. H. (2019) 'Platforms in the peer-to-peer sharing economy'. *Journal of Service Management*, 30(4), 452– 483; de Reuver, M., Sørensen, C. and Basole, R. C. (2018) 'The digital platform: A research agenda'. *Journal of Information Technology*, 33(2), 124–135.

24 McIntyre, D. P. and Srinivasan, A. (2017) 'Networks, platforms, and strategy: Emerging views and next steps'. *Strategic Management Journal*, 38(1), 141–160; Shapiro, C. and Varian, H. R. (1999) *Information Rules: A Strategic Guide to the Network Economy*. Boston, MA: Harvard Business School Press; Eisenmann, T., Parker, G. and Van Alstyne, M. (2006) 'Strategies for two-sided markets'. *Harvard Business Review*, 84(10), 92–101.

25 Gassmann, O. and Ferrandina, F. (2021) 'Die Win-Win-Win Formel'. *Harvard Business Manager*, 6(6), 30–41.

26 Ng, A. (2018) 'AI transformation playbook: How to lead your company into the AI era'. Available at: https://landing.ai/wp-content/uploads/2020/05/LandingAI_Transformation_Playbook_11-19.pdf (accessed August 2023).

27 Ng, A. (2018) 'AI transformation playbook: How to lead your company into the AI era'. Available at: https://landing.ai/wp-content/uploads/2020/05/LandingAI_Transformation_Playbook_11-19.pdf (accessed August 2023); Hagiu, A. and Wright, J. (2020) 'When data creates competitive advantage'. *Harvard Business Review*, 98(1), 94–101; Currier, J. (2020) 'What makes data valuable: The truth about data network effects'. Available at: https://www.nfx.com/post/truth-about-data-network-effects (accessed August 2023).

28 Gregory, R. W., Henfridsson, O., Kaganer, E. and Kyriakou, H. (2021) 'The role of artificial intelligence and data network effects for creating user value'. *Academy of Management Review*, 46(3), 534–551; Gregory, R. W., Henfridsson, O., Kaganer, E. and Kyriakou, H. (2022) 'Data network effects: Key conditions, shared data, and the data value duality'. *Academy of Management Review*, 47(1), 189–192; Parker, G., Van Alstyne, M. and Choudary, S. (2016) *Platform Revolution: How Networked Markets Are Transforming the Economy and How to Make Them Work for You*. New York: W. W. Norton & Company.

29 Ng, A. (2018) 'AI transformation playbook: How to lead your company into the AI era'. Available at: https://landing.ai/wp-content/uploads/2020/05/LandingAI_Transformation_Playbook_11-19.pdf (accessed August 2023); Hagiu, A. and Wright, J. (2020) 'When data creates competitive advantage'. *Harvard Business Review*, 98(1), 94–101; Currier, J. (2020) 'What makes data valuable: The truth about data network effects'. Available at: https://www.nfx.com/post/truth-about-data-network-effects (accessed August 2023).

30 Moore, J. F. (1993) 'Predators and prey: A new ecology of competition'. *Harvard Business Review*, 71(3), 75–86.

31 Gassmann, O. and Ferrandina, F. (2021) 'Die Win-Win-Win Formel'. *Harvard Business Manager*, 6(6), 30–41.

32 Adner, R. (2021) *Winning the Right Game: How to Disrupt, Defend, and Deliver in a Changing World*. Cambridge, MA: The MIT Press.

33 Adner, R. (2017) 'Ecosystem as structure: An actionable construct for strategy'. *Journal of Management*, 43(1), 39–58; Jacobides, M. G., Cennamo, C. and Gawer, A. (2018) 'Towards a theory of ecosystems'. *Strategic Management Journal*, 39(8), 2255–2276.

34 Fuller, J., Jacobides, M. and Reeves, M. (2019) 'The myths and realities of business ecosystems'. *MIT Sloan Management Review*; Hein, A., Schreieck, M., Riasanow, T., Setzke, D. S., Wiesche, M., Böhm, M. and Krcmar, H. (2020) 'Digital platform ecosystems'. *Electronic Markets*, 30(1), 87–98.

35 Jacobides, M. G., Cennamo, C. and Gawer, A. (2018) 'Towards a theory of ecosystems'. *Strategic Management Journal*, 39(8), 2255–2276; Thomas, L. D. W. and Autio, E. (2014) 'Innovation ecosystems'. *Research Technology Management*, 57(6), 10–14.

36 Parker, G., Van Alstyne, M. and Choudary, S. (2016) *Platform Revolution: How Networked Markets Are Transforming the Economy and How to Make Them Work for You*. New York: W. W. Norton & Company.

37 Adner, R. (2017) 'Ecosystem as structure: An actionable construct for strategy'. *Journal of Management*, 43(1), 39–58.

38 Gassmann, O. and Ferrandina, F. (2021) 'Die Win-Win-Win Formel'. *Harvard Business Manager*, 6(6), 30–41.

39 Adner, R. (2021) *Winning the Right Game: How to Disrupt, Defend, and Deliver in a Changing World*. Cambridge, MA: The MIT Press.

Chapter 2

1 Cusumano, M., Gawer, A. and Yoffie, D. B. (2019) *The Business of Platforms: Strategy in the Age of Digital Competition, Innovation, and Power*. New York: Harper Business; Evans, P. C. and Gawer, A. (2016) *The Rise of the Platform Enterprise: A Global Survey*. The Center for Global Enterprise. Available at: https://openresearch.surrey.ac.uk/esploro/outputs/report/The-Rise-of-the-Platform-Enterprise-A-Global-Sur-vey/99516671002346 (accessed August 2023).

2 Gurley, B. (2012) 'All markets are not created equal: 10 factors to consider when evaluating digital marketplaces'. *Above the Crowd*. Available at: https://abovethecrowd.com/2012/11/13/all-markets-are-not-created-equal-10-factors-to-consider-when-evaluating-digital-marketplaces/ (accessed August 2023).

3 Pavlou, P. A. and Gefen, D. (2004) 'Building effective online marketplaces with institution-based trust'. *Information Systems Research*, 15(1), 37–59.

4 Jin, L. and Chen, A. (2018) 'What's next for marketplace startups?' Available at: https://a16z.com/2018/11/27/services-marketplaces-service-economy-evolution-whats-next/ (accessed August 2023).

5 Dealroom.co. (2020) 'Online marketplaces entering the next phase'. Available at: https://dealroom.co/uploaded/2020/06/Marketplaces-2020-vFINAL.pdf (accessed August 2023); Coolica, D., Barros, B., Jordan, J., Chen, A., Jin, L. and Murrow, L. (2021) *A16zMarketplace100*. Available at: https://info.a16z.com/rs/382-JZB-798/images/marketplace-100-2021.pdf (accessed August 2023); Hockenmaier, D. (2021) 'The future of marketplaces: Coordination, capital, and creativity'. Available at: https://www.danhock.com/posts/the-future-of-marketplaces (accessed August 2023); Horev, G. (2020) 'Sequencing business models: The types of marketplaces'. Available at: https://www.giladhorev.com/posts/sequencing-business-models-the-types-of-marketplaces (accessed August 2023); Cicero, S. (2021) 'Seeking sustainable growth in platform-marketplaces'. Available at: https://stories.platformdesigntoolkit.com/seeking-sustainable-growth-in-platform-marketplaces-cc1d5112cec4 (accessed August 2023).

6 Gawer, A. and Cusumano, M. A. (2014) 'Industry platforms and ecosystem innovation'. *Journal of Product Innovation Management*, 31(3), 417–433.

7 Wulf, J. and Blohm, I. (2020) 'Fostering value creation with digital platforms: A unified theory of the application programming interface design'. *Journal of Management Information Systems*, 37(1), 251–281; Dal Bianco, V., Myllärniemi, V., Komssi, M. and Raatikainen, M. (2014) 'The role of platform boundary resources in software ecosystems: A case study'. *2014 IEEE/IFIP Conference on Software Architecture*, Sydney, NSW, Australia, pp. 11–20.

8 Sandoval, K. (2016) 'What is the difference between an API and an SDK?' Available at: https://nordicapis.com/what-is-the-difference-between-an-api-and-an-sdk/ (accessed August 2023).

9 Wulf, J. and Blohm, I. (2020) 'Fostering value creation with digital platforms: A unified theory of the application programming interface design'. *Journal of Management Information Systems*, 37(1), 251–281; Dal Bianco, V., Myllärniemi, V., Komssi, M. and Raatikainen, M. (2014) 'The role of platform boundary resources in software ecosystems: A case study'. *2014 IEEE/IFIP Conference on Software Architecture*, Sydney, NSW, Australia, pp. 11–20.

10 Foerderer, J., Kude, T., Schuetz, S. W. and Heinzl, A. (2019) 'Knowledge boundaries in enterprise software platform development: Antecedents and consequences for platform governance'. *Information Systems Journal*, 29(1), 119–144; Gawer, A. (2021) 'Digital platforms' boundaries: The interplay of firm scope, platform sides, and digital interfaces'. *Long Range Planning*, 54(5), 102045.

11 Ghazawneh, A. and Henfridsson, O. (2013) 'Balancing platform control and external contribution in third-party development: The boundary resources model'. *Information Systems Journal*, 23(2), 173–192.

12 O'Mahony, S. and Karp, R. (2022) 'From proprietary to collective governance: How do platform participation strategies evolve?' *Strategic Management Journal*, 43(3), 530–562.

13 Huber, T. L., Kude, T. and Dibbern, J. (2017) 'Governance practices in platform ecosystems: Navigating tensions between cocreated value and governance costs'. *Information Systems Research*, 28(3), 563–584.

14 Zhang, Y., Li, J. and Tong, T. W. (2022) 'Platform governance matters: How platform gatekeeping affects knowledge sharing among complementors'. *Strategic Management Journal*, 43(3), 599–626.

15 Cusumano, M. A., Yoffie, D. B. and Gawer, A. (2020) 'The future of platforms'. *MIT Sloan Management Review*, 61(3), 46–54.

16 Vouillon, C. (2019) 'A landscape of the major SaaS app stores'. *Medium*. Available at: https://medium.com/point-nine-news/a-landscape-of-the-major-saas-app-stores-4c48b103e69b (accessed August 2023).

17 Markfort, L., Arzt, A., Kögler, P., Jung, S., Gebauer, H., Haugk, S., Leyh, C. and Wortmann, F. (2022) 'Patterns of business model innovation for advancing IoT platforms'. *Journal of Service*

Management, 33(1), 70–96; Iansiti, M. and Lakhani, K. R. (2014) 'Digital ubiquity: How connections, sensors, and data are revolutionizing business'. *Harvard Business Review*, 92(11).

18 Porter, M. E. and Heppelmann, J. E. (2014) 'Smart, connected products are transforming competition'. *Harvard Business Review*, 11, 64–88; Porter, M. E. and Heppelmann, J. E. (2015) 'How smart, connected products are transforming companies'. *Harvard Business Review*, 10, 96–112.

19 Parker, G., Van Alstyne, M. and Choudary, S. (2016) *Platform Revolution: How Networked Markets Are Transforming the Economy and How to Make Them Work for You*. New York: W. W. Norton & Company; Porter, M. E. and Heppelmann, J. E. (2014) 'Smart, connected products are transforming competition'. *Harvard Business Review*, 11, 64–88.

20 Jung, S., Wortmann, F., Bronner, W. and Gassmann, O. (2021) 'Platform economy: Converging IoT platforms and ecosystems'. In O. Gassmann and F. Ferrandina (Eds.), *Connected Business: Create Value in a Networked Economy* (pp. 35–54). Springer, Cham; Porter, M. E. and Heppelmann, J. E. (2014) 'Smart, connected products are transforming competition'. *Harvard Business Review*, 11, 64–88; Porter, M. E. and Heppelmann, J. E. (2015) 'How smart, connected products are transforming companies'. *Harvard Business Review*, 10, 96–112.

21 Mercedes-Benz. (2023) 'Architects of desire: Coding the future of Mercedes-Benz'. Available at: https://group.mercedes-benz.com/dokumente/investoren/praesentationen/mbsu-os-2023-presentation-markus-schaefer-magnus-oestberg.pdf (accessed August 2023).

Chapter 3

1 Hodapp, D., Hawlitschek, F., Wortmann, F., Lang, M. and Gassmann, O. (2022) 'Key lessons from Bosch for incumbent firms entering the platform economy', *MIS Quarterly Executive*, 21(2); Boudreau, K. and Lakhani, K. R. (2008) 'How to manage outside innovation'. *MIT Sloan Management Review*, 50(4), 69–76.

2 Hodapp, D., Hawlitschek, F., Wortmann, F., Lang, M. and Gassmann, O. (2022) 'Key lessons from Bosch for incumbent firms entering the platform economy', *MIS Quarterly Executive*, 21(2).

3 Hodapp, D., Hawlitschek, F., Wortmann, F., Lang, M. and Gassmann, O. (2022) 'Key lessons from Bosch for incumbent firms entering the platform economy', *MIS Quarterly Executive*, 21(2).

4 Porter, M. (1985) *Competitive Advantage*. New York: The Free Press.

5 Cusumano, M. A., Yoffie, D. B. and Gawer, A. (2020) 'The future of platforms'. *MIT Sloan Management Review*, 61(3), 46–54.

6 Statista. 'Amazon's share of online retail sales in selected regions as of September 2020'. Available at: https://www.statista.com/statistics/1183515/amazon-market-share-region-worldwide/ (accessed August 2023).

7 Hagiu, A. (2014) 'Strategic decisions for multisided platforms'. *MIT Sloan Management Review*, 55(2), 4–13; Dealroom.co. (2020) 'Online marketplaces entering the next phase'. Available at: https://dealroom.co/uploaded/2020/06/Marketplaces-2020-vFINAL.pdf (accessed August 2023); Van Alstyne, M. W., Parker, G. and Choudary, S. P. (2016). 'Pipelines, platforms, and the new rules of strategy'. *Harvard Business Review*, 94(4), 54–62.

8 Eisenmann, T., Parker, G. and Van Alstyne, M. (2009) 'Opening platforms: How, when and why?' In A. Gawer (Ed.), *Platforms, Markets and Innovation* (pp. 131–162). Glos, UK: Edward Elgar Publishing; Hein, A., Schreieck, M., Riasanow, T., Setzke, D. S., Wiesche, M., Böhm, M. and Krcmar, H. (2020) 'Digital platform ecosystems'. *Electronic Markets*, 30(1), 87–98; Gawer, A. (2021) 'Digital platforms' boundaries: The interplay of firm scope, platform sides, and digital interfaces'. *Long Range Planning*, 54(5), 102045.

9 Hein, A., Schreieck, M., Riasanow, T., Setzke, D. S., Wiesche, M., Böhm, M. and Krcmar, H. (2020) 'Digital platform ecosystems'. *Electronic Markets*, 30(1), 87–98.

10 Parker, G., Van Alstyne, M. and Choudary, S. (2016) *Platform Revolution: How Networked Markets Are Transforming the Economy and How to Make Them Work for You*. New York: W. W. Norton & Company.

11 Open Handset Alliance. (2007) 'Industry leaders announce open platform for mobile devices'. Available at: http://www.openhandsetalliance.com/press_110507.html (accessed August 2023).

12 Parker, G., Van Alstyne, M. and Choudary, S. (2016) *Platform Revolution: How Networked Markets are Transforming the Economy and How to Make Them Work for You*. New York: W. W. Norton & Company.

13 Karhu, K. and Ritala, P. (2021) 'Slicing the cake without baking it: Opportunistic platform entry strategies in digital markets'. *Long Range Planning*, 54(5), 101988.

14 Papadopoulos, T. (2021) 'A timeline of MySpace, your ex-social medium'. Available at: https://thanasispapadopoulos.medium.com/a-timeline-of-myspace-your-ex-social-medium-b2e29fa9aa18 (accessed June 2023); Statista. (2021) 'Facebook keeps on growing'. Available at: https://www.statista.com/chart/10047/facebooks-monthly-active-users/ (accessed June 2023).

15 Eisenmann, T., Parker, G. and Van Alstyne, M. (2011) 'Platform envelopment'. *Strategic Management Journal*, 32(12), 1270–1285; Gawer, A. (2021) 'Digital platforms' boundaries: The interplay of firm scope, platform sides, and digital interfaces'. *Long Range Planning*, 54(5), 102045.

16 Trischler, M., Meier, P. and Trabucchi, D. (2021) 'Digital platform tactics: How to implement platform strategy over time'. *Journal of Business Models*, 9(1), 67–76.

17 Statista. (2023) 'PayPal – statistics & facts'. Available at: https://www.statista.com/topics/2411/paypal/#topicOverview (accessed January 2023).

Part Two

Chapter 1

1 Porter, M. (1985) *Competitive Advantage*. New York: The Free Press.

2 Jeff Bezos, The Power of Invention, amazon.com. Retreived from https://s2.q4cdn.com/299287126/files/doc_financials/annual/letter.PDF

3 Ordanini, A., Miceli, L., Pizetti, M. and Parasuman, A. (2011) 'Crowd-funding: Transforming customers into investors through innovative service platforms'. *Journal of Service Management*, 22(4).

4 Statista Research Department. (2023) 'Kickstarter – statistics & facts'. Available at: https://www.statista.com/topics/2102/kickstarter/#dossierSummary (accessed June 2023).

5 The story of Patreon. Available at: https://www.patreon.com/en-GB/about (accessed June 2023).

6 Crowdfunding.de (2020) '"Unser Mut und die ständige Experimentierfreude haben sich über zehn Jahre ausgezahlt" – Interview zu 10 Jahren Startnext' [Translated from German, written interview]. Available at: https://www.crowdfunding.de/magazin/interview-zu-10-jahre-startnext/ (accessed August 2023).

7 Gassmann, O. and Enkel, E. (2004) 'Towards a theory of open innovation: Three core process archetypes'. R&D Management Conference (RADMA).

8 Allio, R. (2004) 'CEO Interview: The InnoCentive model of open innovation'. *Strategy & Leadership*, 32(4). Available at: https://www.emerald.com/insight/content/doi/10.1108/10878570410547643/full/html (accessed August 2023).

9 Chesbrough, H. (2003) 'The era of open innovation'. *MIT Sloan Management Review*, 44(3), 35–41; Chesbrough, H. (2010) 'Business model innovation: Opportunities and barriers'. *Long Range Planning*, 43(2–3), 354–363; Enkel, E., Gassmann, O. and Chesbrough, H. (2009) 'Open R&D and open innovation: Exploring the phenomenon'. *R&D Management*, 39(4), 311–316.

10 Medal, A. (2014) 'The story of how GitHub supplied software its teeth'. Available at: https://www.linkedin.com/pulse/20141029195334-25909192-the-story-of-how-github-supplied-software-its-teeth/ (accessed August 2023).

11 https://app.playtestcloud.com/signup (accessed June 2023).

12 (2023) 'Hugging Face collaborates with Microsoft to launch Hugging Face model catalog on Azure'. Available at: https://huggingface.co/blog/hugging-face-endpoints-on-azure (accessed August 2023).

13 Iansiti, M. and Lakhani, K. R. (2014) 'Digital ubiquity: How connections, sensors, and data are revolutionizing business'. *Harvard Business Review*, 92(11).

14 EuroSecurity TV aktuell. (2018) 'SAST, neues Startup der Bosch Gruppe geht an den Start' [Translated from German, video interview]. Available at: https://www.youtube.com/watch?v=mY8Ri1oNB2s (accessed August 2023).

15 365FarmNet. https://www.365farmnet.com/en/365partner/ (accessed June 2023).

16 Jaeschke, H. (2020) [Translated from German, audio interview]. Available at: https://anchor.fm/hauke-jaeschke/episodes/Agrora-6---Maximilian-von-Lbbecke-von-365FarmNet-AgTech-Avantgarde-Wie-365FarmNet-Landwirte-untersttzt--Betriebsprozesse-zu-digitalisieren-und-dadurch-profitabler-zu-werden-eietnd (accessed August 2023).

17 Figure adapted from Ng, A. (2018) 'AI transformation playbook: How to lead your company into the AI era'. Available at: https://landing.ai/wp-content/uploads/2020/05/LandingAI_Transformation_Playbook_11-19.pdf (accessed August 2023).

18 Parker, G., Van Alstyne, M. and Choudary, S. (2016) *Platform Revolution: How Networked Markets Are Transforming the Economy and How to Make Them Work for You*. New York: W. W. Norton & Company.

19 Bardin, N. (2018) 'Keeping cities moving – How Waze works'. *Medium*. Available at: https://medium.com/@noambardin/keeping-cities-moving-how-waze-works-4aad066c7bfa (accessed June 2023).

20 Levy-Weiss, G. (2021) 'The insider story of Waze'. Available at: https://www.nfx.com/post/the-insider-story-of-waze (accessed August 2023).

21 Goedegebuure, D. (2016) 'You are helping Google AI image recognition'. *Medium*. Available at: https://medium.com/@thenextcorner/you-are-helping-google-ai-image-recognition-b24d89372b7e (accessed August 2023); Malley, O. (2018) 'Captcha if you can: How you've been training AI for years without realising it'. *Techradar*. Available at: https://www.techradar.com/news/captcha-if-you-can-how-youve-been-training-ai-for-years-without-realising-it (accessed August 2023).

22 Einav, L., Farronato, C. and Levin, J. (2016) 'Peer-to-peer markets'. *Annual Review of Economics*, 8, 615–635; Pavlou, P. A. and Gefen, D. (2004) 'Building effective online marketplaces with institution-based trust'. *Information Systems Research*, 15(1), 37–59.

23 Pavlou, P. A. and Gefen, D. (2004) 'Building effective online marketplaces with institution-based trust'. *Information Systems Research*, 15(1), 37–59.

24 Teubner, T. and Dann, D. (2018) 'How platforms build trust'. *SSRN*. Available at: https://ssrn.com/abstract=3266472 (accessed August 2023).

25 MIPIM world. (2015) 'Meet the players – Allianz and Airbnb discuss the sharing economy'. Available at: https://www.youtube.com/watch?v=AJ40c4X8ahM (accessed August 2023).

26 Wind Turbine.com "About Us", Retrieved from https://en.wind-turbine.com/impressum.html

27 Futurebrains. (2022) 'Bernd Weidmann über Community Building im B2B' [translated from German, video interview] Available at: https://www.youtube.com/watch?v=TJwHFtrkjWc&t=174s (accessed August 2023).

28 Casadesus-Masanell, R. and Namrata, A. (2017) 'Jumia Nigeria: From retail to marketplace (A)'. Harvard Business School Case 718-401.

29 Chen, M., Mao, S. and Liu, Y. (2014) 'Big data: A survey'. *Mobile Networks and Applications*, 19(2), 171–209.

30 Bergman, R., Abbas, A. E., Jung, S., Werker, C. and de Reuver, M. (2022) 'Business model archetypes for data marketplaces in the automotive industry'. *Electronic Markets*, 32(2), 747–765.

31 Budimir, M. (2021) 'Bosch Rexroth's crtlX store offers automation and control apps'. Available at: https://www.motioncontroltips.com/bosch-rexroths-ctrlx-store-offers-automation-and-control-apps/ (accessed August 2023).

32 The history of Uber, Newsroom, Uber. Retrieved from https://www.uber.com/newsroom/history/ (accessed June 2023).

33 Kren, S. (2019) 'Die digitale Spedition' [translated from German, written interview]. Available at: https://www.it-zoom.de/mobile-business/e/die-digitale-spedition-24457/ (accessed August 2023).

34 Wermke, I. (2023) 'Digitale Plattform für die Baubranche – Schüttflix verdoppelt Umsatz'. *Handelsblatt*. Available at: https://www.handelsblatt.com/technik/thespark/bau-start-up-digitale-plattform-fuer-die-baubranche-schuettflix-verdoppelt-umsatz/29096280.html (accessed June 2023).

35 Copley, C. (2014) 'Mila sees big firms using web to outsource customer support'. Available at: https://www.reuters.com/article/us-mila-sharingeconomy-idUSBREA2U0UK20140331 (accessed August 2023).

36 Stock Exchange inc , Retrieved from https://stackexchange.com/sites?view=list#questions

37 Statista. 'Daily time spent on social networking by internet users worldwide from 2013 to 2023'. Available at: https://www.statista.com/statistics/433871/daily-social-media-usage-worldwide/ (accessed August 2023).

38 Langley, P. and Rieple, A. (2021) 'Incumbents' capabilities to win in a digitized world: The case of the fashion industry'. *Technological Forecasting and Social Change*, 167, 1–13.

39 PatientsLikeMe"About Us", Retrieved from https://www.patientslikeme.com/about

40 Howell, J. (2020) '"Interns helped save my firm"'. *bbc.com*. Available at: https://www.bbc.com/news/business-55229148 (accessed June 2023).

41 Inkitt. (2017) 'Ali Albazaz, founder and CEO, Inkitt, on BBC' [video interview]. Available at: https://www.youtube.com/watch?v=cHuPshSqTQE (accessed August 2023).

42 Coursera inc, Retrieved from https://www.coursera.org/about/partners

43 Littleton, C. (2021) 'How MasterClass CEO David Rogier brought star power to online learning'. *Variety*. Available at: https://variety.com/2021/digital/news/masterclass-classes-covid-ceo-david-rogier-1234951028/ (accessed August 2023).

44 'See how Fiverr uses Zendesk Support to serve its thriving marketplace'. Available at: https://www.zendesk.com/customer/fiverr/ (accessed August 2023).

45 uTest, Inc. 'uTest: The alternative to outsourced software testing'. Available at: https://dsimg.ubm-us.net/envelope/135123/301372/1376402375_uTest_eBook_Crowdsourcing_vs_Outsourced_Testing.pdf (accessed June 2023).

46 Warwick, M. (2021) 'Digital banking service M-Pesa is now the biggest fintech platform in Africa'. *TelecomTV*. Available at: https://www.telecomtv.com/content/digital-platforms-services/branchless-banking-service-m-pesa-is-now-the-biggest-fintech-platform-in-africa-42322/amp/ (accessed June 2023).

47 Vodafone. (2022) 'M-Pesa – Africa's leading fintech platform – marks 15 years of transforming lives'. Available at: https://www.vodafone.com/news/inclusion/mpesa-marks-15-years (accessed June 2023).

48 Warwick, M. (2021) 'Digital banking service M-Pesa now the biggest fintech platform in Africa'. Telecom TV. Available at: https://www.telecomtv.com/content/digital-platforms-services/branchless-banking-service-m-pesa-is-now-the-biggest-fintech-platform-in-africa-42322/ (accessed August 2023).

49 Klein, G., Shtudiner, Z. and Zwilling, M. (2023) 'Why do peer-to-peer (P2P) lending platforms fail? The gap between P2P lenders' preferences and the platforms' intentions'. *Electronic Commerce Research*, 23(2), 709–738.

50 Funding Societies. (2021) 'Funding Societies: Survey reveals 72% of MSMEs in SEA boosted revenue with digital financing'. Available at: https://fundingsocieties.com/economic-impact-survey (accessed June 2023).

51 Funding Societies. (2021) 'Funding Societies: Survey reveals 72% of MSMEs in SEA boosted revenue with digital financing'. Available at: https://fundingsocieties.com/economic-impact-survey#:~:text=Funding%20Societies%20%7C%20Modalku%20is%20the,Thailand%2C%20and%20registered%20in%20Malaysia (accessed August 2023).

52 (2022). 'Seedmatch Interview – Die bisherigen Erfolge soqie kritisch gesehene Fundings der Anleger' [translated from German, written interview]. Available at: https://crowdinvesting-compact.de/journal/seedmatch-interview_2022-02/ (accessed August 2023).

53 Chnar, M. and Subhi, Z. (2021) 'Sufficient comparison among cloud computing services: IaaS, PaaS, and SaaS: A review'. *International Journal of Science and Business*, 5(2), 17–30; Giessmann, A. and Stanoevska-Slabeva, K. (2013) 'Business models of platform as a service (PaaS) providers: Current state and future directions'. *Journal of Information Technology Theory and Application*, 13(4), 4.

54 Amazon Web Services Launches, March 14, 2006. Retrieved from [Quote on para. 1] https://press.aboutamazon.com/news-releases/news-release-details/amazon-web-services-launches-amazon-s3-simple-storage-service (accessed August 2023).

55 Long, K. A. (2021) 'In the 15 years since its launch, Amazon Web Services transformed how companies do business'. *The Seattle Times*. 13 March, 2021. Available at: https://www.seattletimes.com/business/amazon/in-the-15-years-since-its-launch-amazon-web-services-has-transformed-how-companies-do-business/ (accessed August 2023).

56 Long, K. K. (2021) 'In the 15 years since its launch, Amazon Web Services transformed how companies do business'.*TechXplore*. Available at: https://techxplore.com/news/2021-03-years-amazon-web-companies-business.html (accessed August 2023).

57 Chnar, M. and Subhi, Z. (2021) 'Sufficient comparison among cloud computing services: IaaS, PaaS, and SaaS: A review'. *International Journal of Science and Business*, 5(2), 17–30; Giessmann, A. and Stanoevska-Slabeva, K. (2013) 'Business models of platform as a service (PaaS) providers: Current state and future directions'. *Journal of Information Technology Theory and Application*, 13(4), 4.

58 Reminnyi, S. (2021) 'UiPath marketplace: Enhanced for the enterprise'. UiPath. Available at: https://www.uipath.com/blog/product-and-updates/uipath-marketplace-enhanced-for-enterprise (accessed August 2023).

59 Worsham, A. (2008) 'Interview with James Lindenbaum, CEO of Heroku'. sazbean.com. Available at: https://sazbean.com/2008/05/29/interview-with-james-lindenbaum-ceo-of-heroku/ (accessed August 2023).

60 Casadesus-Masanell, R. and Llanes, G. (2015) 'Investment incentives in open-source and proprietary two-sided platforms'. *Journal of Economics & Management Strategy*, 24(2), 306–324; West, J. (2003) 'How open is open enough? Melding proprietary and open source platform strategies'. *Research Policy*, 32(7), 1259–1285; O'Mahony, S. and Karp, R. (2022) 'From proprietary to collective governance: How do platform participation strategies evolve?' *Strategic Management Journal*, 43(3), 530–562.

61 Levine, P. and Li, J. (2019) 'Open source: From community to commercialization'. *A16z*. Available at: https://a16z.com/2019/10/04/open-source-from-community-to-commercialization/ (accessed August 2023).

62 Cassel, D. (2021) 'Linus Torvalds on why open source solves the biggest problems'. *The New Stack*. Available at: https://thenewstack.io/linus-torvalds-on-why-open-source-solves-the-biggest-problems/ (accessed August 2023).

Chapter 2

1 Cusumano, M. A., Yoffie, D. B. and Gawer, A. (2020) 'The future of platforms'. *MIT Sloan Management Review*, 61(3), 46–54.

2 Lutwak, T. and Chung, Y. (2013) 'The lion, the platform, and the lesson'. *a16z.com*. Available at: https://a16z.com/2013/12/18/the-lion-the-platform-and-the-lesson/ (accessed August 2023).

3 Gassmann, O., Frankenberger, K. and Choudury, M. (2020) *The Business Model Navigator: The Strategies Behind the Most Successful Companies* (2nd ed.). FT Publishing.

4 By 2036 – Alibaba wants 2 billion customers, 10 million businesses, 100 million staff, Mumbrella Asia, 2018. Retreived from https://www.mumbrella.asia/2018/10/by-2036-alibaba-is-aiming-for-2-billion-customers-10-million-profitable-businesses-and-100-million-staff [letter to shareholders] (accessed August 2023).

5 Schilling, M. (2013) *Strategic Management of Technological Innovation* (4th ed.). New York: McGraw-Hill.

6 Currier, J. (2019) '19 tactics to solve the chicken-or-egg problem and grow your marketplace'. Available at: https://www.nfx.com/post/19-marketplace-tactics-for-overcoming-the-chicken-or-egg-problem (accessed August 2023).

7 Gerhardt, J. (2022) 'Instafreight raises US$40 million'. Available at: https://www.startbase.com/news/instafreight-sammelt-40-millionen-us-dollar-ein/ (accessed August 2023).

8 Akerlof, Stiglitz and Spence received in 2001 the Nobel prize for their work on asymmetric information, e.g. 'The market for "lemons": Quality uncertainty and the market mechanism' is one of Akerlof's seminal papers.

9 Teubner, T. and Dann, D. (2018) 'How platforms build trust'. *SSRN*. Available at: https://ssrn.com/abstract=3266472 (accessed August 2023).

10 Jacobides, M. G., Sundararajan, A. and Van Alstyne, M. (2019) 'Platforms and ecosystems: Enabling the digital economy'. In WEF Briefing Paper. Available at: https://www3.weforum.org/docs/WEF_Digital_Platforms_and_Ecosystems_2019.pdf (accessed August 2023).

11 Interview of Christian Bertermann by Stephan Knieps in *Wirtschaftswoche* (1 December, 2020). Available at: https://www.wiwo.de/erfolg/gruender/auto1-mitgruender-christian-bertermann-im-jahr-2000-hat-man-ja-auch-ueberlegt-ob-jemand-ein-buch-online-kaufen-wuerde-/26654048-2.html (accessed August 2023).

12 Vidra, E. (2009) 'Utest defines the future of quality assurance: CEO interview'. Available at: https://www.vccafe.com/2009/04/08/utest-defines-the-future-of-quality-assurance-ceo-interview/ (accessed August 2023).

13 Teubner, T. and Dann, D. (2018) 'How platforms build trust. *SSRN*. Available at: https://ssrn.com/abstract=3266472 (accessed August 2023).

14 Corporate Valley. (2013) 'Exclusive interview with Pierre Omidyar – Founder of eBay Inc.' Available at: https://www.youtube.com/watch?v=Yy-p5i4Vimo (accessed August 2023).

15 Butcher, M. (2022) 'As our populations age, this startup is turning li-in care into a gig-economy platform'. Available at: https://techcrunch.com/2022/08/23/as-our-populations-age-this-startup-is-turning-live-in-care-into-a-gig-economy-platform/ (accessed August 2023).

16 Achilles Information. (2021) 'International Finance Corporation selects Achilles Information to deliver digital platform'. Available at: https://www.achilles.com/media-centre/press-release/ifc-selects-achilles-western-balkans/ (accessed August 2023).

17 Jin, L. and Chen, A. (2018) 'What's next for marketplace startups?' Available at: https://a16z.com/2018/11/27/services-marketplaces-service-economy-evolution-whats-next/ (accessed August 2023).

18 Oates, G. (2016) 'Airbnb CTO and 3 tech CTOs discuss the digital platform economy at Davos'. Available at: https://skift.com/2016/01/31/airbnb-cto-and-3-tech-ceos-discuss-the-digital-platform-economy-at-davos/ (accessed August 2023).

19 McDonald, J. (2022) 'Fitbit expands enterprise ambitions with Google Cloud-powered software platform'. *Tech Brew*. Available at: https://www.emergingtechbrew.com/stories/2022/10/18/fitbit-expands-enterprise-ambitions-with-google-cloud-powered-software-platform (accessed August 2023).

20 Bittner, C. (2020) 'Von APIs zu Ökosystemen: Neue Chancen für Banken'. *Der Bank Blog*. Available at: https://www.der-bank-blog.de/api-oekosysteme-commerzbank/digital-banking/37666255/ (accessed August 2023).

21 Johnsen, M. (2016) 'The long game: Fitbit positioning to be key digital health partner'. Available at: https://drugstorenews.com/news/long-game-fitbit-positioning-be-key-digital-health-partner (accessed August 2023).

22 Wulf, J. and Blohm, I. (2020) 'Fostering value creation with digital platforms: A unified theory of the application programming interface design'. *Journal of Management Information Systems*, 37(1), 251–281.

23 Kogut, B. and Metiu, A. (2001) 'Open-source software development and distributed innovation'. *Oxford Review of Economic Policy*, 17(2), 248–264; Walli, S. (2016) 'There is NO open source business model'. *Medium*. https://medium.com/@stephenrwalli/there-is-no-open-source-business-model-cdc4cc20238 (accessed August 2023); Boudreau, K. and Lakhani, K. R. (2008) 'How to manage outside innovation'. *MIT Sloan Management Review*, 50(4), 69–76.

24 Starting an Open Source Project, The Linux Foundation. Retreived from https://www.linuxfoundation.org/resources/open-source-guides/starting-an-open-sourceproject (accessed August 2023).

25 Digital Commerce 360. (2021) 'A European chemicals marketplace eyes the U.S. market'. Available at: https://www.digitalcommerce360.com/2021/03/29/a-european-chemicals-marketplace-plans-a-gradual-u-s-rollout/ (accessed June 2023).

26 Tiwana, A. (2014) *Platform Ecosystems: Aligning Architecture, Governance, and Strategy*. Burlington, MA: Morgan Kaufmann; Eisenmann, T., Parker, G. and Van Alstyne, M. (2011) 'Platform envelopment'. *Strategic Management Journal*, 32(12), 1270–1285.

27 Scherkamp, H. (2019) 'Warum Nutzer diesem Gründer Geld zahlen? Um ihre Nachbarn kennenzulernen' [translated from German, written interview]. Available at: https://www.businessinsider.de/gruenderszene/business/christian-vollmann-nebenan-de-interview/ (accessed August 2023).

28 Zhu, F. and Iansiti, M. (2019) 'Why some platforms thrive and others don't'. *Harvard Business Review*, 97(1), 118–125.

29 Eisenmann, T., Parker, G. and Van Alstyne, M. (2006) 'Strategies for two-sided markets'. *Harvard Business Review*, 84(10), 92–101.

30 David, R. (2015) Trouble selling grandma's cards led to $1 billion start-up'. Bloomberg. Available at: https://www.bloomberg.com/news/articles/2015-07-06/trouble-selling-grandma-s-cars-sowed-seed-for-1-billion-startup#xj4y7vzkg (accessed June 2023).

31 Walt, V. (2022) 'It's expensive to be poor. This CEO wants to reduce "antiquated" bank fees and wait times'. *Time*. Available at: https://time.com/6132715/dan-schulman-ceo-paypal-interview/ (accessed August 2023).

32 Buchak, G., Matvos, G., Piskorski, T. and Seru, A. (2020) 'iBuyers: Liquidity in real estate markets?' *SSRN*, March, 1–81; Helgaker, E., Oust, A. and Pollestad, A. J. (2022) 'Adverse selection in iBuyer business models – don't buy lemons!' *Zeitschrift für Immobilienökonomie*.

33 Homag Group AG. (2017) 'World premiere: The digital platform for the wood industry's value chain.' Available at: https://www.homag.com/en/news-events/news/article/world-premiere-the-digital-platform-for-the-wood-industrys-value-chain (accessed February 2023).

34 Schenker, J. L. (2020) 'Interview of the week: Joerg Hellwig'. Available at: https://innovator.news/interview-of-the-week-joerg-hellwig-26637edb59a3 (accessed August 2023).

35 Devine, D. A., Dugan, C. B., Semaca, N. D. and Speicher, K. J. (2001) 'Building enduring consortia'. *McKinsey Quarterly*, 8, 26–33.

36 Businesswire. (2022) 'Richemont, FARFETCH and Alabbar cement partnership to advance the digitalization of the luxury industry'. Available at: https://www.businesswire.com/news/home/20220823005877/en/Richemont-FARFETCH-and-Alabbar-cement-Partnership-to-advance-the-Digitalisation-of-the-Luxury-Industry (accessed June 2023).

37 Grant, R. (2013) 'GE invests $105M in Pivotal to build the Industrial Internet'. Available at: https://venturebeat.com/entrepreneur/ge-invests-105m-in-pivotal-to-build-the-industrial-internet/ (accessed June 2023).

38 Lardinois, F. (2018) 'Cloud Foundry Foundation looks east as Alibaba joins as a gold member'. Available at: https://techcrunch.com/2018/04/18/cloud-foundry-foundation-looks-east-as-alibaba-joins-as-a-gold-member/ (accessed June 2023).

39 Hein, A., Schreieck, M., Riasanow, T., Setzke, D. S., Wiesche, M., Böhm, M. and Krcmar, H. (2020) 'Digital platform ecosystems'. *Electronic Markets*, 30(1), 87–98.

40 (2022) 'Richemont, FARFETCH and Alabbar cement partnership to advance the digitalisation of the luxury industry'. Available at: https://www.richemont.com/en/home/media/press-releases-and-news/richemont-farfetch-and-alabbar-cement-partnership-to-advance-the-digitalisation-of-the-luxury-industry/ (accessed August 2023).

41 Zutshi, A., Grilo, A. and Nodehi, T. (2021) 'The value proposition of blockchain technologies and its impact on digital platforms'. *Computers & Industrial Engineering*, 155.

42 The Linux Foundation. 'Starting an open source project'. Available at: https://www.linuxfoundation.org/resources/open-source-guides/starting-an-open-source-project?hsLang=en (accessed June 2023).

43 Hein, A., Schreieck, M., Riasanow, T., Setzke, D. S., Wiesche, M., Böhm, M. and Krcmar, H. (2020) 'Digital platform ecosystems'. *Electronic Markets*, 30(1), 87–98.

44 Urgo, J., Lestan, M. and Khoriaty, A. (2017) 'District0X network'. Available at: https://district0x.io/docs/district0x-whitepaper.pdf (accessed August 2023).

45 Dealroom.co. (2020) 'Online marketplaces entering the next phase'. Available at: https://dealroom.co/uploaded/2020/06/Marketplaces-2020-vFINAL.pdf (accessed August 2023).

46 Cusumano, M. A., Yoffie, D. B. and Gawer, A. (2020) 'The future of platforms'. *MIT Sloan Management Review*, 61(3), 46–54.

47 Jin, L. and Chen, A. (2018) 'What's next for marketplace startups?' Available at: https://a16z.com/2018/11/27/services-marketplaces-service-economy-evolution-whats-next/ (accessed August 2023).

48 Oates, G. (2016) 'Airbnb CTO and 3 tech CTOs discuss the digital platform economy at Davos'. Available at: https://skift.com/2016/01/31/airbnb-cto-and-3-tech-ceos-discuss-the-digital-platform-economy-at-davos/ (accessed August 2023).

49 Dealroom.co. (2020) 'Online marketplaces entering the next phase'. Available at: https://dealroom.co/uploaded/2020/06/Marketplaces-2020-vFINAL.pdf; Jin, L. and Chen, A. (2018) 'What's next for marketplace startups?' Available at: https://a16z.com/2018/11/27/services-marketplaces-service-economy-evolution-whats-next/ (accessed August 2023).

50 Buchak, G., Matvos, G., Piskorski, T. and Seru, A. (2020) 'iBuyers: Liquidity in real estate markets?' *SSRN*, March, 1–81.

51 (2022) 'An interview with Opendoor CEO Eric Wu about building a marketplace in a real estate slowdown'. Available at: https://stratechery.com/2022/an-interview-with-opendoor-ceo-eric-wu-about-building-a-marketplace-in-a-real-estate-slowdown/ (accessed August 2023).

52 Stokel-Walker, C. (2021). Why Zillow couldn't make algorithmic house pricing work. *Wired*. Available at: https://www.wired.com/story/zillow-ibuyer-real-estate/ (accessed June 2023).

53 E-commerce is not a platform business model, but can be seen as a complementary one.

54 Gassmann, O., Frankenberger, K. and Choudury, M. (2020) *The Business Model Navigator: The Strategies Behind the Most Successful Companies* (2nd ed.). FT Publishing.

55 Alaei, A. M., Taleizadeh, A. A. and Rabbani, M. (2022) 'Marketplace, reseller, or web-store channel: The impact of return policy and cross-channel spillover from marketplace to web-store'. *Journal of Retailing and Consumer Services*, 65, 1–17.

56 Direct to customer is not a platform business model, but can be seen as a complementary one. See also Gassmann, O., Frankenberger, K. and Choudury, M. (2020) *The Business Model Navigator: The Strategies Behind the Most Successful Companies* (2nd ed.). FT Publishing.

57 Albrecht, C. (2020) 'Beyond Meat now sells directly to consumers'. The Spoon. Available at: https://thespoon.tech/beyond-meat-now-sells-directly-to-consumers/ (accessed June 2023).

58 Eisenmann, T., Parker, G. and Van Alstyne, M. (2009) 'Opening platforms: How, when and why?' In A. Gawer (Ed.), *Platforms, Markets and Innovation* (pp. 131–162). Glos, UK: Edward Elgar Publishing; Hein, A., Weking, J., Schreieck, M., Wiesche, M., Böhm, M. and Krcmar, H. (2019) 'Value co-creation practices in business-to-business platform ecosystems'. *Electronic Markets*, 29(3), 503–518; Hein, A., Schreieck, M., Riasanow, T., Setzke, D. S., Wiesche, M., Böhm, M. and Krcmar, H. (2020) 'Digital platform ecosystems'. *Electronic Markets*, 30(1), 87–98.

59 Swartz, J. (2022) 'Apple has spent decades building its walled garden. It may be starting to crack'. Available at: https://www.marketwatch.com/story/apple-has-spent-decades-building-its-walled-garden-it-may-be-starting-to-crack-11651762698 (accessed June 2023).

60 Weintraub, S. (2022) 'Tesla App Store concept is so real you can almost touch it'. Available at: https://electrek.co/2022/02/16/tesla-app-store-concept-is-so-real-you-can-almost-touch-it/ (accessed June 2023).

61 Weintraub, S. (2022) 'Tesla App Store concept is so real you can almost touch it'. Available at: https://electrek.co/2022/02/16/tesla-app-store-concept-is-so-real-you-can-almost-touch-it/ (accessed June 2023).

62 Casadesus-Masanell, R. and Llanes, G. (2015) 'Investment incentives in open-source and proprietary two-sided platforms'. *Journal of Economics & Management Strategy*, 24(2), 306–324.

63 Katz, B. M. L. and Shapiro, C. (1985) 'Network externalities, competition, and compatibility'. *The American Economic Review*, 75(3), 424–440.

64 https://android.googleblog.com/2012/09/the-benefits-importance-of-compatibility.html (accessed June 2023).

65 Gawer, A. and Cusumano, M. A. (2002) *Platform Leadership: How Intel, Microsoft, and Cisco Drive Industry Innovation*. Boston, MA: Harvard Business School Press.

66 Starting an Open Source Project, The Linux Foundation. Retreived from https://www.linuxfoundation.org/resources/open-source-guides/starting-an-open-sourceproject (accessed June 2023).

67 Eisenmann, T., Parker, G. and Van Alstyne, M. (2009) 'Opening platforms: How, when and why?' In A. Gawer (Ed.), *Platforms, Markets and Innovation* (pp. 131–162). Glos, UK: Edward Elgar Publishing.

68 Statista. (2023) 'Share of Apple's revenue by product category from the 1st quarter of 2012 to the 3rd quarter of 2023'. Available at: https://www.statista.com/statistics/382260/segments-share-revenue-of-apple/ (accessed June 2023).

69 Wiggers, K. (2019) 'The Alexa Skills Store now has more than 100,000 voice apps'. Available at: https://venturebeat.com/ai/the-alexa-skills-store-now-has-more-than-100000-voice-apps/ (accessed June 2023).

70 CNet. (1997) 'Jobs touts "very cool technology"'. Available at: https://www.cnet.com/news/jobs-touts-very-cool-technology/ (accessed June 2023).

71 Piller, C. (1997) 'Apple may be ready to cease cloning about'. *Los Angeles Times*. 4 August 1997. Available at: https://www.latimes.com/archives/la-xpm-1997-aug-04-fi-19214-story.html//; https://www.macobserver.com/features/power.shtml (accessed June 2023).

72 Hein, A., Schreieck, M., Riasanow, T., Setzke, D. S., Wiesche, M., Böhm, M. and Krcmar, H. (2020) 'Digital platform ecosystems'. *Electronic Markets*, 30(1), 87–98; Hein, A., Weking, J., Schreieck, M., Wiesche, M., Böhm, M. and Krcmar, H. (2019) 'Value co-creation practices in business-to-business platform ecosystems'. *Electronic Markets*, 29(3), 503–518.

73 Statista. (2023) 'Number of Xiaomi IoT connected devices worldwide from 2018–2023'. Available at: https://www.statista.com/statistics/967485/worldwide-xiaomi-number-of-connected-devices/ (accessed June 2023).

74 Tong, W., Guo, Y. and Chen, L. (2021) 'How Xiaomi redefined what it means to be a platform'. *Harvard Business Review*. Available at: https://hbr.org/2021/09/how-xiaomi-redefined-what-it-means-to-be-a-platform (accessed June 2023).

75 Tong, W., Guo, Y. and Chen, L. (2021) 'How Xiaomi redefined what it means to be a platform'. *Harvard Business Review*. Available at: https://hbr.org/2021/09/how-xiaomi-redefined-what-it-means-to-be-a-platform (accessed June 2023).

76 Hein, A., Weking, J., Schreieck, M., Wiesche, M., Böhm, M. and Krcmar, H. (2019) 'Value co-creation practices in business-to-business platform ecosystems'. *Electronic Markets*, 29(3), 503–518.

77 This is just the beginning!, Ctrix Automation. Retreived from https://apps.boschrexroth.com/microsites/ctrlx-automation/en/news-stories/story/this-is-just-the-beginning/ (accessed August 2023).

78 Hein, A., Weking, J., Schreieck, M., Wiesche, M., Böhm, M. and Krcmar, H. (2019) 'Value co-creation practices in business-to-business platform ecosystems'. *Electronic Markets*, 29(3), 503–518.

79 Karhu, K., Gustafsson, R. and Lyytinen, K. (2018) 'Exploiting and defending open digital platforms with boundary resources: Android's five platform forks'. *Information Systems Research*, 29(2), 479–497.

80 Dexheimer, M. J. (2021) 'Strategic complement certification in platform-based markets'. [PhD thesis]. University of St Gallen, Switzerland.

81 Udin, E. (2021) 'Tim Cook explains why Apple will not open up the iOS system'. Gizchina. Available at: https://www.gizchina.com/2021/10/29/tim-cook-explains-why-apple-will-not-open-up-the-ios-system/ (accessed August 2023).

82 Huber, T. L., Kude, T. and Dibbern, J. (2017) 'Governance practices in platform ecosystems: Navigating tensions between cocreated value and governance costs'. *Information Systems Research*, 28(3), 563–584.

83 Cusumano, M., Gawer, A. and Yoffie, D. B. (2019) *The Business of Platforms: Strategy in the Age of Digital Competition, Innovation, and Power*. New York: Harper Business.

84 Budimir, M. (2021) 'Bosch Rexroth's ctrlX store offers automation and control apps'. Available at: https://www.motioncontroltips.com/bosch-rexroths-ctrlx-store-offers-automation-and-control-apps/ (accessed June 2023).

85 https://developer.android.com/distribute/marketing-tools/alternative-distribution (accessed June 2023).

Chapter 3

1 Albergotti, R. (2014) 'Instagram CEO Systrom: "We can't be just a hedge" for Facebook'. *The Wall Street Journal*. 10 December 2014. Available at: https://www.wsj.com/amp/articles/instagram-ceo-systrom-we-cant-be-just-a-hedge-for-facebook-1418227334 (accessed August 2023).

2 https://www.apple.com/newsroom/2020/11/apple-announces-app-store-small-business-program/ (accessed June 2023).

3 Airbnb. (2020) 'How much does Airbnb charge hosts?' Available at: https://www.airbnb.co.uk/resources/hosting-homes/a/how-much-does-airbnb-charge-hosts-288 (accessed June 2023).

4 CNBC. (2018) 'Steve Jobs 1997 interview: Defending his commitment to Apple'. Available at: https://www.youtube.com/watch?v=xchYT9wz5hk (accessed August 2023).

5 https://create.roblox.com/docs/art/marketplace/marketplace-fees-and-commissions# (accessed June 2023).

6 Meier, P. (2019) 'How do digital platforms make their money?' Alexander von Humboldt Institute for Internet and Society. Available at: https://www.hiig.de/en/how-do-digital-platforms-make-their-money/ (accessed August 2023).

7 Arrington, M. (2009) 'Davos interviews: Etsy founder Robert Kalin'. Available at: https://techcrunch.com/2009/02/01/davos-interviews-etsy-founder-robert-kalin/ (accessed August 2023).

8 Bloom, S. (2017) 'Craigslist: A platform eroded by platforms'. Available at: https://digital.hbs.edu/platform-digit/submission/craigslist-a-platform-eroded-by-platforms/ (accessed August 2023).

9 Indeed.com (2023) 'Indeed pricing: Job posting costs'. Available at: https://www.indeed.com/hire/resources/howtohub/how-pricing-works-on-indeed (accessed January 2023).

10 (2010) 'Interview: Indeed.com founder discusses online recruitment'. Available at: https://huntscanlon.com/interview-indeed-com-founder-discusses-online-recruitment/ (accessed August 2023).

11 Schurter, D. (2021) 'Threema ist das neue Whats-App – und schlägt die Konkurrenz um Längen'. Available at: https://www.watson.ch/!298079852 (accessed August 2023).

12 Raveling, J. (2022) 'Der Duft Asiens in einer Dose'. *Starthaus*. Available at: https://www.starthaus-bremen.de/de/page/mediathek/stories/yummy-organics (accessed August 2023).

13 Gassmann, O., Frankenberger, K. and Choudury, M. (2020) *The Business Model Navigator: The Strategies Behind the Most Successful Companies* (2nd ed.). FT Publishing.

14 https://www.babylonhealth.com/en-gb/pricing (accessed January 2023).

15 (2005) 'LinkedIn launches premium service for recruiters and researchers'. Available at: https://news.linkedin.com/2005/08/linkedin-launches-premium-service-for-recruiters-and-researchers (accessed August 2023).

16 Bringing Our Customer Promise to the Next Level, Annual Report 2017, Zalando. Retreived from https://annual-report.zalando.com/2017/magazine/zalando-plus-bringing-our-customer-promise-to-the-next-level/ (accessed August 2023).

17 Meier, P. (2019) 'How do digital platforms make their money?' Alexander von Humboldt Institute for Internet and Society. Available at: https://www.hiig.de/en/how-do-digital-platforms-make-their-money/ (accessed August 2023).

18 Rodriguez, A. (2017) 'Ten years ago, Netflix launched streaming video and changed the way we watch everything'. Available at: https://qz.com/887010/netflix-nflx-launched-streaming-video-10-years-ago-and-changed-the-way-we-watch-everything (accessed January 2023).

19 Zhu, F. (2018) 'Friends or foes? Examining platform owners' entry into complementors' spaces'. *Journal of Economics & Management Strategy*, 28(1), 23–28.

20 Bean, J. (2022) 'The bottom line: The analytics behind the economics of an iBuyer'. *Medium*. Available at: https://medium.com/alpha-beta-blog/the-economics-of-an-ibuyer-an-opendoor-case-study-ddd497d0af08 (accessed June 2023).

21 Oakland, T. (2022) 'Opendoor: The art of winning an unfair game'. *Seeking Alpha*. Available at: https://seekingalpha.com/article/4490583-opendoor-the-art-of-winning-an-unfair-game (accessed August 2023).

22 TechCrunch. (2011) 'Tr'pAdvisor's Stephen Kaufer – Founder stories'. Available at: https://www.youtube.com/watch?v=5JBa9ZH1i1M (accessed August 2023).

23 Recode. (2018) 'Full interview: Susan Wojcicki, CEO of YouTube, at Code Media'. Available at: https://www.youtube.com/watch?v=klQZLssoyl4&t=1063s (accessed August 2023).

24 Gassmann, O., Frankenberger, K. and Choudury, M. (2020) *The Business Model Navigator: The Strategies Behind the Most Successful Companies* (2nd ed.). FT Publishing; https://www.ahrq.gov/workingforquality/priorities-in-action/patientslikeme.html (accessed January 2023).

25 Collins, L. (2018). 'Farmobile launches nationwide data marketplace for "the infinite commodity"'. *Kansas City Business Journal*. Available at: https://www.bizjournals.com/kansascity/news/2018/07/18/farmobile-launches-nationwide-data-marketplace.html (accessed August 2023).

26 Gassmann, O., Frankenberger, K. and Choudury, M. (2020) *The Business Model Navigator: The Strategies Behind the Most Successful Companies* (2nd ed.). FT Publishing.

27 Quest Means Business, Transcripts. Retreived from https://transcripts.cnn.com/show/qmb/date/2015-03-02/segment/01 (accessed August 2023).

28 Gassmann, O., Frankenberger, K. and Choudury, M. (2020) *The Business Model Navigator: The Strategies Behind the Most Successful Companies* (2nd ed.). FT Publishing.

29 Rachitsky, L. (2019) 'Accelerating growth at scale: Phase 2 of kickstarting and scaling a marketplace business'. *Lenny's Newsletter*. Available at: www.lennysnewsletter.com/p/accelerating-growth-at-scale-phase (accessed August 2023).

30 Irwin, I. (2014) 'Uber's Travis Kalanick explains his pricing experiment'. *New York Times*. 11 July 2014. Available at: https://www.nytimes.com/2014/07/12/upshot/ubers-travis-kalanick-explains-his-pricing-experiment.html (accessed August 2023).

Chapter 4

1 Caillaud, B. and Jullien, B. (2003) 'Chicken & egg: Competition among intermediation service providers'. *The RAND Journal of Economics*, 34(2), 309–328; Parker, G., Van Alstyne, M. and Choudary, S. (2016) *Platform Revolution: How Networked Markets Are Transforming the Economy and How to Make Them Work for You*. New York: W. W. Norton & Company; Veisdal, J. (2020) 'The dynamics of entry for digital platforms in two-sided markets: A multi-case study'. *Electronic Markets*, 30(3), 539–556.

2 Peter Thiel: Escape the Competition, The Podcase. Retreived from https://s3.amazonaws.com/he-product-images/docs/Podcase_transcript_A.pdf?elqTrackId=f086091397a74b1d82f8a23d4ebb0fba&elqaid=124&elqat=2 (accessed August 2023).

3 Parker, G., Van Alstyne, M. and Choudary, S. (2016) *Platform Revolution: How Networked Markets Are Transforming the Economy and How to Make Them Work for You*. New York: W. W. Norton & Company.

4 https://press.opentable.com/news-releases/news-release-details/opentable-waives-fees-and-updates-features-help-restaurants/ (accessed June 2023); Dixler Canavan, H. and Forbes, P. (2014) 'OpenTable by the numbers: From launch to $2.6 billion'. Available at: https://www.eater.com/2014/6/13/6207641/opentable-by-the-numbers-from-launch-to-2-6-billion (accessed June 2023).

5 Come for the tool, stay for the network, Cdixon January 1,2015. Retreived from https://cdixon.org/2015/01/31/come-for-the-tool-stay-for-the-network (accessed June 2023).

6 Rachitsky, L. (2019) 'How to kickstart and scale a marketplace business'. Available at: https://www.lennysnewsletter.com/p/how-to-kickstart-and-scale-a-marketplace (accessed August 2023).

7 Parker, G., Van Alstyne, M. and Choudary, S. (2016) *Platform Revolution: How Networked Markets Are Transforming the Economy and How to Make Them Work for You*. New York: W. W. Norton & Company.

8 Parker, G., Van Alstyne, M. and Choudary, S. (2016) *Platform Revolution: How Networked Markets Are Transforming the Economy and How to Make Them Work for You*. New York: W. W. Norton & Company.

9 Rachitsky, L. (2019) 'How to kickstart and scale a marketplace business'. Available at: https://www.lennysnewsletter.com/p/how-to-kickstart-and-scale-a-marketplace-911?s=r (accessed August 2023).

10 Cheredar, T. (2012) 'Cheating and lying are at Reddit's core, founder reveals'. Available at: https://venturebeat.com/2012/06/22/reddit-fake-users/ (accessed June 2023).

11 Apple's Find My network now offers new third-party finding experiences, Newsroom, Apple 2021. Retreived from https://www.apple.com/newsroom/2021/04/apples-find-my-network-now-offers-new-thirdparty-finding-experiences/ (accessed August 2023).

12 Rachitsky, L. (2019) 'How to kickstart and scale a marketplace business'. Available at: https://www.lennysnewsletter.com/p/how-to-kickstart-and-scale-a-marketplace (accessed August 2023).

13 Boudreau, K. and Hagiu, A. (2008) 'Platform rules: Multi-sided platforms as regulators'. *SSRN*, 163–191; Veisdal, J. (2020) 'The dynamics of entry for digital platforms in two-sided markets: A multi-case study'. *Electronic Markets*, 30(3), 539–556; Parker, G., Van Alstyne, M. and Choudary, S. (2016) *Platform Revolution: How Networked Markets Are Transforming the Economy and How to Make Them Work for You*. New York: W. W. Norton & Company.

14 Google Announces $10 Million Android Developer Challenge, Google news from Google. Retreived from http://googlepress.blogspot.com/2007/11/google-announces-10-million-android_12.html (accessed August 2023).

15 Boudreau, K. and Hagiu, A. (2008) 'Platform rules: Multi-sided platforms as regulators'. *SSRN*, 163–191.

16 Khan Academy. Elon Musk – CEO of Tesla Motors and SpaceX. Interview. Available at: https://www.youtube.com/watch?v=vDwzmJpI4io&t=680s (accessed August 2023); https://www.crunchbase.com/search/funding_rounds/field/organization.has_investor.reverse/num_funding_rounds/paypal (accessed June 2023).

17 CBInsights. (2020) 'How Uber makes money now'. Available at: https://www.cbinsights.com/research/report/how-uber-makes-money/ (accessed January 2023).

18 Zhou, C. (2023) 'China's JD.com to offer big subsidies in price war with Pinduoduo'. *Nikkei Asia*. Available at: https://asia.nikkei.com/Business/Consumer/China-s-JD.com-to-offer-big-subsidies-in-price-war-with-Pinduoduo (accessed June 2023).

19 Cennamo, C. and Santalo, J. (2013) 'Platform competition: Strategic trade-offs in platform markets'. *Strategic Management Journal*, 34(11), 1331–1350; Parker, G., Van Alstyne, M. and Choudary, S. (2016) *Platform Revolution: How Networked Markets Are Transforming the Economy and How to Make Them Work for You*. New York: W. W. Norton & Company.

20 Open Handset Alliance. (2007) 'Industry leaders announce open platform for mobile devices'. Available at: http://www.openhandsetalliance.com/press_110507.html (accessed January 2023).

21 Gassmann, O. and Ferrandina, F. (2021) 'Die Win-win-win Formel' [translated from German]. Available at: https://www.alexandria.unisg.ch/server/api/core/bitstreams/78ebcba9-f857-4435-9bcd-05c9923f4540/content (accessed August 2023).

22 Parker, G., Van Alstyne, M. and Choudary, S. (2016) *Platform Revolution: How Networked Markets Are Transforming the Economy and How to Make Them Work for You*. New York: W. W. Norton & Company.

23 Roblox Corporation"Earning on Roblox", Retrieved from https://create.roblox.com/docs/production/monetization/economics

24 Rachitsky, L. (2019) 'Accelerating growth at scale: Phase 2 of kickstarting and scaling a marketplace business'. *Lenny's Newsletter*. Available at: www.lennysnewsletter.com/p/accelerating-growth-at-scale-phase (accessed August 2023).

25 Parker, G., Van Alstyne, M. and Choudary, S. (2016) *Platform Revolution: How Networked Markets Are Transforming the Economy and How to Make Them Work for You*. New York: W. W. Norton & Company.

26 (2021) 'Gisbert Rühl: Leading digital transformation at a century old German steel distributor'. Available at: https://web.archive.org/web/20220118041815/https://kreatize.com/blog/launchpad/gisbert-ruehl-interview-digital-transformation/ (accessed August 2023).

27 Porsche Consulting. 'B2B platform play'. Available at: https://newsroom.porsche.com/dam/jcr:456d1e10-84cc-47f4-83e9-274c08970c54/B2B%20Platform%20Play%20C%20Porsche%20Consulting%202022.pdf (accessed June 2023).

28 https://www.quora.com/How-did-eBay-process-payments-before-PayPal (accessed June 2023); O'Connell, B. (2020) 'Hisotry of PayPal: Timeline and facts'. Available at: https://www.thestreet.com/technology/history-of-paypal-15062744 (accessed June 2023).

29 Lomas, N. (2022) 'Babylon Health dials back some services in the UK'. Available at: https://techcrunch.com/2022/08/09/babylon-health-nhs-contracts-ended/ (accessed August 2023).

30 Stummer, C., Kundisch, D. and Decker, R. (2018) 'Platform launch strategies'. *Business & Information Systems Engineering*, 60(2), 167–173; Zhu, F. and Iansiti, M. (2019) 'Why some platforms thrive and others don't'. *Harvard Business Review*, 97(1), 118–125.

31 *Red Herring.* (2020) 'German healthcare jobs startup Medwing wins $30m seires B round'. Available at: https://www.redherring.com/europe/german-healthcare-jobs-startup-medwing-wins-30m-series-b-round/ (accessed June 2023).

32 Vidra, E. (2009) 'Utest defines the future of quality assurance: CEO interview'. Available at: https://www.vccafe.com/2009/04/08/utest-defines-the-future-of-quality-assurance-ceo-interview/ (accessed August 2023).

33 Rachitsky, L. (2019) 'How to kickstart and scale a marketplace business'. Available at: https://www.lennysnewsletter.com/p/how-to-kickstart-and-scale-a-marketplace-911?s=r (accessed August 2023).

34 Büge, M. and Ozcan, P. (2021) 'Platform scaling, fast and slow'. *MIT Sloan Management Review.* Further reading: *MIT Sloan Management Review*, Special Collection on new strategies for the platform economy (Spring 2021).

35 Zhu, F. and Iansiti, M. (2019) 'Why some platforms thrive and others don't'. *Harvard Business Review*, 97(1), 118–125.

36 Tong, T. W., Guo, Y. and Chen, L. (2021) 'How Xiaomi redefined what it means to be a platform'. *Harvard Business Review.* Available at: https://hbr.org/2021/09/how-xiaomi-redefined-what-it-means-to-be-a-platform (accessed August 2023).

37 May, K. (2022) 'Online travel giants ramped up marketing spend in 2021'. *PhocusWire.* Available at: https://www.phocuswire.com/Marketing-spend-2021-online-travel (accessed August 2023).

38 Rachitsky, L. (2019) 'Accelerating growth at scale: Phase 2 of kickstarting and scaling a marketplace business'. *Lenny's Newsletter.* Available at: https://www.lennysnewsletter.com/p/accelerating-growth-at-scale-phase (accessed August 2023).

39 Karhu, K. and Ritala, P. (2021) 'Slicing the cake without baking it: Opportunistic platform entry strategies in digital markets'. *Long Range Planning*, 54(5), 101988.

40 Chen, A. (n.d.). 'Growth Hacker is the new VP Marketing'. Available at: https://andrewchen.com/how-to-be-a-growth-hacker-an-airbnbcraigslist-case-study/ (accessed August 2023).

41 Chen, A. (n.d.). 'Growth Hacker is the new VP Marketing'. Available at: https://andrewchen.com/how-to-be-a-growth-hacker-an-airbnbcraigslist-case-study/ (accessed August 2023).

42 Karhu, K. and Ritala, P. (2021) 'Slicing the cake without baking it: Opportunistic platform entry strategies in digital markets'. *Long Range Planning*, 54(5), 101988.

43 Victor, H. (2012) 'Here is why Google blocked Acer's Aliyun smartphone launch'. Phone Arena. Available at: https://www.phonearena.com/news/Here-is-why-Google-blocked-Acers-Aliyun-smartphone-launch_id34535 (accessed August 2023).

44 Karhu, K. and Ritala, P. (2021) 'Slicing the cake without baking it: Opportunistic platform entry strategies in digital markets'. *Long Range Planning*, 54(5), 101988; Ghazawneh, A. and Henfridsson, O. (2013) 'Balancing platform control and external contribution in third-party development: The boundary resources model'. *Information Systems Journal*, 23(2), 173–192.

45 Karhu, K. and Ritala, P. (2021) 'Slicing the cake without baking it: Opportunistic platform entry strategies in digital markets'. *Long Range Planning*, 54(5), 101988; Ghazawneh, A. and Henfridsson, O. (2013) 'Balancing platform control and external contribution in third-party development: The boundary resources model'. *Information Systems Journal*, 23(2), 173–192.

46 Rutnik, M. (2020) 'Did you know: Android was originally designed for digital cameras not phones'. Available at: https://www.androidauthority.com/android-history-digital-cameras-1111795/ (accessed January 2023).

47 Google LLC v. Oracle America Inc. (2021) Available at: https://www.supremecourt.gov/opinions/20pdf/18-956_d18f.pdf (accessed January 2023).

48 Chestukhin, D. (2021, April) 'U.S. Supreme Court finds Google's copying of Oracle's Java API code a non-infringing fair use'. *Cowen Liebowitz and Latman*. Available at: https://www.cll.com/CopyrightDevelopmentsBlog/u-s-supreme-court-finds-googles-copying (accessed August 2023).

Chapter 5

1 (2017) 'Full transcript: Instagram CEO Kevin Systrom on. Recode decode'. Vox. Available at: https://www.vox.com/2017/6/22/15849966/transcript-instagram-ceo-kevin-systrom-facebook-photo-video-recode-decode (accessed August 2023).

2 Zhao, Y., von Delft, S., Morgan-Thomas, A. and Buck, T. (2020) 'The evolution of platform business models: Exploring competitive battles in the world of platforms'. *Long Range Planning*, 53(4), 101892.

3 Michelli, J. (2021) 'Customer experience excellence: The Airbnb way'. Customer Think. Available at: https://customerthink.com/create-belonging-customer-experience-excellence-the-airbnb-way/ (accessed August 2023).

4 CNBC Television. (2020) 'Watch CNBC's full interview with PayPal CEO Dan Schulman at Davos'. Available at: https://www.youtube.com/watch?v=nAM9uKJpDxM (accessed August 2023).

5 Schenker, J. L. (2020) 'Interview of the week: Joerg Hellwig'. Available at: https://innovator.news/interview-of-the-week-joerg-hellwig-26637edb59a3 (accessed August 2023).

6 Tabaka, M. (2019) 'Amazon's 4 keys to success, according to Jeff Bezos'. Available at: https://www.inc.com/marla-tabaka/jeff-bezos-says-these-4-principles-are-key-to-amazons-success-they-can-work-for-you-too.html (accessed August 2023).

7 Zhao, Y., von Delft, S., Morgan-Thomas, A. and Buck, T. (2020) 'The evolution of platform business models: Exploring competitive battles in the world of platforms'. *Long Range Planning*, 53(4), 101892.

8 Spolsky, J. (2018) 'The stack overflow age'. *Joel on Software*. Available at: https://www.joelonsoftware.com/2018/04/06/the-stack-overflow-age/ (accessed June 2023).

9 Rose, C. (2006) 'Preview of interview with YouTube co-founders'. Available at: https://www.youtube.com/watch?v=7E6E9q8Jebw (accessed August 2023).

10 Associated Press. (2013) 'Number of active users at Facebook over the years'. Available at: https://news.yahoo.com/number-active-users-facebook-over-230449748.html (accessed June 2023); https://about.fb.com/news/2007/05/facebook-unveils-platform-for-developers-of-social-applications/ (accessed June 2023).

11 Tan, B., Pan, S., Xianghua, L. and Huang, L. (2015) 'The role of IS capabilities in the development of multi-sided platforms: The digital ecosystem strategy of Alibaba.com'. *Journal of the Association for Information Systems*, 16(4).

12 Apple's Find My network now offers new third-party finding experiences, Newsroom, Apple 2021. Retrieved from https://www.apple.com/newsroom/2021/04/apples-find-my-network-now-offers-new-thirdparty-finding-experiences/ (accessed August 2023).

13 Porter, M. (2008) 'The five competitive forces that shape strategy'. *Harvard Business Review*, 57(1), 57–71.

14 Porter, M. (1985) *Competitive Advantage*. New York: The Free Press.

15 Tiwana, A. (2014) *Platform Ecosystems: Aligning Architecture, Governance, and Strategy*. Burlington, MA: Morgan Kaufmann; Allen, B. J., Chandrasekaran, D. and Gretz, R. T. (2021)

'How can platforms decrease their dependence on traditional indirect network effects? Innovating using platform envelopment'. *Journal of Product Innovation Management*, 38(5), 497–521.

16 Statista. (2022) 'Number of Apple Music subscribers worldwide from October 2015 to June 2021'. Available at: https://www.statista.com/statistics/604959/number-of-apple-music-subscribers/ (accessed June 2023).

17 Eisenmann, T., Parker, G. and Van Alstyne, M. (2011) 'Platform envelopment'. *Strategic Management Journal*, 32(12), 1270–1285.

18 Adeleke, D. (2015) 'How Facebook "owned" MySpace'. Tech Cabal. Available at: https://techcabal.com/2015/11/10/how-facebook-owned-myspace/ (accessed August 2023).

19 Choudary, S. (2015) 'Uber vs. Lyft: How platforms compete on interaction failure'. *Medium*. Available at: https://medium.com/platform-thinking/uber-vs-lyft-how-platforms-compete-on-interaction-failure-30f59fdca137 (accessed August 2023).

20 Salem, T. (2018) 'Why some cities have had enough of Waze'. *U.S. News & World Report*. Available at: https://www.usnews.com/news/national-news/articles/2018-05-07/why-some-cities-have-had-enough-of-waze (accessed August 2023).

21 (2021) 'China verhängt Milliardenstrafe gegen Internetriese Alibaba – angeblich wegen Verstoß gegen Wettbewerbsrecht'. *Neue Zürcher Zeitung*. Available at: https://www.nzz.ch/wirtschaft/china-verhaengt-milliardenstrafe-gegen-internetriese-alibaba-ld.1611231?reduced=true (accessed August 2023).

22 (2021) 'China verhängt Milliardenstrafe gegen Internetriese Alibaba – angeblich wegen Verstoß gegen Wettbewerbsrecht'. *Neue Zürcher Zeitung*. Available at: https://www.nzz.ch/wirtschaft/china-verhaengt-milliardenstrafe-gegen-internetriese-alibaba-ld.1611231?reduced=true (accessed August 2023).

23 Trischler, M., Meier, P. and Trabucchi, D. (2021) 'Digital platform tactics: How to implement platform strategy over time'. *Journal of Business Models*, 9(1), 67–76.

24 McIntyre, D., Srinivasan, A., Afuah, A., Gawer, A. and Kretschmer, T. (2021) 'Multisided platforms as new organizational forms'. *Academy of Management Perspectives*, 35(4), 566–583.

25 Trischler, M., Meier, P. and Trabucchi, D. (2021) 'Digital platform tactics: How to implement platform strategy over time'. *Journal of Business Models*, 9(1), 67–76.

26 Gawer, A. (2020) 'Digital platforms' boundaries: The interplay of firm scope, platform sides, and digital interfaces'. *Long Range Planning*, 54(5), 102045.

27 Staub, N., Haki, K., Aier, S., Winter, R. and Magan, A. (2021) 'Acquisition of complementors as a strategy for evolving digital platform ecosystems'. *MIS Quarterly Executive*, 20(4), 237–258.

28 https://www.govinfo.gov/content/pkg/CPRT-117HPRT47832/pdf/CPRT-117HPRT47832.pdf (accessed August 2023).

29 Roberts, M. (2022) 'Killer acquisitions and the death of competition in the digital economy'. *Transactions: The Tennessee Journal of Business Law*, 24(1), 3. Available at: https://ir.law.utk.edu/cgi/viewcontent.cgi?article=1623&context=transactions (accessed June 2023).

30 Lawsuits Filed by the FTC and the State Attorneys General Are Revisionist History, Jennifer Newstead (2020), Meta. https://about.fb.com/news/2020/12/lawsuits-filed-by-the-ftc-and-state-attorneys-general-are-revisionist-history/ (accessed August 2023).

31 Roberts, M. (2022) 'Killer acquisitions and the death of competition in the digital economy'. *Transactions: The Tennessee Journal of Business Law*, 24(1), 3. Available at: https://ir.law.utk.edu/cgi/viewcontent.cgi?article=1623&context=transactions (accessed June 2023).

32 Staub, N., Haki, K., Aier, S., Winter, R. and Magan, A. (2021) 'Acquisition of complementors as a strategy for evolving digital platform ecosystems'. *MIS Quarterly Executive*, 20(4), 237–258.

33 Bond, S. (2020) '"The wrath of Mark": 4 takeaways from the government's case against Facebook'. NPR. Available at: https://www.npr.org/2020/12/11/945234491/the-wrath-of-mark-takeaways-from-the-governments-case-against-facebook?t=1660722432117 (accessed August 2023).

34 Trischler, M., Meier, P. and Trabucchi, D. (2021) 'Digital platform tactics: How to implement platform strategy over time'. *Journal of Business Models*, 9(1), 67–76.

35 Somerville, H. (2015) 'Lyft's CEO Logan Green: On why being nice pays off, and getting back to its roots'. *The Mercury News*. 12 February 2015. Available at: https://www.mercurynews.com/2015/02/12/lyfts-ceo-logan-green-on-why-being-nice-pays-off-and-getting-back-to-its-roots/ (accessed August 2023).

36 Trischler, M., Meier, P. and Trabucchi, D. (2021) 'Digital platform tactics: How to implement platform strategy over time'. *Journal of Business Models*, 9(1), 67–76.

37 Jacobides, M. G., Sundararajan, A. and Van Alstyne, M. (2019) 'Platforms and ecosystems: Enabling the digital economy'. In WEF Briefing Paper. Available at: https://www3.weforum.org/docs/WEF_Digital_Platforms_and_Ecosystems_2019.pdf (accessed August 2023).

38 CNBC Television. (2020) 'Watch CNBC's full interview with PayPal CEO Dan Schulman at Davos'. Available at: https://www.youtube.com/watch?v=nAM9uKJpDxM (accessed August 2023).

39 Statista. (2023) 'PayPal – statistics & facts'. Available at: https://www.statista.com/topics/2411/paypal/#topicOverview (accessed January 2023).

40 Parker, G., Van Alstyne, M. and Choudary, S. (2016) *Platform Revolution: How Networked Markets Are Transforming the Economy and How to Make Them Work for You*. New York: W. W. Norton & Company.

41 Perez, S. (2016) '117 million LinkedIn emails and passwords from a 2012 hack just got posted online'. Available at: https://techcrunch.com/2016/05/18/117-million-linkedin-emails-and-passwords-from-a-2012-hack-just-got-posted-online/ (accessed August 2023).

42 https://twitter.com/tim_cook/status/1487100529251520512?ref_src=twsrc%5Etfw%7Ctwcamp%5Etweetembed%7Ctwterm%5E1487100529251520512%7Ctwgr%5E663a97d57b02ef0ddf0d8f69fc6ef058eb2cc96c%7Ctwcon%5Es1_&ref_url=https%3A%2F%2F www.redditmedia.com%2Fmediaembed%2Fseusxn%3Fresponsive%3Dtrueis_nightmode%3Dfalse (accessed August 2023).

43 Boehm, J., Grennan, L., Singla, A. and Smaje, K. (2022) 'Why digital trust truly matters'. McKinsey & Company. Available at: https://www.mckinsey.com/capabilities/quantumblack/our-insights/why-digital-trust-truly-matters (accessed August 2023); Casadesus-Masanell, R. and Hervas-Drane, A. (2015) 'Competing with privacy'. *Management Science*, 61(1), 229–246.

44 Statt, N. (2020) 'Apple launches new App Store privacy labels so you can see how iOS apps use your data'. Available at: https://www.theverge.com/2020/12/14/22174017/apple-app-store-new-privacy-labels-ios-apps-public (accessed January 2023).

45 Fitzpatrick, J. (2023) 'Protecting people's privacy on health topics'. Available at: https://blog.google/technology/safety-security/protecting-peoples-privacy-on-health-topics/ (accessed January 2023).

46 Wong, Q. (2021) 'Why WhatsApp users are pushing family members to Signal'. Available at: https://www.cnet.com/tech/services-and-software/why-whatsapp-users-are-moving-their-family-members-to-signal/ (accessed August 2023).

47 Jacobides, M. G., Sundararajan, A. and Van Alstyne, M. (2019) 'Platforms and ecosystems: Enabling the digital economy'. In WEF Briefing Paper. Available at: https://www3.weforum.org/docs/WEF_Digital_Platforms_and_Ecosystems_2019.pdf (accessed August 2023).

48 Braun, J. (2019) 'Die WeChat-App – Die Chinesische Wunder-App mit einem Haken'. Available at: https://www.boxcryptor.com/de/blog/post/wechat-chinese-wunder-app-with-a-catch/ (accessed January 2023).

49 Suresh, H. (2021) '"We have no data with us to sell to anyone": Signal CEO Aruna Harder to TNM'. *The News Minute*. 18 January 2021. Available at: https://www.thenewsminute.com/article/we-have-no-data-us-sell-anyone-signal-coo-aruna-harder-tnm-141678 (accessed August 2023).

50 Interview with Ben Heywood, CEO of PatientsLikeMe (transcript), health Business Group. Retreived from https://www.healthbusinessgroup.com/blog/2008/01/interview-with-ben-heywood-ceo-of-patientslikeme-transcript (accessed August 2023).

51 The New York Times. (2017) 'Full interview: Uber C.E.O Dara Khosroshahi'. Available at: https://www.youtube.com/watch?v=Mo2-4sXYZxU (accessed August 2023).

52 Statista. (2023) 'Monthly time spent on the YouTube mobile app per user in selected markets worldwide in 2022'. Available at: https://www.statista.com/statistics/1287283/time-spent-youtube-app-selected-countries/ (accessed January 2023).

53 Chen, A. and Fu, X. (2017) 'Data + intuition: A hybrid approach to developing product North Star metrics'. *26th International World Wide Web Conference*, 617–625; Ellis, S. (2017, June). 'What is a North Star metric?' Growth Hackers Blog. Available at: https://blog.growthhackers.com/what-is-a-north-star-metric-b31a8512923f (accessed August 2023).

54 Parker, G., Van Alstyne, M. and Xiaoyue, J. (2016) 'Platform ecosystems: How developers invert the firm'. *MIS Quarterly*.

55 Pangambam, S. (2014) 'Apple CEO Tim Cook keynote at WWDC June 14 Transcript'. *The Singju Post*. Available at: https://singjupost.com/apple-ceo-tim-cook-keynote-wwdc-june-2014-transcript/?singlepage=1 (accessed August 2023).

56 Fireside chat with Nate Moch VP product teams at zillow and morgan brown coo at inman news defining true growth how do you find your north star metric, Retrieved from https://www.slideshare.net/growthhackers/growthhacker-conference-16-fireside-chat-with-nate-moch-vp-product-teams-at-zillow-and-morgan-brown-coo-at-inman-news-defining-true-growth-how-do-you-find-your-north-star-metric#5

57 Hodapp, D., Hawlitschek, F., Wortmann, F., Lang, M. and Gassmann, O. (2022) 'Key lessons from Bosch for incumbent firms entering the platform economy', *MIS Quarterly Executive*, 21(2).

58 Wessel, M., Levie, A. and Siegel, R. (2017) 'Why some digital companies should delay profitability for as long as they can'. *Harvard Business Review*; Sterk, F., Heinz, D., Peukert, C., Fleuchaus, F., Kölbel, T. and Weinhardt, C. (2022) 'Fostering value co-creation in incumbent firms: The case of Bosch's IoT ecosystem landscape'. *Forty-Third International Conference on Information Systems (ICIS)*, 1–17.

59 Statista. (2023) 'Most popular social networks worldwide as of January 2023, ranked by number of monthly active users'. Available at: https://www.statista.com/statistics/272014/global-social-networks-ranked-by-number-of-users/ (accessed June 2023).

60 Jingli, S. (2019) 'Despite widening losses, Pinduoduo continues to prioritize user engagement over monetization (updated)'. KrAsia. Available at: https://kr-asia.com/pinduoduo-hits-123-year-on-year-revenue-growth-narrows-gap-with-alibaba-in-user-count (accessed August 2023).

61 Interview of Christian Bertermann by Stephan Knieps in *Wirtschaftswoche* (1 December, 2020) [translated from German, written interview]. Available at: https://www.wiwo.de/erfolg/gruender/auto1-mitgruender-christian-bertermann-im-jahr-2000-hat-man-ja-auch-ueberlegt-ob-jemand-ein-buch-online-kaufen-wuerde-/26654048-2.html (accessed August 2023).

62 https://web.archive.org/web/20130113204630/http://www.newscorp.com/news/news_251.html (accessed June 2023), Jackson, N. and Madrigal, A. C. (2011) 'The rise and fall of Myspace'. *The Atlantic*. Available at: https://www.ft.com/content/fd9ffd9c-dee5-11de-adff-00144feab49a (accessed June 2023).

63 Investment Knowledge. (2019) 'Jeff Bezon explains why Amazon makes no profit (2014)'. Available at: https://www.youtube.com/watch?v=Ue9uW1K_RJw (accessed August 2023).

Index